Application of Library Science

Application of Library Science

M. Ram

RANDOM PUBLICATIONS
NEW DELHI (INDIA)

Application of Library Science

ISBN 978-93-5111-945-6

Published in 2016 in India by

RANDOM PUBLICATIONS

4376-A/4B, Gali Murari Lal, Ansari Road
New Delhi-110 002
Phone : +9111-43580356, 011-23289044, 011-43142548
e-mail: sales@randompublications.com,
info@randompublications.com, randomexports@gmail.com

Reprint 2021

Type Setting by : Friends Media, Delhi-110089
Printed at : Replika Press Pvt. Ltd.

Preface

Library science (often termed library studies or library and information science) is an interdisciplinary or multidisciplinary field that applies the practices, perspectives, and tools of management, information technology, education, and other areas to libraries; the collection, organization, preservation, and dissemination of information resources; and the political economy of information.

Library and Information Science is a profession that is full of people passionate about making a positive change in the world & they tend to be wildly happy about what they do. According to one recent survey, over 85% of information professionals questioned said if they had the choice, they'd do it again.

Modern practices of maintaining books have become complex. Evolution of printing press made it possible to produce more and more books. A librarian has to deal with a number of jobs procurement of books, categorisation and cataloguing, etc. He has to maintain a file of reference, periodical section and record of new arrivals.

Librarians, in the truest sense, are the custodians of information. Whether in the public library or in corporate, faculty, or professional facilities, they provide the community with the knowledge, skills, and resources to find more information on virtually any topic. From the future novelist who spends his childhood immersed in fiction to the doctoral candidate preparing a dissertation on medical treatments, the best source for any recorded material, including CD-ROMs, web sites, virtual libraries, and remote access to a wide range of resources, is the library.

The publication will be useful to students, practicing librarians, teachers of library and information science, planners, policy makers in the field.

– Author

Contents

1

Introduction

INFORMATION SCIENCE

What is information science? The question, while seemin-gly simple, begs another, more complex one: *How is information science, or for that matter any field, to be defined?* This is a complex problem dealt with at length in philosophy and in other fields. Lexical definitions are necessary for providing a broad description and boundaries of the subjects covered by a field, but they cannot provide for a deeper understanding. Webster does not a field define. This is not to reject clear lexical definitions—not at all—just to establish their limitations.

In approaching the discussion of information science, I am taking the problem point of view as elaborated by Popper who argued that:

- [S]ubject matter or kind of things do not, I hold, constitute a basis for distinguishing disciplines. . . .*We are not students of some subject matter, but students of problems*. Any problem may cut right across the border of any subject matter or discipline.

Our emphasis is on problems addressed by information science. Although we provide definitions of information science and other fields in interdisciplinary relations with information science later in the chapter, we are doing this solely to advance the understanding of problems addressed by different fields and their relation to information science problems.

Debates over the "proper" definition of information science, as of any field, are fruitless, and in expectations naive. Information science, as a science and as a profession, is defined by the problems it has addressed and the methods it has used for their solutions over time.

Any advances in information science depend on whether the field is indeed progressing in relation to problems addressed and methods used. Any "fixing," if in order, will have to be approached by redefining or refocusing either the problems addressed, or the methods for their solutions, or both. Information science has three general characteristics that are the leitmotif of its evolution and existence. These are shared with many modern fields. They can also be viewed as problem areas with which infor-mation science has to deal on a general level:

- First, information science is interdisciplinary in nature; however, the relations with various disciplines are changing. The interdisciplinary evolution is far from over.
- Second, information science is inexorably connected to information technology. A technological imperative is compelling and constraining the evolution of information science, as is the evolution of a number of other fields, and moreover, of the information society as a whole.
- Third, information science is, with many other fields, an active participant in the evolution of the infor-mation society. Information science has a strong social and human dimension, above and beyond technology.

A number of works that I freely consulted dealt with various historical aspects of information science.

Among those works are:

- Shera and Cleveland,
- Bourne,
- Herner,
- Salton,
- Cleverdon,
- Swanson,
- Lilley and Trice,
- Farkas-Conn,
- Buckland and Liu, and
- Rayward.

Still, a comprehensive history of information science is a project for a future historian of science. As yet only historical pieces and different perspectives of pieces exist. A history of any field is a history of a few powerful ideas. I suggest that information science has three such powerful ideas, so far. These ideas deal with processing of information in a radically different way than was done previously or elsewhere. The first and the original idea, emerging in 1950s, is *information retrieval*, providing for processing of information based on formal logic. The second, emerging shortly thereafter, is *relevance*, directly orienting and associating the process with human information needs and assessments.

The third, derived from elsewhere some two decades later, is *interaction*, enabling direct exchanges and feedback between systems and people engaged in IR processes. So far, no powerful ideas have emerged about *information*, as the underlying phenomenon, or *"literature"*, as the object of processing.

However, one can argue that the idea of mapping of "literature," that started with exploitation of citation indexes in 1960s, may also qualify as a powerful idea. In a non-historical sense this stage deals with these powerful ideas and with leitmotifs. They form a framework for understanding the past, present, and future of information science.

WHAT IS "INFORMATION" IN INFORMATION SCIENCE

In a scientific sense, the answer to the question is "We don't know." Yes, we can and do provide various lexical definitions of information, and we have an intuitive understanding of its meaning that we apply daily and widely. Thus, we do understand the message-sense in which we deal with information in information science. But that does not provide for a deeper and more formal understanding and explanation. Information is a basic phenomenon. For all basic phenomena—energy or gravity in physics, life in biology, justice in jurisprudence—the same "we-don'tknow" answer applies.

However, the investigation of the basic phenomena is proceeding—that is the basic point of all these fields. It is proceeding by investigating the *manifestations, behaviour,* and *effects* of phenomena under question. While we do not know what information is, or what some of its derivative notions, such as relevance, may be, over the years we have learned a lot about their various manifestations, behaviours, and effects. And we are continuing to learn about them through scientific investigations. "Information" has a variety of connotations in different fields. For instance, from the standpoint of physics and biology, a number of highly ambitious attempts have undertaken to explore information as a basic property of the universe.

In psychology, information is used, at times, as a variable dealing with sensory perception, comprehension, or other psychological processes. These senses of information are very different than the one in information science. In some fields, information science included, the notion of information is broadly associated with messages. For this sense, a number of interpretations exist, which are assumed in different theoretical and pragmatic treatments of information. We can present them as related, but differing manifestations of information in an ordered sequence or a continuum of increasing complexity.

Narrow Sense

Information is considered in terms of *signals or messages for decisions* involving little or no cognitive processing, or such processing that can be expressed in algorithms and probabilities. Information is treated as the property of a message, which can be estimated by some probability. Examples are information in terms of uncertainty in information theory, "perfect infor-mation" in game theory, or information as related to decision-making and market equilibrium in the theory of uncertainty and information in economics of information.

The latter has been surveyed by Hirshleifer and Riley, who provide this illustrative explanation: In the economics of uncertainty, an individual is assumed to act on the basis of current *fixed beliefs*, *e.g.*, deciding whether to carry an umbrella based on one's present estimate of the chance of rain, while in the economics of information a person typically is trying to arrive at *improved beliefs*, *e.g.*, by studying a weather report before deciding to take an umbrella.

Information may be considered as causing a difference between fixed and improved beliefs. The value of information is calculated as the difference between the decision maker's expected utility of the decision made without the information, and the expected utility of the best possible choice in decision made after receiving and analysing the information. The huge, and sometimes insurmountable, problem, of course, is estimating appropriate probabilities. A number of pragmatic applications follow this interpretation, such as computerized trading.

Broader Sense

Information is treated as directly involving *cognitive processing and understanding.* It results from interaction of two cognitive structures, a "mind" and a "text." Information is that which affects or changes the state of a mind. In cases of information services, information is most often conveyed through the medium of a text, document, or record, *e.g.*, what a reader may understands from a text or document.

The interpretation by Tague-Sutcliff fits:

- Information is an intangible that depends on the conceptualization and the understanding of a human being. Records contain words or pictures absolutely, but they contain information relative only to a user... Information is associated with a transaction between text and reader, between a record and user.

Broadest Sense

Information is treated in a context. That is, information involves not only messages that are cognitively processed but also *a context*—situation, task, problem-at-hand, and the like. Using information that has been cognitively processed for a given task is an example. In addition to other senses, it involves motivation or intentionality, and therefore it is connected to the expansive social context or horizon, such as culture, work, or problemat-hand.

In information science, we must consider the third and broadest sense of information, because information is used in a context and in relation to some reasons.

The point was implicitly understood from the beginning of information science, particularly as reflected in the practice of information retrieval. This interpretation of "information" in information science is not new. Such a broad interpretation of information that explicitly incorporates cognition and context was, among others, elaborated by Wersig and Neveling and Belkin and Robertson. It is also implicit in the social role of information science.

ORIGIN AND SOCIAL CONTEXT OF INFORMATION SCIENCE

Information science is a field that emerged in the after-math of the Second World War (WW II), along with a number of new fields, with computer science being but one example. The rapid pace of scientific and technical advances that were accumu-lating since the start of the 20th century, produced by mid-century a scientific and technical revolution. A most visible manifestation of this revolution was the phenomenon of "information explosion," referring to the exponential and unabated growth of scientific and technical publications and information records of all kinds, so masterfully synthesized and illuminated by de Solla Price.

In a remarkable turn of events, the impetus for the development of information science, and even for its very origin and agenda, a respected MIT scientist and, even more importantly, the head of the U.S. scientific effort during WW II.

Bush did two things:

- He succinctly defined a critical and strategic problem that was on the minds of many, and
- Proposed a solution that was a "technological fix", and thus in tune with the spirit of the times.

Both had wide appeal and Bush was listened to because of his stature. He defined the problem in almost poetic terms as "the massive task of making more accessible a bewildering store of knowledge". In other words, Bush addressed the problem of information explosion. The problem is still with us. His solution was to use the emerging computing and other information technology to combat the problem. But he went even further. He proposed a machine named Memex, incorporating a capability for "association of ideas," and duplication of "mental processes artificially." A prescient anticipation of information science and artificial intelligence is evident.

Memex, needless to say, was never built, but to this day is an ideal, a wish list, an agenda, and, some think, a utopia. We are still challenged by the ever-worsening problem of the information explosion, now universal and in a variety of digital formats.

We are still trying to fix things techno-logically. We are still aspiring to incorporate Memex's basic ideas in our solutions. A number of scientists and professi-onals in many fields around the globe listened and took up Bush's challenge.

Governments listened as well and provided funding. The reasoning went something like this: Because science and technology are strategically important for society, efforts that help them, information activities in particular, are also important and need support. In the U.S., the *National Science Foundation* (NSF) Act of 1950 established NSF and provided a number of mandates, among them "to foster the interchange of scientific information among scientists in the U.S.

and foreign countries" and "to further the full dissemination of information of scientific value consistent with the national interest".

The 1958 National Defence Education Act enlarged the mandate:

"The National Science Foundation shall..undertake programme to develop new or improved methods, including mechanized systems, for making scientific information available".

By those mandates, an NSF division, which after a number of name and direction changes is now called the Division of *Information and Intelligent Systems* (IIS), has supported research in these areas since the 1950s. Importantly, the field-defining studies that NSF supported included, among others, Cranfield IR evaluation studies in the 1950s and 1960s, large chunks of SMART studies from the 1960s to 1990s, and now the Digital Libraries Initiatives.

In the U.S., information science developed and began flourishing on its own in a large part due to government support by a host of agencies, as did many other fields. Historically, the support was a success—it was instrumental in creation of the whole enterprise of information science and even of the information online industry based on IR. But to the credit of information science it kept growing on its own even after government support slackened substantially. This cannot be said of a number of other fields or areas that floundered after government stopped being their main source and resource.

Social Context

It is a truism to state that information was always important for any society in any historical period. But the role of information and its degree of importance differed. With the evolution of the social order to a "post-industrial" society, or "post-capitalist" society or what we now commonly also call "information society," knowledge and information is assuming an increasing central role in every aspect of life. The classic study by Machlup, followed by a number of similar studies, documented the startling structural changes in the economy and society as driven by the growth of information and knowledge production and processing.

Popularly, they were summarized by Drucker:

The change in the meaning of knowledge that began two hundred fifty years ago has transformed society and economy. Formal knowledge is seen as both the key personal and the key economic resource. . . [K]nowledge proves itself in action. What we now mean by knowledge is information effective in action, information focused on results.... The actual products of the pharmaceutical industry is knowledge; pill and prescription ointment are no more than packaging for knowledge.

Addressing the problem of information explosion, information science found a niche within the broader context in the evolution of the information society.

In its various manifestations and attempted solutions, the niche is getting broader and bigger. But by no means does information science hold a monopoly in that niche. As the importance of infor-mation is increasing in society, more and more resources and expenditures are channeled into various information-related activities. More and more research funds, projects, and initia-tives are devoted to information in various disguises. It is not surprising then that more and more fields, researchers, professionals, and businesses are turning to information, and even "discovering" information. There is gold in information. Information science has many competitors—it may be even swamped by them.

2

Multimedia Applications in Libraries

Hypermedia, not only helps the users in providing information from different media on one platform but also saves on space, money, maintenance, operational inconveniences, etc.

The other advantages of multimedia in libraries are:

- It can help satisfying different information needs such as reference, enrichment, entertainment, leisure, etc.
- It can help meeting various types of information preferences of the users, such as scholarly, scientific, vocational, ' artistic, recreational, etc.
- Being in digital format, information can also be accessed by remote users on a network. It also helps in over coming the barriers of boundaries, proximity and physical rapacity of a library to accommodate users.
- It is interesting and easy to use over the existing form such as print, microforms, online, etc.
- Its control and interactivity helps the users and provides the benefits of books and human beings.

Electronic information, and multimedia in general, is about to become a vital part of our cultural heritage. Libraries have throughout the history ensured a democratic, independent and free access to the knowledge and intellectual value represented by conventional books. It is evident that this principle is also valid for electronic information and multimedia. The availability of multimedia information through,data networks may also open completely new ways for the libraries to obtain information for the common users.

AMERICAN AND EUROPEAN LIBRARIES

Many big libraries including the *Library of Congress* (LC), British Library, OCLC, etc. are building their collections in multimedia form. Apart from multimedia collection development in 1990, LC began the American Memory Project, aided by Annenberg Fund; the David and Lucile Packard Foundation; and others, for preparing multimedia CDs. This covered several kinds of information including country's historical books, pamphlets, photographs, folk songs, movies, genealogical works, etc. LC brought out the first part of this project America at the start of a New Century 1880-1920, as a CD. Similarly, Elmer E Rasmussen Library and 'University of Alaska started a Project Jukebox-a Hypercard-based Multimedia Archival System.

Project jukebox is used for archiving as well as providing access to recordings of oral history archives. For the past five years, many libraries in the developed countries started various projects such as archiving different forms of information, multimedia databases, multimedia catalogues, walk-through programmes, Instructional packages, electronic books, and digital libraries. There are a few surveys in the literature that are focused on the usage of multimedia technology in public libraries, academic libraries and special libraries. These studies primarily cover the use of multimedia CD-ROMs in libraries and also the use of world wide web and Internet.

INDIAN SCENARIO

Nowadays many librarians feels that the multimedia should be integrated into the regular services by the libraries. Even in advanced countries, libraries do not have a separate department or personnel responsible for multimedia products or services. For the past 2-3 years, use of electronic resources, particularly multimedia, in libraries has improved considerably. However, budget for multimedia products still seems to be less, but it is growing for bigger libraries situated in metropolitan cities.

Generally, for selecting multimedia products, libraries depend on retail stores displays, publisher's catalogues, reviews, advertisements, trade shows, demos, computer magazines and catalogues. The main type of multimedia products being sought in libraries are reference and educational. Other related categories include databases, electronic books, software and their training packages, entertainment, leisure, etc. Most of th'e libraries are using multimedia resources for reference service and instructional purpose. In this connection, a survey was undertaken by the author on the use of multimedia in Delhi libraries to have a clear picture of usage in Indian libraries particularly in Delhi. So far published results are not available in the literature. Overall, inspite of cost reduction in the multimedia hardware and software, use of the multimedia resources is limited to some of the national level institutions or organisations. However, the majority of the libraries are now setting up such facilities for their users.

After the availability of internet in a very large scale in the offices, libraries, and houses, multimedia has become more popular, with the result most of the decision makers/financial authorities are realising the importance of multimedia in the daily life and particularly in libraries. American Centre Library, British Council Libraries and a few other libraries in Delhi are having good number of *multimedia PCs* (MPCs) for using Internet and multimedia resources to their users.

LIMITATIONS OF MULTIMEDIA

Even though Multimedia systems have many advantages introducing such systems into offices, schools, colleges, universities, and homes is not easy task. The problems or limitations of multimedia technology are in two areas.

Technology

- The requisite hardware/software to setup a multimedia content creating facility is still very expensive and requires large investments.
- A wide range of multimedia software is not available to integrate, control, coordinate, manage and adapt different media for the latest human computer interfaces.
- There is a lack of support software facilitating the authoring, composition and production of multimedia content.
- Poor support technology in the area of, multimedia data and document storage and manipulation.
- Lack of proper search and pattern recognition capability for locating information from multimedia databases.
- Lack of software support technology for group decision making and cooperative work, especially in application of multimedia technology to cooperative decision making and work.
- Converting all the multimedia resources into digital multimedia and storing is difficult.
- Time being, there is no full-fledged established hardware/software multimedia technology solution for design and development of a large size realtime multimedia digital library.
- Existing distributed networks do not support real time multimedia services.

Skilled Manpower

- Lack of trained manpower for the development and management of multimedia databases
- Vast amount of work required to create an hour interactive multimedia content
- Good multimedia content creation requires multi-disciplinary disciplinary knowledge, multi-technological skills and experience.

The main barrier to the widespread use of multimedia technology is the absence of standardisation among the various platforms and between hardware and software. For the time being there is no full-strength application of the multimedia information system, however, several universities are working in exploiting the full strengths of multimedia, such as natural language processing, realtime A-V content retrieval along with text and date, and implementing such a system in a network environment.

The market is dominated by multimedia CD-ROMs, multimedia databases, reference tools, etc.

The effectiveness of these systems will depend on various factors such as well developed software programmes, information content and development of new information handling skills. The requirements of the effective management are the support of the senior manager, the professional qualifications, knowledge about IT technology, interpersonal skills and learning models and frameworks and how to use these new resources and to be effective in the information needs of an organisation.

APPLICATIONS OF MULTIMEDIA

Multimedia systems are being used for many purposes by different people in different organisations/offkes/environment. The main functions include media integration, storing, organisation and dissemination at different places in different ways. This chapter attempted in reviewing the use of multimedia for library and information services in various countries from the published literature.

Some of the general applications of multimedia are given below:

- Instruction/training and technical presentations
- Multimedia communications such as multimedia e-mail, personal conferencing, video phones, video conferencing, etc.
- Public information points/kiosks for libraries, museums, hospitals, tourists sites, monuments, etc.
- Medical information systems
- Multimedia databases, multimedia information banks
- Multimedia newsletters, multimedia books, other information resources
- Reference tools, *e.g.* Encyclopaedias, directories, etc.
- Archival systems
- Geographical information systems
- Electronic publishing and bookselling
- Point-of-sale displays,
- Product information catalogues
- Technical documentation, including engineering drawings, specifications, etc.
- Architectural information displays for example walk-through programmes for the new buildings or constructions/already constructed buildings/ monuments,

- Entertainment, leisure, home
- Exhibitions such as conferences, trade shows, new product, facilities, museums, libraries, etc.
- Interactive displays in museums, hospitals, libraries, etc.

Tourism is one of the industries that has exploited the full strength of multimedia for developing tourist information systems for public and libraries.

Glasgow Online is one of the best tourist information systems designed by the University of Strathclyde during 1989 using Hypercard software. Afterwards several commercial multimedia information products were introduced in the market.

BUILDING A MULTIMEDIA DIGITAL LIBRARY

Multimedia knowledge resources as document surrogates and as significant knowledge sources in a library needs no emphasis. In the present academic and special library setting the educational videos, instructional visual aids and audio learning resources form a significant collection. Time is fast catching up the world over that the traditional forms of collection development techniques and collection maintenance strategies need replacements with the upcoming trends in the profession.

Consequently, the traditional information service options are no longer acceptable to a large majority of the users or that there is a strong demand for newer forms of services which are not so familiar to the libraries. Libraries therefore are now forced to be friendly and familiarised themselves with all relevant and current popular multimedia formats.

As technology marches past at a tremendous pace, the traditional meaning and definitions of a library's collection range also undergo a great deal of change.

Interactive and multimedia learning resources are one of the most rapidly changing and exciting areas of education in the world today. The recent entrants are computer-based training (CBTs) materials/Web-based training (WBTs) materials, especially interactive multimedia programmes that run on personal computers.

These new technologies offer students, teachers and researchers access to materials as never before. Multimedia can deliver large amounts of information in ways that make it manageable, approachable, and useful. And by making it possible to access illustrations and photographs, sound and video, as well as large amounts of text, interactive multimedia programmes present learning information to teachers, students, and scholars in newly engaging and meaningful ways.

The integration of multimedia programmes into libraries and classrooms promises not only to change the kinds of information that is available for learning, but the in which that learning takes place.

MULTIMEDIA COLLECTION: FEATURES, PROBLEMS AND PROSPECTS

Predominantly multimedia collection of a library comprise video resources (educative as well as entertainers), audio recordings, computer-based training materials (CBTs), Web-Based Training materials (WBTs), illustrations, photographs, etc. Depending on the nature of the parent institution's goals, academic focus, research thrust its resource allocations and financial capabilities, their collection strength may considerably vary. In most cases, the collection-building process of the multimedia resources may follow the normal traditional mode. In the case of e-Resources the purchase may be restricted to licensing and only online access to the product may be available to the library.

Publishers usually enforce stringent copyright and IPR restrictions to multimedia resources. Multimedia collection, especially the analogue knowledge resources, poses a variety of practical and operational constraints to libraries. One of the major limitations is their sole dependency on a host of gadgets such as media players, viewers, etc.

They also suffer from reach and visibility limitations as they can be viewed or listened to by a single or fewer number of viewers/listeners simultaneously. Further more, there are shortcomings with respect to resource discovery possibilities other than the basic indexing offered by their catalolgues (traditional as well as digital). Collection maintenance and long-term preservation of these special collections are always a concern for librarians. Multimedia resources in the newer breeds of media formats such as the CBTs, WBTs, digital videos/ audios, etc., have the added advantage of being dynamic and mobile with respect to their flexibility, portability and efficiency of access/dissemination. The current information environment also unequivocally prompts libraries to leverage on the latest digital technologies towards building multimedia digital libraries and in setting up dynamic electronic information systems.

These newer information services offer lots of power and visibility to libraries and the user community without compromising on their quality and performance. Yet, they also pose a multitude of problems in the course of their preparations while submitting them in a digital library. Swift developments in mediarelated technologies, rapid obsolescence and their redundancy, time-to-time media and format migrations, resource intensive maintenance, etc., add up the complexity and complications of these collections. This chapter attempts to share the IIMK experience in developing, implementing and maintaining the multimedia collection as a part of its digital library development activities which comprise the entire publication types, formats and media.

OPEN SOURCE PHILOSOPHY OF IIMK

IIMK is an ardent proponent of the Open Access and the Open Source Software philosophies which is sweeping the world now. It was a chosen decision not to go in for a proprietary software for its digital library applications. Accordingly we evaluated some of the popular Open Source Software for digital libraries, which were in use internationally. 'Dienst', 'Eprints', 'Fedora', 'Greenstone', etc., were the candidates for the preferred software. Obviously Greenstone outscored the group and we formally adopted the software for creating the IIMK digital library (Greenstone). The Greenstone Digital Library Software (GSDL) is a top of the line and internationally renowned Open Source Software system for developing digital libraries, promoted by the New Zealand Digital Library project research group at the University of Waikato, headed by Dr. Ian H. Witten, and is sponsored by the UNESCO [Witten]. Greenstone software (versions starting from 2.30) along with Java Run Time Environment (JRE) were deployed for the purpose. The software suite is available at the open source directory 'Sourceforge' [Sourceforge].

DIGITAL LIBRARY AT IIMK

The primary objective of the IIMK digital library was to enhance the digital collection in a substantial way, by strategically sourcing digital materials, conforming to copyright permissions, in all possible standards/formats so that scalability and flexibility is guaranteed for the future and advanced information services and are assured to the user community right from beginning.

The digital library was planned in such a way that it would integrate and aggregate the existing collections and services with an outstanding user interface. Accordingly, necessary strategies were adopted towards working out the digital library system.

This implied that the digital library system should have a strong collection interface capable of embracing almost all the popular digital standards, digital formats and software platforms, in line with the underlying digital library technologies in vogue. This was crucial in the case of multimedia integration, which was again important as it was planned to host a digital audio and video library as part of the core library collection.

The Digital Library Project at IIMK took off during September 2001. The first few months were mainly devoted to infrastructure build-up such as hardware and software, digitisation strategies, strategies regarding collection building, and finalisation of the variety of content categories. Since, the campus intranet and the Internet connectivity were robust, there were no worries on those fronts. The IIMK DL was slated to be populated with e-Books, ('born digital' as well as digitised), e-Journals, management cases, technical reports, working papers, faculty publications, teaching notes, CBTs, WBTs, educational videos/audios, value adding the existing OPAC, speeches, presentations, etc. It took around two/three months for us to install and get proper command over the software. The collection comprises multiple digital formats such as HTML, XML, PDF, PS, RTF, JPG, CIF, MPEG, etc.

The DL has now got a sizable collection of over 500 e-Books covering almost all areas of business and management, literature, classics, and Information Technology.

Cross collection pointers were given to project Gutenberg (classics and literature) and to other GSDL example collections (social science, environmental science) and hence, the virtual collection strength is over 15000 e-Books. IIMK has plans to host the IIM Consortium (led by the six IIMs in India) digital archive and studies are underway on the feasibility of putting the IIM Consortium digital content under Greenstone (IIM Consortium).

A rigourous collection development drive is being worked out with most of the popular electronic publishers specialising in business and management. One of the major bottlenecks to the speedy collection development is the non-availability of proprietary and trade literature in Greenstone acceptable formats such as HTML, Word, or PDF. Most of these publishers put their materials in their own proprietary e-Book reader formats, from which the text extraction becomes almost impossible.

RESOURCE DISCOVERY

Leading edge technical skills and technology backing on campus demand sophisticated human resource requirements and high-end IT infrastructure. The quality and performance of a digital library is measured in terms of its information retrieval logistics. Multimedia digital libraries also indeed require the strong footings of Resource Description Framework (RDF) vision supplemented with descriptive metadata standards such as Dublin Core, Metadata Object Description Schema (MODS) or Metadata Encoding and Transmission (METS). They also need the strength of Extensible Markup Language (XML) encoding schemas, related Document Type Definitions (DTDs) and Extensible Stylesheet Language (XSL) transformations between the non-traditional datastreams and the Hypertext Markup Language (HTML) front-end.

MULTIMEDIA DIGITAL LIBRARY WORKFLOW METHODOLOGY

One of the salient features of this collection is that the multimedia digital library is carved exclusively out of open source software (except for the media conversion utility) and open digital library standards. The untiring support and hard work of the IIMK's Digital Library team in the Library and the Computer Center need special mention.

COLLECTION STRATEGY

The videos/audios multimedia collection was planned as a 'metadata' collection. The digital objects (video file) were stored in a separate media server so that the digital library server is not overloaded or overburdened. Hyperlinks were given to the Streaming Server where the audio/video objects were kept in JPEG format.

SOFTWARE AND STANDARDS

As discussed earlier, the Greenstone Digital Library Software (GSDL) was deployed for the digital library application. "PlayTV-USB-Pro" software was used for converting the analog videos to digital files. Videos were first converted to AVI files and subsequently made to JPEG format. "Unreal Media Server" software was used for streaming the videos from the media server. "Streaming Media Player" software was given with all the retrieved pages for the users to download and stream/view the file. Each Video file was built as an HTML embedded page and XML was used for metadata encoding purposes. "Dublin Core" was the metadata standard used.

DUBLIN CORE METADATA AND XML TAGGING

To create indexes for section and sub-section (document hierarchy and structuring) in Greenstone the document should be in HTML format. Obviously now the Source File has to be edited as a HTML file structure.

For the section and sub-sections, the source file has to be edited appropriately, giving XML tags passed as comments in the body of the HTML file. Unqualified version of Dublin Core Metadata standard was deployed for resource description of the multimedia digital library. The Section Tagging pattern used for the video collection is given in fig.

```
<Section> <Description>

<Metadata name="Title"><a HREF="ums:\\TCP:streamserver:5119\video\V83.mpg">l. 20
        Steps to better management : Solving problems and thinking creatively(NEIF)
        V201 </a></Metadata>
<Metadata name="Subject" mode="accumulate"><font size=l>
        Creativity<Ifont><JMetadata>
<Metadata name="Subject" mode="accumulate"><font size=l >Strategic
        Management</font></Metadata>
<Metadata name="Subject" mode="accumulate"><font size=l>
        Strategy</font></Metadata>
<Metadata name="Subject" mode="accumulate"><font size=1> Innov
        ation</font></Metadata>
<Metadata name="Subject" mode="accumulate"><font size=l ><Ifont></Metadata> <Metadata
        name="Publisher" mode="accumulate"><font size=l> NEIF</font></Metadata>
<Metadata name="Resource Identifier" mode="accumulate"><font size=1> V 201
        </font></Metadata>
<Metadata name="Source" mode="accumulate"><font size=l>
        </font>NEIF</Metadata>

</Description> </Section>
```

Fig. XML based Section Tagging of Dublin Core Metadata.

Unreal Media Server is an open source server software which ensures efficient multimedia deliver over the network, LAN as well as WAN. UMediaServer is a streaming server for Windows operatin systems.

Unreal scores high over its proprietary counterparts such as Microsoft and Real, with it efficiency in streaming high quality content.

SYSTEM ARCHITECTURE

Transmission Control Protocol (TCP), Hypertext Transfer Protocol (HTTP) and Real Transpo] Protocol (RTP) and Multicast transport protocols are used for streaming content from Media Server t clients. Incoming content is not stored on the client computer's hard disk and the user is not allowe to save media locally, thus author's rights are fully protected. User authentication and access restriction enable trusted access to media resources. User logging provides the means to track user activity. For the client workstations, Unreal Media Player client software was provided. The System Architectur of the multimedia digital library is given in fig.

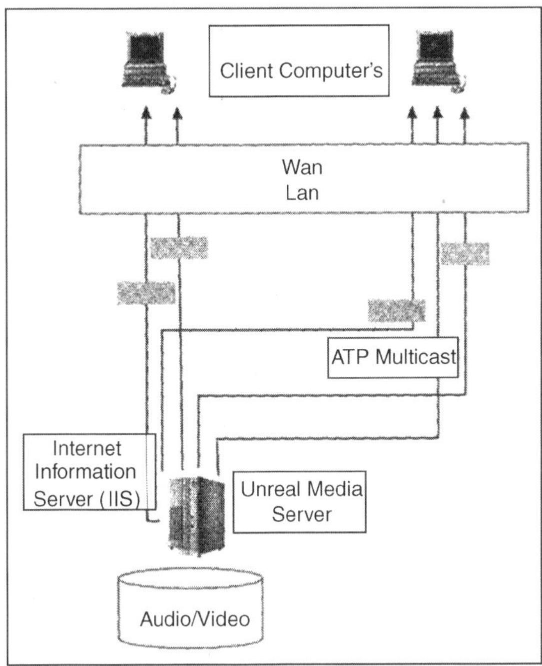

Fig. System Architecture of the Multimedia Digital Library.

CREATING LINKS TO MEDIA RESOURCE

While setting up the Streaming Media Player it registers a custom URL protocol on the user's machine. This is a UMS protocol, allowing launching Streaming Media Player directly from the hyperlink on the web page. Though the most comfortable way for the users to access remote media is to click on a link in the Web browser, for this application we gave the hyperlink embedded in the Dublin Core metadata element 'title' as follows:

```
<Metadata name="Title"><a HREF="ums:\\TCP: streamserver:5119\video
\V83.mpg">1. 20 Steps to better management: Solving problems and
thinking creatively (NEIF) V201</a></Metadata>
```

In the Metadata Tag, 'UMS' is the custom protocol of the UMediaServer Software. Streaming is achieved using the 'TCP' protocol. 'Streamserver' is the media server holding the multimedia digital objects. TCP's default port '5119' is the port utilised. For HTTP, default 80 is the port specified. Using Media Server Configuration tool, you can create virtual folders and map them to the different physical locations on the server machine.

Alternatively, the physical location can be anywhere in the server machine's LAN. 'Video' is the folder where the digital videos are located and 'V83.mpg' is the object being streamed to the client.

ACCESS METHODS

The multimedia collection is one of the important and appreciated services of the IIMK Library Portal. Users are able to visit the multimedia digital library and select the videos/audios of their choice by browsing alphabetically or by searching the author, title/free text, keyword, source or publisher. The Dublin Core metadata description facilitates efficient subject approach to information retrieval of the important resources with fanciful titles too, such as 'Eye of the Beholder', 'Just in Time' etc. Retrieval of cross collection resources is another special feature which is seldom achieved through traditional methods. The digital library at IIMI< has been able to strike great impact amongst the user community on campus. The academic quality of the resources coupled with flexibility, convenience and efficiency of access across the entire campus are the major reasons for this scenario. User education and product orientation sessions held at regular intervals by the library, both online as well as live, have paid rich dividends in the increased awareness and resource utility. The usage and usability of the digital resources have increased extensively as per server logs and monitoring statistics. The multimedia collection now streams out over hundreds of world-class educational videos, as well as audio resources.

The distinction of this work is that it has used only open source digital library softwares and open digital library standards across the entire workflow and operations. This has significant impact and implications as the proprietary softwares and standards are exorbitantly expensive and beyond the reach of most of the academic and special libraries in developing countries.

MULTIMEDIA/HYPERMEDIA

Multimedia is a combination of some or all forms such as text, data, images, photographs, animation, audio and video, which are converted from different formats into a uniformat digital media and is delivered by computers. Unlike the analogue media the digital media which allows users to manipulate according to the needs, use at their pace, and interact at any point of the programme.

When a multimedia programme is developed in a hypertext environment, the resulting product is called 'hypermedia'. *So* multimedia would then be a part of the hypermedia. All hypermedia products are multimedia products but not vice versa. The basic difference between hypermedia and multimedia is in the organisation and linkages of the information fragments. The information chunks/fragments in multimedia are organised linearly whereas in hypermedia, these are organised Non-linearly with links to each other.

The main elements of the multimedia are:

- *Text*: Information about an object/event, etc; notes, captions, subtitles, contents, indexes, dictionaries, and help facilities.
- *Data*: Tables, charts, graphs, spreadsheets, statistics, and raw data.
- *Graphics*: Both traditional and computer, generated such as drawings, prints, maps, etc.
- *Photographic images*: Negatives, slides, prints.
- *Animation*: Including both computer generated, video, etc.
- *Audio*: Including speech and music digitised from cassettes, tapes, CDs, etc.
- *Video*: Either converted from analogue film or entirely created within a computer.

A multimedia system records, processes, stores and delivers all types of information in binary code the same way as a computer does. This is quite different from the traditional analogue technology of radio, TV, A-V tapes, gramophone records, or the combination of digital audio and analogue video in interactive video discs. The main advantage of a digital format is the flexibility in combining, transmitting, manipulating and customising the elements of the multimedia according to the needs of the user. Basically, a multimedia system with have a powerful PC with high-end graphics processor, a sound card, CD drive, and multimedia extensions and drivers for playing digital audio and video.

Nowadays, major systems that are used for desktop multimedia design include IBM's PS/2, Apple's PowerMac, Commodore's Amiga, NeXT's Nextstation Colour, and Silicon Graphics IRIS Indigo. There are a wide variety of application software commercially available for all computer platforms. The most popular and inexpensive among all these are the Hypercard on Mac, and ToolBook on PC compatibles.

On the other hand, there are a number of authoring packages for high-end multimedia design. The popular ones include Macromedia's Director for both Mac and PC platforms and Icon Author for PC. Hypercard is a popular Hypermedia toolkit for Mac and is being used extensively in libraries for designing various applications during post 1980s and early 1990s.

MULTIMEDIA LIBRARY INFORMATION KIOSKS/WALK-THROUGH PROGRAMMES

Improving accessibility to both collections and services has always been a concern of libraries. Several libraries made attempts to create plans and guides to help users. In this connection, multimedia is one of the best tools for creating electronic library guides or web library guides or electronic tours for their users. Many libraries in the US and Europe have started using hypermedia for designing library walk-through programmes for their users.

Reference service is one of the most visible services that can be provided by these systems. 1.1 one study, it was found that 44 per cent of reference questions were directional, 18 per cent were instructional, 32 per cent actual reference and 6 per cent were extended reference. In another study, it was found that 34 per cent of the queries are actual reference and 66 per cent are directional. So, Librarians designed Hypermedia Library information Kiosks for their users to provide quick reference and redeployed the reference staff in other library activities. Andruss Library Hypercard tour is one such hypermedia walk-through programme designed for library users to provide ready made reference. This programme does not tell the users where to find books on a specific topic, one has to still use the online or card catalogues which are briefly explained in this system, and also it is not an index to periodical or newspaper articles. However, these are described and their locations are given in this tour programme.

The Andruss Library has two catalogues for library material: a card catalogue for books, phone records, tapes, maps, and music scores; and a computerised catalogue called PALS. This tour programme helps the users by giving all the basic information that the library users require to use PALS. Sweet Briar College Library's Hvpermedra walk-through programme is another of this kind designed for the staff and students to provide information about the collection, catalogue, archives, services, and locations of various collections and responsible persons of various library services showing on the floor layout.

Some other important examples of multimedia library guide web library guides/electronic tours are:

- Electronic Library Guide in the University of Birmingham's main library, created 'using ToolBook
- Guide to South Bank University's Centenary Library, developed with HyperCard
- Guide to the Dickens House Museum Library, designed using Guide
- Multimedia Database of Tourist information developed using HyperCard by the Public Library of Gateshead Libraries and Arts Service
- Guide to the Edinburgh University Computer Services, designed using Guide
- Multimedia Library Tour of the Wayne State University Library, designed using HyperCard
- Multimedia Library Tour of the Sweet Briar College Library, designed using HyperCard

- Drexel Disk is a hypermedia walk-through programme to the Drexel University students, designed using Hypercard
- Multimedia Library Kiosk of the Defence Science Library, DESIDOC, designed using Hypercard.

INSTRUCTION/TRAINING

The role of multimedia in instruction has been well documented in several research experiments done in various discipline. So, librarians have started using multimedia as a tool to train their staff in the new library technologies/ applications and also to the users to provide training about using library resources. The main advantage of using multimedia for training is its interactivity Hence,, it is being used by several schools, colleges, and universities for designing individualised library instructional packages for providing training to their users and also to provide in-depth subject training to their staff. The Paul Leonard Library at San Francisco State University desrgned a multimedia-based instructional programme on library skills to teach their users. This package is intended to serve as a prototype For subject tutorials using computing technology. This was integrated in the library skills modules being developed by the HyperCard Library Instructional Project. University of Tennessee, Knoxville libraries have made another hypermedia-based *computer-based training* (CBT) package for their new staff. To make this training more interesting, they have used pictures, animation, sound and graphics and iniplemented on Mac platform. The training programme covers library services, online catalogue, orientation to the libraries, circulation policy, access to journals literature, preservation of library materials, introduction to reference work, using e-mail, technical services, integrated online systems for libraries, and acquisition and processing library material's.

A few multimedia-based CAI packages designed using HyperCard used for library staff training/instruction are:

- *Illuminate* - a Multimedia-based CAI project about the University of Minnesota Library's OPACs.
- *Tour of the Internet* - a quick tour about the Internet
- *Information Access* - a library research skills tutorial for the university students
- *Hypercard-basedAACR2* - a self teaching CAI package for preparing catalogue cards
- *Hypercard-based University of Hawaii OPAC tutorial*
- *CatSkills* - an interactive Multimedia package to teach AACR2. It is a good professional training tool for students, beginners in cataloguing and working librarians. This multimedia CD is available in both Mac and Windows platforms. The Library Association, London is marketing this tool for $495

- *UGE 100 Library Skills* - designed by the Wayne State University Library
- *Teaching Mini Medline* - a training tool for Library users
- *STAR (Student Tutorial Access and Resources)* - CAI package designed for OSU Libraries
- *Hypermedia-based CBT package* for training the new staff of University of Tennessee, Knoxville libraries

SELF-LEARNING TOOLS

For people who need practical education in areas such as home ownership, vehicles repairing, etc, the multimedia CD-ROMs are a good medium for presenting the nuts-and-bolts tasks required to keep the house/machine functioning. For example, the House Repair Encyclopaedia provides a thorough compendium of well-illustrated repair guidelines, covering essential tasks such as stopping water leak, performing electrical wiring, pouring concrete, fixing a roof and patching the damaged walls and ceilings. Individual tasks are' depicted in animation, sound, video and providing far better information than the static pages of a book. The lnternet Resource Guide is an online book about lnternet that describes the various services available on it. Similarly many more commercial multimedia self learning tools are available in the market. Some of the important training applications available in libraries are National Geographic's Animal Samplings, ABC Golf, Music Data City, Cartoon Jukebox and Magic Flute, etc. These are self learning tools that any library can purchase and provide free education/instruction to their library users. The linking capabilities of hypertext with multimedia provides an ideal learning environment for foreign languages. Addition of graphics, photographs, music, speech and video play a lot of impact on the learner's interest, speed of learning and retaining of information in their brain. Several popular multimedia packages were' designed for learning most of the European languages by foreigners, such as Think and Talk French/Spanish/German and Introduction to Russian and Chinese, etc.

DIGITAF/ELECTRONIC LIBRARIES

Digital libraries are basically decentralised and easily extensible, able to support interoperability between different tools, applications and systems; support heterogeneity both in terms/forms of data and systems/tools supported; able to support a rich information seeking environment; and scaleable in terms of the size of the system. Digital information may include digital books, scanned images, graphics, data, digitised A-V clips, etc.

The first *Digital Libraries* (DL) project initiative was started, in 1995 in the following Universities in USA:

- University of Illinois Urbana-Champaign,
- Carnegie-Mellon University,
- Stanford University,

- University of California at Berkeley,
- University of California at Santa Barbara and
- University of Michigan.

Later on several organisations/universities/libraries in different countries started such projects. In the UK, an important DL projects were started by British Library is ELINOR-Electronic Library Project of De Montfort University, University of East Anglia, University of Bath, University College London, University of Wales, University of Ulster and University of Surrey. Some Digital Library related projects are listed below:

- IBM Digital Library provides a hardware/software solution for the libraries to develop their own multimedia digital libraries or multimedia archival systems. It is an integrated system for capturing, indexing, storage and retrieval of tabular, textual, audio, still images, and video data at compressed and full resolutions. A search engine that can combine parametric queries, free text searches, and Query by Image Content. Workflow processing to manage approvals and routing of data is also provided. !t has an integrated rights management including electronic watermarking, encryption, licensing, accounting, metering, and authentication. It is scaleable storage and network management system that allows libraries to grow without sacrificing the convenience of anytime, anywhere access. It also provides a hierarchical storage system to protect the assets from loss and ensure fast access to most frequently used media. A world-wide web client that facilitates the multi-search capability and delivers ranked results. This system has an integrated frame-accurate VTR control of continuous media. IBM Digital Library provides a way for libraries and users of content to store and retrieve multimedia information along with textual information that describes it. Regardless of who the end user is, IBM Digital Library allows the users to capture information and images quickly, find them when needed, and build them into new products quickly, whether it is today's broadcast, a new multimedia CD-ROM, magazine, or Internet product.

Some other important Digital Library:
Initiative projects and their site information.

- The Networked Computer Science Technical Reports Library - a collection of computer science technical reports from CS departments and industrial and government research laboratories.
- The Networked Digital Library of Theses and Dissertations - a project which aims to increase the availability of theses and dissertations by placing them online with the content in an accessible form. The works may be accessed through the Electronic Thesis and Dissertation Library.

- Library Without Walls - a broad based digital library project to make information available to researchers on their desktops on a network environment.
- Thesaurus Linguarum Hiberni - an interactive on-line searchable database archive of literary and historical materials in the various languages of early, mediaeval and modern Ireland.
- The Perseus Project - a collection on ancient Greek and Roman world. Perseus contains texts in Greek and its translation.
- The RYHINER - consists of more than 15,000 maps, charts, plans and views from the 16th to the 18th century, covering the whole globe.
- Project Bartleby - a public library on the Internet.
- Digital Libraries - a collection papers discussing digital libraries and their research efforts.
- The Visible Human Project - a complete, anatomically detailed, three dimensional representations of the male and female human body.
- National Digital Library the American 'Memory project, Special American Collections at the LC and Country Studies.
- Digital Library Programme at Tilburg University is to provide staff and students with excellent support facilities for teaching, learning and research.

MULTIMEDIA DATABASES

Now-a-days a large number of photographs, artifacts, audio recordings and textual $material in various collections are available in libraries. Multimedia is helping the librarians in integrating all the information from various forms/sources subject-wise and making meaningful multimedia databases both for day-to-day use and archiving. Mendocino County Library, Ukiah has developed a multimedia database of historical and cultural information that is relevant to the Californian Indians in that area. In addition to the historical photographs, this database is also having parts of oral histories from the state and local archives. Ultimately this library is trying to bring out a CD-ROM on 'Gathering together a Native American History'. Ancient Biblical Manuscript Centre in Claremont; California has ancient texts, photographs, negatives, related to the Bible. This centre has undertaken an ambitious programme 'Dead Sea Scroll Imaging Project', which involves digitising and reformatting photographic negatives for the past four years. The Centre has converted this collection into a comprehensive digital library and it has sophisticated search/sort enquiries on Dead Sea Scrolls.

MULTIMEDIA INFORMATION RETRIEVAL SYSTEM

Hypermedia Information Retrieval System (HIRS) is a hypertext version of a large and comprehensive annotated bibliography of hypertext/hypermedia information. Compiled from a variety of sources including periodicals, academic journals and online informational databases, it is intended for educational and training purposes only and no warranty is made as to the suitability of anything included in this stack for any specific purpose. HIRS was created in association with Project Rivendell, at the University of Toledo. Rivendell focuses on the application of hypertext/hypermedia research to address training and educational needs. It is an interdisciplinary centre for applied hypermedia research serving as the focal point for the collection, synthesis, evaluation, and dissemination of the most current research available for using hypermedia to solve instructional problems in a variety of learning settings. HyperKRS is another commercial package being used for developing hypermedia-based information retrieval systems.

MULTIMEDIA CATALOGUES

Interactive multimedia Catalogues are electronic forms of catalogues distributed in the mail-order catalogue market. Printed catalogues are one of the important information sources particularly in technical libraries. These catalogues consume large percentage of postal carrier bags. Today, the interactive multimedia catalogues offer a high volume of information on a small disk. Several international publishing companies are also bringing out their catalogues in interactive multimedia CD-ROMs. For example, CD-ROM Catalogue Shopping, SW. Catalogues, Macromedia Showcase, Silverplatter Directory of Electronic Resources, etc. Under the *Colorado Alliance of Research Libraries* (CARL) System, Denver Public Library has designed a Kid's Catalogue is for children. The Kid's Catalogue designed to capture the imagination and the natural curiosity of children and connect them with intellectual and emotional delights of information. This catalogue was designed in *graphical user interface* (GUI) using Hypercard software. It was found that this catalogue made a considerable impact on the children's usage of the library collection. The Hans Helgesen Elementary School Library, British Columbia, Canada have also developed a Hypercard-based school card catalogue for the school children. Hypercataloguer is a Hypercard-based cataloguing tool. It can take text, graphics, animation, audio and video information for preparing multimedia-based digital catalogues. Several libraries are using multimedia Catalogues and OPACS' in their libraries for various purposes.

MULTIMEDIA INFORMATION RESOURCES

The kinds of multimedia systems/information resources available in libraries and information centers include:

- CD-ROMs.
- Video discs.
- Laser discs.

- Audio 8 video cassettes.
- Web.
- Databases on servers.
- Digital video.

Many big publishers have now converted their reference books including, Encyclopaedias, dictionaries, handbooks, etc. from the traditional print form to multimedia format. Thus libraries have a choice of selecting either print or multimedia publications.

Some of the multimedia publications are listed below:

- *Encyclopaedias*:Crompton's lnteractive Encyclopaedia, 1998; Britannica CD 98 and Britannica Video CD; Encyclopaedia Americana 98; Grolier Multimedia Encyclopaedia, 1998; World Book Multimedia Encyclopaedia; Microsoft Encarta 98, etc.
- *Dictionaries and Directories*: Oxford English Dictionary; Webster English Dictionary; The Dictionary of Living World; National Geograpic's Mammals; British Birds; Microsoft Dinosatlrs, etc.
- *Reference Manuals*: MIT Movie Manual; interactive Graphics Documents; The Manual of Medical Therapeutics, etc.
- *Year Books*: The Guiness Disk of Records
- *Reference Book*s: Earth Quest; World Climate Disc; interactive Periodic Table, etc.
- *Electronic Books*: Manual of Medical Therapeutics; The Electronic Whole Earth Catalogue; Microsoft Musical Instruments; Introduction to Classical Music; The Oxford Textbook of Medicine on CD-ROM, etc.
- *Electronic Newspapers/Journals*: The Times/Sunday Times/The Guardian; Times, Newsweek; Multimedia Tech for Electronic Newspapers; Integrated Multimedia Environment; Music and Multimedia Publishing; ST and Medical Publishing for Electronic Delivery, etc.
- *Multimedia Fiction*: Nowadays several Multimedia fiction books/packages are available for all levels of people. For example, The Manhole, a children fiction takes the kids to a fantasy world with talking animals and dragons where magic bean stalks grow into the sky.

GEOGRAPHICAL INFORMATION SYSTEMS (GIS)

Additional multimedia information, visuals, audio and video can be associated along with landmarks and other points of interest in a Geographical Information system?. For example, GIs multimedia application in The National Capital Planning Commission (NCPC), Washington, DC, uses online video clips and images of buildings along with their maps. In India, Bangalore Online, is a multimedia GIS applications designed with Maplnfo software. Similarly Escorts,

India developed multimedia GIS for several cities in India. Number of commercial GIs reference tools are available in the market for libraries for their ready reference..

ELECTRONIC PUBLISHING

The emergence of CD-writers and recordable CDs has solved some of the problems at the libraries in storing/archiving their less used materials. Multimedia tools along with CD-writers made possible in publishing information from different sources in a most easy to use and acceptable form to the library users. Now several big libraries started publishing their special collections, image databases, OPACs, etc on multimedia CD-ROMs. It is one of the most viable alternatives to paper-based publishing.

MULTIMEDIA ARCHIVAL SYSTEM

Multimedia Archival System are mostly developed by the national museums, publishing houses, movie production companies, etc. The Design Museum located in Butler's Wharf in London has stored information regarding 250 artifacts, 40 designers, 25 manufactures and 11 monuments on Mac using Hypercard. The museum of London has over *3* million archaeological files on 7 gigabite storage space. Similarly ABC News has a very large size Mac-based video archival library for developing hypermedia applications. Project Jukebox is another Hypercard-based multimedia archival system for archiving multimedia information resources in the library.

MULTIMEDIA USE IN MUSEUM LIBRARIES

Multimedia systems allow images, sounds and text to be combined in imaginative new ways to be transmitted in digitised formats and to be stored and reproduced or networked for wide public access and use. To accelerate the multimedia digitalisation of collections, to ensure their accessibility to the public and to stress its value as a learning resource for schools and universities. Global co-operation will help museums and galleries to increase public interest in their collections and to exploit their resources for the benefit of further enrichment.

The target users will be students, teachers, researchers, general public as well as curators and the end-users of the multimedia services provided by museums and galleries. Many American, European and Indian libraries are already using Multimedia in their libraries for providing information services to their users and interactive museums displays.

Examples of Indian multimedia museum guides are:

- An interactive Multimedia guide of the National Museum of Natural History designed using Director

- An interactive Multimedia guide of the National Rail Museum designed using ToolBook.

CALL NUMBER DIRECTORIES

A Call Number Directory programme was designed using Macintosh's Hypercard at the Science and Engineering Library. The Science and Engineering Library houses materials pertaining to the life and physical sciences, computing, mathematics, and nursing on seven floors. This programme helps the users in locating the information and also the physical locations of the books in different floors showing the pictures of those floors, stacks, etc.

MULTIMEDIA TRENDS IN LIBRARY AND INFORMATION SERVICES

After the introduction of e-mail and internet in libraries, use of information in digital form has increased many folds. There is a considerable change in-libraries in their acquisition of library collection, organisation and providing services to users. The prospects for the development of a multimedia market have been transformed in the past two years by the explosive emergence of the internet and the digital revolution in the converging, IT, telecoms and entertainment sectors.

There will be major changes in distribution networks and the implications of multimedia on the economy will be profound. The Internet has shown that there is a huge market for multimedia applications. The most exciting developments will come. from what is known as networked multimedia-the distribution of information using both telecommunication and broadcast technologies.

It is currently multimedia packages/products such as CD-ROMs and hand-held videogames-which are the favoured methods of distributing multimedia, mainly because communications networks cannot deliver the same level of functionality. However networks are rapidly being upgraded to distribute graphics, sound and video and should soon take over from packaged multimedia. Products which can be transmitted digitally such as CDs and books are already facing major challenges. Paper publishing may never be completely replaced by electronic distribution but the cost savings for content producers may be too large to ignore. Value in the multimedia market will move away from infrastructure provision, where the network operators are strong, towards service provision and packaging which require innovation and new skills for libraries and information services. Consequently, new types of companies are poised to wrench control of the multimedia market from the network operators who will have to act quickly to gain the skills necessary to compete in the higher value areas of the market. Their alternative is to be left with high volume, but low profitability infrastructure provision.

CONCLUSION

Now many inexpensive hypermedia software are available in the market for Macs and PCs. The cost of both the hardware and software are also going down considerably. However, in India, introduction of computers and latest technologies such as multimedia, CD-ROMs, etc., is limited to the big and affluent libraries in the metropolitan cities only. It may be due to the unawareness of these technologies, insufficient funds, lack of skilled manpower, etc. Unless all the Indian Library Schools introduce the latest,technologies in their: syllabi and the teachers get trained, it will not be possible to change the present scenario of the libraries.

Multimedia is a boon to the libraries, it is up to the Indian librarians how they use it in their libraries to improve the services. DESIDOC has designed a Multimedia Library information Kiosk for its user. Similarly others can also start designing for their libraries. Since, it is proven technology, it is up to Indian librarians/libraries to implement these technologies in their libraries and make optimum use to improve the user services as early as possible. In this information technology society, the future users require to access a variety of multimedia information sources in a manner that is simple, easy, and independent of time, place and subject discipline, for the purpose ranging from augmenting and refreshing memory, to learning, decision-making, and creating or uncovering new knowledge. The time is not too far in this cyber world and all these dreams will be realities in the coming 21st century.

3

Information Retrieval in Library Science

In the early and mid-1950s, a critical mass of scientists, engineers, librarians, and entrepreneurs started working enthusiastically on the problem and solution defined by Bush. By 1960s this became a large and relatively well-funded effort and organized activity. Often, there were heated arguments and controversies about the "best" solution, technique, or system.

These arguments brought on the tradition of evaluation, a major staple of IR research and development. What is now TREC started with Cranfield evaluations in the late 1950s and early 1960s. Remarkably, the basic evaluation principles developed then are still the underpinning of TREC today. Calvin Mooers, an active and highly visible pioneer of information science, coined the term *information retrieval* in 1951. The term took hold, and today is a part of the English language.

At that time, Mooers not only coined the term, but also defined the problems to be addressed:

> "Information retrieval embraces the intellectual aspects of the description of information and its specification for search, and also whatever systems, techniques or machines that are employed to carry out the operation.

Today, we would add that IR also and particularly involves interaction in all of these, with all the contextual-cognitive, affective, situational—aspects that interaction embraces. An expanded Mooers' conception is still valid. As it advanced, IR produced a number of theoretical, empirical, and pragmatic concepts and constructs. Numerous IR systems were developed and successfully deployed.

A great many historical examples can be given to illustrate the remarkable evolution of IR systems and techniques, adapting the ever-evolving information technology, from punch cards in the midcentury to the Internet at its close. Based on IR, an online information industry emerged in the 1970s, and grew through its own version of information explosion, as chronicled by Hahn. IR is one of the most widely spread applications of any information system worldwide. It has a proud history. Surely, information science is more than IR, but many of the problems raised by IR or derived from objects and phenomena involved in IR, are at its core.

Approaches and Paradigm Split

The approach taken by Mooers was to concentrate on the building of systems. This systems emphasis which was formulated early in the 1950s, was the sole approach to IR for some decades. It still predominates in a good part of IR research to this day.

Consequently, most of the IR research and practice concentrated on retrieval systems and processes. However, starting in the late 1970s and gaining steam in the 1980s, a different line of reasoning and research evolved-one that concentrates on the cognitive, interactive, and contextual end of the process. It addressed users, use, situations, context, and interaction with systems, rather than IR systems alone as a primary focus.

The retrieval cluster started splitting into subclusters, as noted by White and McCain, and before by others such as Saracevic and Harter. We now have two distinct communities and approaches to research in the retrieval cluster. They became commonly known as *systems-centred* and *user-centred.* Both address retrieval, but from very different ends and perspectives. The split is not only conceptual, looking very differently at the same process, but also organizational. The systemscentered side is now mostly concentrated in the *Special Interest Group on Information Retrieval* (SIGIR) of the *Association for Computing Machinery* (ACM), while the user-centered cluster congregates around the *American Society for Information Science* (ASIS).

Each has its own communication outlets-journals, proceedings, and conferences. There is less and less overlap of authors and works between the two outlets. We have two camps, two islands, with, unfortunately, relatively little traffic in-between. The systems-centered approach is exemplified by work on algorithms and evaluation based on the traditional IR model, a model that does not consider the users or interaction. The massive research that evaluates a variety of IR algorithms and approaches within TREC is a culmination of this approach.

In contrast, cognitive, situational, and interactive studies and models, involving the use of retrieval systems exemplify the human-centered approach. Following that approach, interactive models, differing significantly from the traditional IR model, started to emerge. Even in TREC, a group of researchers started an interaction track, but so far have a hard time conceptually and methodologically, thus demonstrating the difficulty in merging the traditional and interactive models and approaches. Let me characterize, in a simplified way, the relationship between the two approaches or subclusters addressing different sides of retrieval. On the one hand, the human-centred side was often highly critical of the systems side for ignoring users and use, and tried valiantly to establish humans as the proper center of IR work. The mantra of human-centred research is that the results have implications for systems design and practice. Unfortunately, in most human-centred research, beyond suggestions, concrete design solutions were not delivered. On the other hand, the systems side, by and large, ignores the human side and user studies, and is even often completely ignorant of them. As to design, the stance is "tell us what to do and as suggested, do it." But nobody is really telling, or if telling, nobody is listening.

As a rule, in systems-oriented projects, people and users are absent. Thus, there are not many interactions between the two camps. Let me provide some examples. A rough analysis of the 1997 SIGIR proceedings found only 3 papers of some 34 that dealt in some way with people and users; in the ACM's Digital Libraries 1997 conference proceedings, of 25 papers only 3 mentioned people and users. If one reads authors such as Dervin and Nilan, and many of their successors, who champion the human centered approach, one gets the impression that there is a real conflict between the two sides and approaches, and that there is an alternative way to the "dreadful" systems approach.

In a way, this stance is a backlash caused by the excesses, failures, and blind spots of systems-centered approaches not only in IR, but also in great many other technological applica-tions. Unfortunately, sometimes the backlash is justified. All of us who work on the humancentered side are not that dismissive of the systems side. But the issue is not whether we should have systems-*or* humancentered approaches. The issue is even less of human*versus* systems-centered. *The issue is how to make human*and *systems-centered approaches work together.* In this sense, a number of works have addressed integrating usercentered and systems-centered approaches in IR, but this has been discussed mostly by researchers from the usercentered side.

Examples are works by:

- Bates,
- Belkin,
- Cool,
- Stein,
- Thiel,
- Fidel
- Efthimidiadis,
- Robertson and
- Beaulieu.

To reiterate, it is not one camp against the other but how can we incorporate the best features of both approaches and make them work jointly. The issue is how to deliver and incorporate the desired design features that will improve systems orientations towards users, integrate them with systems features, and use advantages provided by both, humans and technology. In other words, the issue is *putting the human in the loop* to build better algorithms and to exploit computational advantages. Real progress in information science, and by extension in IR, will come when we achieve this. Lately, the NSF has championed human-centered design involving an interdisciplinary approach to information systems. Hopefully, this will go beyond rhetoric. It is not easy to do. But, that is what research is for—to address difficult, not only easy problems.

Proprietary IR

By the 1980s, the commercial information industry based on IR became successful and profitable. Out of academe, grants, and government, IR became a money-making propo-sition. This, of course, is another and important sign of success. Not surprisingly, a number of former IR researchers, practitioners, and graduates of IR programmes ventured out to become IR entrepreneurs.

Sure enough, throughout information science history there were many entrepreneurs, and they were highly significant in development of the field. But this generation of entrepre-neurs was different. They ventured to develop and market a variety of IR procedures based on algorithms, applicable and scalable to large files, multiple applications, and/or various advanced technologies. It was knowledge industry at its purest. But, as in all commercial knowledge industries, the product was proprietary. While it was not that hard to guess the base of these various proprietary algorithms and how they worked—after all they were derived from publicly available knowledge and experiences, such as those that came from SMART experi-ments—they remain unpublished and "secret."

A new kind of IR evolved, separate from the rest, not communicating as to intellectual advances with the rest. None of these ventures became a high commercial success, as measured by Silicon Valley standards. But the World Wide Web, emerging in the first half of the 1990s, changed all this. The acceleration of the growth of the Web is an information explosion of the like never before seen in history. Not surprisingly then, the Web is a mess. No wonder that everybody is interested in some form of IR as a solution to fix it.

A number of academic-based efforts were initiated to develop mechanisms, search engines, "intelligent" agents, crawlers, and so forth, to help control the Web. Some of these were IR scaled, and adapted to the problem; others were a variety of extensions of IR. Many had few, if any original, developments, besides new packaging or labeling; and a good number were just the usual hype. The wheel was reinvented a number of times. But out of this, and fast, came commercial ventures, such as the pioneering Yahoo!, whose basic objective is to provide search mechanisms for finding something of relevance for users on demand.

And to make a lot of money. These enterprises pride themselves on having proprietary methods by which they are accomplishing the retrieval tasks. The connection to the information science community is tenuous, and almost non-existent. The flow of knowledge, if any, is onesided, from IR research results into proprietary engines. The reverse contribution to public knowledge is zero. A number of evaluations of these search engines have been undertaken simply by comparing some results between them or comparing of their retrieval against some benchmarks. Some evaluations were done within, others outside of information science. Results were not complimentary. The Web-based proprietary IR is expanding and flourishing outside of the field. It is addressing a vexing problem, the like we have not seen before. But as yet, the success is elusive and questionable.

RELEVANCE

As information science pioneers developed IR processes and systems in the 1950s, they defined as the main objective retrieval of *relevant* information. Effectiveness was expressed in terms of relevance. From then to now, IR is explicitly geared not towards any old kind of information, but towards *relevant information*.

Various IR approaches, algorithms, and practices were, and still are, evaluated in relation to relevance. Thus, relevance became a key notion in information science. It is also a complex phenomenon with a long and turbulent history in information science transcending IR, going back to early 1950s. Of course, there was a choice.

Relevance did not have to emerge as the key notion. Uncertainty was one choice suggested by a number of theorists to be the base of IR, and thus to reflect effectiveness. But it did not take. In contrast, uncertainty is the basic notion underlying expert systems. If the pioneers had not embraced relevance, but instead, let's say, uncertainty, as the base for IR, we would have today a very different IR, and probably not that successful. In general, relevance, according to *Webster*, means having significant bearing on matter at hand. As with many other concepts, relevance assumes related but more specific meaning in more specific contexts and applications.

In the context of information science, relevance is the attribute or criterion reflecting the effectiveness of exchange of information between people and IR systems in communi-cation contacts based on valuation by people. With relevance as the criterion, and human judgements of relevance of retrieved objects as the measuring instrument, the measures of precision and recall are widely used in evaluation of IR systems. The strength of these measures is that they involve people—users—as judges of effectiveness of performance. The weakness is the same: it involves judgement by people, with all the perils of subjectivity and variability. Relevance indicates a relation. For relevance, many relations have been investigated.

An consensus has emerged in information science that we can distinguish between several differing relations that account for different manifestations or types of relevance:

- *System or Algorithmic Relevance:* Relation between a query and information objects in the file of a system as retrieved, or as failed to be retrieved, by a given procedure or algorithm. Comparative effectiveness in inferring relevance is the criterion for system relevance.
- *Topical or Subject Relevance:* Relation between the subject or topic expressed in a query and topic or subject covered by retrieved texts, or, more broadly, by texts in the system file, or even in existence. Aboutness is the criterion by which topicality is inferred.
- *Cognitive Relevance or Pertinence:* Relation between the state of knowledge and cognitive information need of a user and texts retrieved, or in the file of a system, or even in existence. Cognitive correspondence, infor-mativeness, novelty, information quality, and the like are criteria by which cognitive relevance is inferred.
- *Situational Relevance or Utility:* Relation between the situation, task or problem at hand and texts retrieved by a system, or in the file of a system, or even in existence. Usefulness in decision making, appropriateness of information in resolution of a problem, reduction of uncertainty, and the like are criteria by which situational relevance is inferred.
- *Motivational or Affective Relevance:* Relation between the intents, goals, and motivations of a user and texts retrieved by a system, or in the file of a system, or even in existence. Satisfaction, success, accomplish-ment, and the like are the criteria for inferring motivational relevance.

Practically, IR systems assess systems relevance only-that is, they respond to queries-hoping that the objects retrieved may also be of cognitive relevance, and even more so of utility. However, a user may judge an object by any or all types of relevance-for a user they may interact dynamically. Difficulties arise when an object is of system relevance but not of cognitive relevance or utility, or conversely.

If items are of cognitive relevance or utility, but were not reflected in the query, they are not and cannot be retrieved. At the bottom of IR research is a quest to align systems with other types of relevance. People all over have a strong intuitive understanding of relevance, thus, they intuitively understand, without manuals, what IR is all about. This makes IR systems generally understandable and acceptable-a critical attribute in their widespread application.

DISCIPLINARY RELATIONS

Two things introduced interdisciplinarity in information science. First and foremost, the problems addressed cannot be resolved with approaches and constructs from any single discipline-thus, intedisciplinarity is predetermined, as it is in many modern fields. Second, interdisciplinarity in information science was introduced and is being perpetuated to the present by the very differences in backgrounds of people addressing the described problems. Differences in background are many; they make for richness of the field and difficulties in communication and education. Clearly not every discipline in the background of people working on the problem made an equally relevant contri-bution, but the assortment was responsible for sustaining a strong interdisciplinary characteristic of information science. I will concentrate on interdisciplinary relations with two fields: librarianship and computer science. Obviously, other fields, most notably cognitive science and communication, have also interdisciplinary relations, but these are the most significant and developed ones.

Librarianship

Librarianship has a long and proud history devoted to organization, preservation, and use of graphic records and records in other media. This is done through libraries not only as a particular organization or type of information system, but even more so as an indispensable social, cultural, and educational institution whose value has been proven manifold throughout human history, and across all geographic and cultural boundaries.

Researcher defines the library as:

- . . .Contributing to the total communication system in society. . . Though the library is an instrumentality created to maximize the utility of graphic records for the benefits of society, it achieves that goal by working with the individual and through the individual it reaches society.

The common ground between library science and information science, which is a strong one, is in sharing of their social role and in their general concern with effective utilization of graphic and other records, particularly by individuals.

But there are also very significant differences in several critical respects, among them:

- *Selection of Problems Addressed and the Way they were Defined*: A majority of the problems were not and are not addressed in library science;
- *Theoretical Questions Asked and Frameworks Established*: The theories and conceptual frameworks in librarian-ship have no counterpart in information science, and *vice versa*;
- *The Nature and Degree of Experimentation and Empirical Development and the Resulting Practical Knowledge and Competencies Dderived*: There is very little overlap in experimentation and development between the two, and professional requirements differ as well to a significant degree;

- *Tools and Approaches Used:* A most telling example is the very different approach undertaken in relation to utilization of technology in IR and in library automation; and
- *The Nature and Strength of Interdisciplinary Relations Established and the Dependence of Progress on Inter-disciplinary Approaches*: Librarianship is much more selfcontained.

All of these differences warrant a conclusion that librarian-ship and information science are two different fields in strong interdisciplinary relations, rather than one and the same field, or one being a special case of the other. This is not a matter of turf battles, or of one being better or worse than the other. Such arguments, while common between many fields, matter little to progress of either field. But differences in selection and/or definition of problems addressed, agenda, paradigms, theoretical base, and practical solutions *do* matter. Thus the conclusion that librarianship and information science, while related, are different fields. The differences are most pronounced in the research agenda and directions.

Interestingly, research on OPACs, now that they are incorporating more and more IR features, is bringing the two fields in closer relation. Probably, so will the research in digital libraries, but at this time, it is too early to tell. The conclusion is not without heated controversy.

Among other authors, Vakkari contends on information science and librarianship being one and the same field, with the now commonly used name of "library and information science." Does it matter? Administratively yes, very much so, particularly in universities and professional societies. Otherwise, no. The issue is, and always will be, in the problems addressed and solutions undertaken. I contend that they differ significantly.

Computer Science

The basis of relation between information science and computer science lies in the application of computers and computing in IR, and the associated products, services, and networks. In the last few years, this relation also involves research on the evolving digital libraries, with their strong technological base.

To illustrate the connection, we use a definition by Denning:

- "The discipline of computing is the systematic study of algorithmic processes that describe and transfer information: their theory, analysis, design, efficiency, implementation, and application. The fundamental question underlying all of the computing is: "What can be automated?"

Computer science is about algorithms related to infor-mation interpreted in the first, whereas information science is about the very nature of information and its use by humans, interpreted in the third or broadest sense. Computer science is about symbol manipulation, whereas information science is about content manipulation, where symbol manipulation is the indispensable infrastructure. The two concerns are not in competition, they are complementary—they lead to different basic and applied agendas. Computer science is also many times larger than information science.

A number of computer scientists have been involved in research and development on information and its many spin-offs, to the point of being recognized leaders in information science. Gerard Salton is a prime example. In addition, there are several streams of research and development in computer science that had no connection with the early evolution of information science, but have addressed information problems similar to those in information science. Among others, these include works on expert systems, knowledge bases, hypertext, and human-computer interaction.

More recently, this involves research and development on digital libraries, a "hot", financially heavily supported area by a host of government agencies in the U.S. and many other countries. Bolstered by heavy support, interest in digital library research exploded on the scene in 1990s, attracting the attention of computer scientists from a wide variety of streams, as well as people from many other disciplines. These areas have a significant informational component that is associated with information representation, its intellectual organization, and linkages; meta-information, information seeking, searching, retrieving, and filtering; use, quality, value, and impact of information; evaluation of information systems from user and use perspective; and the like-all traditionally addressed in information science.

Conversely, these streams of computer science research and development provide a different outlook, framework, and approach, and even a different paradigm, not only for information science research and development, but also for its academic and continuing education. Again, as with librarianship, the issue is not about turf. It is about paradigms, theoretical foundations, and pragmatic solutions; and ultimately, it is about their appropriateness to human information problems.

EDUCATION

That education is critical for any field is a truism that hardly needs to be stated. In particular, research lives by education, it cannot be better than the education that researchers receive and then extend and plow back into education. Unfortunately, education in information science has not received the attention that it deserves. This may explain the many difficulties in the field that I have discussed. Educational models that evolved differed to a degree or even substantially from country to country. I am concentrating here on the U.S. models only.

In the United States, two educational models evolved over time. I call them the Shera and Salton models, after those that pioneered them. Both have strengths and weaknesses. Jesse H. Shera was a legendary library school dean from the 1950s until the 1970s at Western Reserve University. Among others, he was instrumental in starting the Center for Documentation and Communication Research in 1955. Shortly thereafter, the library school curriculum started to include courses such as "Machine Literature Searching" and several other more advanced courses and laboratories on the topics of research in the Centre.

The basic approach was to append those courses, mostly as electives, to the existing library school curriculum, without modifications of the curriculum as a whole, and particularly not the required core courses. Information science became one of the specialty areas of library science. The base or core courses that students were taking rested in the traditional library curriculum. Information science education was an appendage to library science. A few attempts to spin off information science as an independent degree and curriculum were not followed widely. But Shera's model was. Library schools in the U.S. and in many other countries imitated Shera's model.

They used the same approach and started incorporating information science courses in their existing curriculum as a specialty. Out of this was borne the current designation "library and information science." Shera's model is still the prevalent approach in schools of library and information science. The strength of the Shera model is that it posits education within a service framework, connects the education to professional practice and to a broader and user-oriented frame of a number of other information services, and relates it to a great diversity of information resources.

The weakness is a lack of a broader theoretical frame-work and a total lack of teaching of any formalism related to systems, such as development and understanding of algori-thms. The majority of researchers in the human-centered side, as I described earlier, came from or are associated with this educa-tional environment. Gerard Salton was first and foremost a scientist, a computer scientist, and the father of modern IR.

As such, he pioneered the incorporation into IR research a whole array of formal and experimental methods from science, as modified for algorithmic and other approaches used so successfully in computer science. His primary orientation was research. For education, he took the time-honoured approach of a close involvement with research. Salton's model was a laboratory and research approach to education.

As Shera's model resulted in information science educa-tion being an appendage to library science education, Salton's model of IR education resulted in it being a specialty of and an appendage to computer science education. Computer science students that were already well-grounded in the discipline, got involved in SMART and other projects directed by Salton, worked and did research in the laboratory, completed their theses in areas related to IR, and participated in the legendary IR seminars.

They also published widely with Salton and with each other, and participated with high visibility in national and international conferences. From Harvard and Cornell, his students went to a number of computer science departments where they replicated Salton's model. Many other computer science departments in the U.S. and abroad took the same approach.

The strength of Salton's model is that it:

"Starts from a base of a firm grounding in formal mathematical and other methods, and in algorithms, and

- Relates directly to research.

The weakness is in that it:

- Ignores the broader aspects of information science, as well as any other disciplines and approaches dealing with the human aspects that have great relevance to both the outcomes of IR research and the research itself, and
- Does not incorporate professional practice where these systems are realised and used. It loses users.

Consequently, this is a successful, but narrowly concen-trated education in IR as a specialty of computer science, rather then in information science. Not surprisingly, the researchers in the systems-centred approach came out of this tradition. The two educational approaches are completely independent of each other. Neither is connected to the other. Neither reflects fully what is going on in the field. While in each model there is an increase in cognizance of the other, there is no educational integration of the systems-and usercentered approaches.

The evident strengths that are provided by Shera and Salton model are not put together. Their weaknesses are perpetuated. It is high time for communities from each model to try to integrate education for information science. It is an open question whether the human-and systems-centered approaches can fruitfully work together as urged in all those calls for human-centered design until an educational inte-gration occurs.

While library education receives formal attention from the *American Library Association* (ALA), and education for computer science from ACM, no such formal attention is paid by any professional/scientific society to education for information science, or for IR in particular. Neither ASIS nor SIGIR, as primary homes for information science, have been involved to any great extent in educational matters, such as setting of standards or devising model curricula. Clearly, there is a need and an opportunity for more substantive involvement by both organizations in educational issues.

STRUCTURE OF INFORMATION SCIENCE

Any field is structured along some distinct, larger areas or subdisciplines of enquiry or practice. Think of a number of areas of medicine, computer science, librarianship, and so forth. Information science is not an exception. It has a distinct, two-partite structure. A number of authors observed that the work in information science falls in two large areas or subdisciplines, each, of course, with further subareas or specialties.

White and McCain conducted a monumental bibliometric study of the domain of information science by providing extensive analysis of co-citation patterns for 120 authors over a period of 23 years. Borrowing from White and McCain, visualize a map of information science as an ellipse with authors inside, distributed or clustered according to their connections. There are two large clusters at each end of the ellipse, with only a few authors spanning both. In other words, there are two major areas or subdisciplines.

I liked their metaphor:

As Things Turn Out, Information Science Looks Rather like Australia:

Heavily coastal in its development, with a sparsely settled interior.

In one of the coastal sections, fall authors that worked on analytical study of literatures; their structures; studies of texts as content-bearing objects; communication in various populations, particularly scientific communication; social context of information; information uses; information seeking and behaviour; various theories of information and related topics. As yet, there is no good label for that cluster. Some call it "information analysis." For simplicity, lets call this the *domain cluster,* as did White and McCain, although "basic" may be a good label. In the other coastal section are authors who concentrated on IR theory and retrieval algorithms; practical IR processes and systems; human-computer interaction; user studies; library systems; OPACs; and related topics.

Let's call this cluster the *retrieval cluster,* although "applied" may also be a good label. Basically, most of the areas in the domain cluster are about study of fundamental manifes-tations and behaviour of phenomena and objects that information science is all about. They are centered on the phenomenon of information and its manifestations in literature. The retrieval cluster deals, by and large, with a variety of implementations, on both practical and theoretical levels. It is about implementation, behaviour, and effects of the interface between literatures and people, including, of course, all kinds of retrieval aspects. Unfortunately, these two main clusters are largely unconnected.

Only a very small number of authors spanned the two clusters. In other words, there are very few integrating works. The last text that undertook an integrative approach encom-passing both clusters. A rare example of such an effort in research is the last work by Tague-Sutcliffe, where she related the notion of informative-ness with evaluation of IR systems.

Several modern texts are specifically aimed at IR but none on information science as a whole. I dare to venture a prediction: fame awaits the researcher who devise a formal theoretical work, bolstered by experimental evidence, that connects the two largely separated clusters, *i.e.*, connecting basic phenomena with their realization in the retrieval world. And a bestseller is awaiting an author that produces an integrative text in information science. Information science will become a full-fledged discipline when the two ends are connected successfully. The two clusters are not equally popu-lated. The retrieval cluster has significantly more authors, not to mention total number of works. As in many other fields, more effort is expanded on the applied side than on the basic side.

In part, this is due to availability of funds for given topics—not surprisingly, research goes after moneyed topics. By and large, over the last decade or so, major granting agencies funded only applied research in information science. For instance, I have been unable to identify a single grant addressing any of the topics in the domain or basic cluster from NSF Division of Information and Intelligent Systems since its preceding Division of Information Science and Technology was reorganized and included in the Directorate for *Computer and Information Science and Engineering* (CISE) in 1985. In de Solla Price's concepts and words, the domain cluster is "little science", while the retrieval cluster is "big science," and the connection between the two has presently no science.

PROBLEMS ADDRESSED

General

Webster routinely defines information science as "the science dealing with the efficient collection, storage, and retrieval of information." It is a general definition of problems addressed by information science.

The definition follows pretty much an early and popular one given by Borko as a part of a wide discussion and controversy about the nature of the field in the 1960s. More specifically, information science is a field of professional practice and scientific enquiry addressing the problem of effective communication of knowledge records—"literature"—among humans in the context of social, organizational, and individual need for and use of information. The key orientation here is the problem of need for and use of information, as involving knowledge records.

To provide for that need, information science deals with specifically, oriented information techniques, procedures, and systems. To elaborate, the specific concentration of information science is on human knowledge records as *content-bearing objects*, in all forms, shapes, and media. The primary emphasis is on content of these objects, in terms of their potential for conveying information. "Literature" may be used as a generic term for these knowledge records, but "literature" has many other connotations, thus requiring a careful restriction in its use in information science. Because of these connotations, "literature" will not become popular in information science.

Realizing this, I am using the term here only as a shorthand, as did White and McCain, when they elegantly stated:

> "The proper study of information science is the interface between people and literature . . . modeling the world of publications with a practical goal of being able to deliver their content to enquirers on demand . . . While many scientists seek to understand communication between persons, information scientists seek to understand communication between persons and certain valued surrogates for persons that literature comprises.

In all of this there is a technological imperative, reflected in efforts to take advantage of modern information technology. While information science is not about technology, the problem of providing effective computer applications pervades the field. Following is a word on the extent and borders of infor-mation science. Focusing information science on the content-bearing properties of literature, and on associated techniques and systems dealing with providing effective access to and use of literature, provides a restriction for information science.

Thus, the field does *not* deal with great many other information systems, such as payroll, inventory, decision support systems, data processing, airline schedules, and a zillion others, nor does it deal with direct communication among and between persons. Information science is about a specific manifestation or type of information that defines its scope and its systems. Information science, as many other fields, also involves a professional component. Starting in 1950s, the profession of information science grew from research and applications in IR, to become a powerful component of the field, and in many ways a leading one in respect to innovation.

As in many other fields, there is an uneasy relation between the scientific or research-oriented component and the professi-onal or practice-oriented one. The profession is responding in its own way to needs of its users and organizations, and chartering its own technological applications, many times independently of research advances, and even in different directions. At present, the connection and feedback between profession and research in information science is not as well established as it is in older fields, such as engineering or medicine. This is a serious inhibitor for progress of both.

More Specific

A number of authors suggested a breakdown of specific areas of information science, beyond the structural analysis offered above. The breakdown among different authors is in significant agreement, although the labels differ somewhat. I will take the breakdown and labels provided by White and McCain. They provided a factor analysis of co-cited authors and extracted 12 factors as specialties.

In descending order of how authors loaded, they labelled the specialties as:

- Experimental *information retrieval* (IR);
- Citation analysis;
- Practical retrieval;
- Bibliometrics;
- General library systems theory;
- Science communication;
- User studies and theory;
- OPACs;
- General imported ideas—other disciplines;
- Indexing theory;
- Citation theory; and
- Communication theory.

While one may quibble with some of the classes and labels, these specialties provide a fairly accurate picture of problem areas in which information scientists worked over the past quarter of a century. Over time, there were shifts in emphasis and there were movements between specialties. Nothing is permanent. But these are the specialties of information science. New areas are clearly on the horizon. For the 1990s, I would suggest that the major new areas include interaction studies; searching of the Internet; multimedia IR; multilanguage IR; and digital libraries.

4

Application of Digital Library

Internet especially the World Wide Web has given thrust to new ways of communication and knowledge sharing. Digital libraries are considered to be a key application of Internet and web technologies. They enable the creation, organization, maintenance, management, access to, sharing and preserving of digital collections. Digital libraries are created today for different communities and in different fields such as education, health, culture and so on. Digital libraries bring significant benefits to the users. Some of them are - Always Available, Improved Access, Wider Access, Improved Information Sharing and Preservation. In 1986, National Informatics Centre (NIC) and Indian Council of Medical Research (ICMR) jointly set up a centre called ICMR-NIC Centre for Biomedical Information. This Centre was recognized as the 17th International MEDLARS Centre in 1990 and now is well known as Indian Medlars Centre (IMC). National Informatics Centre (NIC) has been a pioneer in communicating medical research information through the use of Information Technology. This centre is now emerging as a content creator and aggregator. It has developed three major products that are available over Internet:

- UNcat (http://uncat.nic.in) - union catalogue of journal holdings of medical libraries of India;
- IndMED (http://indmed.nic.in) - A bibliographic database of Indian biomedical journals,
- MedIND (http://medind.nic.in) - full texts of Indian biomedical journals being indexed in IndMED and PubMed. NIC has been providing free access to these databases.

DIGITAL LIBRARY OF INDIAN BIOMEDICAL JOURNALS

Digital Library of Indian Biomedical Journals medIND has many functional and process components.

Selection of Journals

The scope of the Collection development policy is well defined to include only those Indian Medical Journals that are either indexed in IndMED or in

PubMed database. The selection policy of IndMED is to include peer reviewed journals having at least published on time for the last three years.

At present, IndMED covers 77 Indian biomedical journals. All the articles are assigned metadata using data input worksheet based on Common Communication Format of UNESCO. These articles are indexed using controlled vocabulary 'Medical Subject Heading (MeSH) list of US National Library of Medicine.

It is being updating on an ongoing and timely basis can be accessed at <http://indmed.nic.in> which is searchable through web interface. The securing of intellectual rights has been easier due to rapport existing with the publishers of these journals. To remove any ambiguity and to reach clear understanding with the publishers, a formal Memorandum of Understanding (MOU) was signed with the journals [represented by their editors] to make available their contents for the medIND project.

At present, 37 Indian biomedical journals have signed a formal MOU with NIC. The aim of this understanding is to provide a rights framework under which cooperation is established between NIC and joutnals to provide their full content to the end user free of cost.

The journal publishers provide the content and NIC does all the other activities like conversion, organization, hosting and providing access to the end users. The salient features of MOU are given as below:

- The resulting materials will be stored and hosted on NIC server;
- No fee will be payable to either party for providing content to NIC or converting into digitization;
- On termination of the agreement, NIC shall provide continuing access to the digitized completed up to the date of such termination;
- The copyright of the data would remain with the respected Editors.

Acquisition of Source Materials

The acquisition of material is the important part of project management. The content is of three types - printed version, born digital, and online existing journal archives. This heterogeneous material is converted into homogenous digital content as given below:

Converting Existing Print Media into Digital Format

Bulk of the archival and back volume content received is in form of printed copies of the journals. Each article, editorial and case study is scanned and stored as PDF (multi page) files. The files related to issue of a journal is put in a separate folder. File names are assigned as per a file naming policy that is based on bibliographic properties of content. The journal's content page of each issue is scanned, OCR and converted into HTML file. The content page in HTML format has all the links to the respective PDF files holding the articles.

Converting "Born Digital" Journals

These days, it is common to find journals being composed in DTP packages like PageMaker before they are printed. For such journals, the composed material is acquired with the cooperation of the editors/publishers of the journals. This is directly converted into the PDF files without the need of scanning.

The quality of such PDF files is of much better quality. The name of the files is converted in accordance to the file naming convention. The content page of the issues is converted into HTML format and links are provided to the PDF files containing the full text articles.

Archives of On-Line Journals

There are few Indian journals that are already available on-line on the web. However since they are presently hosting on commercial web servers, it may not economical for them for continuing hosting back-volume of the journals.

In such cases the archive can be moved to medIND after suitable conversion according to the policy of file names and file organization. This would ensure unique and persistent address for the contents in such archives.

File Naming and File Organization Policy

Unique and persistent URLs for each article are most desirable for such a project. To achieve this there has to be suitable policy for file names and file organization. Such a policy was formulated and adopted. This formed the core on which cross linking between references in IndMED and their corresponding full text file under medIND has been done. Salient features of the policy is as follows:

Directory Structure

The directory structure is as follows: <http://medind.nic.in>/Journal Folder/.../Year-Folder/.../Issue Folder/...Article Files .../Article Folder/

Journal Folder

There is a folder under the site domain for each journal. The name should be unique for each journal folder. A unique three alphabet code has been created for each journal under MedIND called as MJID. This folder contains Year-Issue Sub-Folders and default (index.html) and other html files constituting the home page for the journal.

Year (Sub) Folder

This folder contains the issue subfolders. The Year folder is of three character format 'cyy' whereas c is for century and yy stands for last two digit of the year. For example, Year 2002 would be t02.

Issue (Sub) Folder

This folder is named as "Inn" format having at least two character long. Each Issue folder contains a table of content html file with same name as folder name.

Article File Naming Policy

The file names of articles are given as per the format given below: *<MJID><Century-Year><Issue No.><Pagination> <DOT><File Extension>*

- <MJID>: It is a unique identifier for each journal in IndMED and MedIND. It is of three alphabetical characters.
- <Century-Year>: It represents the year of publication and of three characters. The first character represents the century and is an alphabet. Next two characters are numeric representing the year (first year would be taken if it is a block year).
- <Issue No.>: A variable length of characters, starting with "i" followed by numerical characters represent the issue number.
- <Pagination>: A variable length of characters, starting with "p" followed by numerical characters represents the starting page number of the article. In case more then one articles starts on the same page then a alphabetic character is suffixed to qualify each article sequentially.
- <DOT>: The name portion of the file ends with a dot (.).
- <File Extension>: Three character extensions are suffixed after the dot to represent the common file types.

DIGITIZATION

Thirty-seven journals have signed MOU till now and given the consent for putting their contents under medIND project. The content is being received in hard as well soft copies formats. Each format requires digitization process. These processes are described below:

Conversion from Hard Copies

Steps Involved in OCR to PDF document

- Scanning the document: Resolution has been fixed for text as 300 dpi whereas for table and image, the resolution is 600 dpi;
- Each table is marked as an image as OCR most often distorts table;
- The remaining document is OCRed and saved as Word Document;
- Necessary corrections are performed such as spellings, special characters, colour changing, layout of the text and references;
- Quality checks: Each document is verified and passing quality test, is converted into PDF using Acrobat.

Steps in creating Table of Contents from scanned document

- Scanning the content pages of a journal, OCR and save in Word;
- Necessary corrections are performed such as spellings, special characters in the Word document;
- To design table of content in the same layout as given in the journal, it is designed in HTML format and saved as per naming convention. Hyperlink is given to each article;
- Quality Checks: Each link is being checked for correctness.

Conversion of Born Digital Contents

Steps in converting born digital contents to PDF document

- Content is being received in the form of Page Maker format;
- Converting from Page Maker format to pdf document and save it as pdf file as per the naming convention adopted;
- Checking the completeness of the document;
- In case, image or page(s) are missing, these are scanned locally for completeness.

DESIGN OF DIGITAL LIBRARY MEDIND WEB SITE

The medIND project is having its own domain name at the Internet (http://medind.nic.in). It has pneumonic value and stands for Medical Journals on Internet [from India]. Home page gives details of the project listing of the participating journals. This listing is hyperlinked to each participating journal home page at the medIND web site. The site provides two approaches to access the journal articles.

Browsing

Journals are hyperlinked and arranged in alphabetical order. Such hyperlinked list leads to pages giving details of selected journals such as editors, instructions to authors, contact address, parent body etc. Further, this leads to listing of issues of the journal by years/volume wise. The content page provides hyperlinks to the individual article.

Searching

The searching is being provided through the bibliographic database IndMED. Each record of the IndMED has been linked to the individual article in the MedIND site. The searching of the articles can be achieved through from http://indmed.nic.in as well as from http://mednic.nic.in web sites.

The references will display icons indicating the availability of the full text. In developing digital collection, issues of intellectual property rights have been dealt to strengthen the cooperation between editors and content service provider to facilitate access to digital content through Internet to end users in the area of biomedicine on non-commercial basis. The design of digital collection should be usable, flexible and simple enough to accommodate future changes and also enables other applications to utilize data for development of future applications.

The naming convention of digital collection is acted as bridge between metadata base and full text of content. This project fulfills the demand of providing full text of documents to health professionals free of cost throughout the world. It serves as a model for the development of similar collections in others S and T areas, medIND is a step in the process of making it as an open archive source where Indian journals covered in Medline database as well in IndMED database will be stored and will be provided access free of cost to health professionals throughout the world.

This will give enough visibility and exposure to Indian biomedical journals and demand for Indian literature would be met through the medIND project. In future, more visibility to articles included in medIND journals would be provided by adopting and exposing metadata in OAI-PMH and RSS protocols.

DIGITAL LIBRARY

A digital library is a collection of documents in organized electronic form, available on the Internet or on CD-ROM (compact-disk read-only memory) disks. Depending on the specific library, a user may be able to access magazine articles, books, papers, images, sound files, and videos.

On the Internet, the use of a digital library is enhanced by a broadband connection such as cable modem or DSL. Dial-up connections can be used to access plain-text documents and some documents containing images, but for complex files and those with animated video content, a downstream data speed of at least several hundred kilobits per second (Kbps) can make the user's experience less tedious, as well as more informative. Internet-based digital libraries can be updated on a daily basis. This is one of the greatest assets of this emerging technology.

On CD-ROM, the amount of data is limited to several hundred megabytes (MB) per disk, but access is generally much faster than on an Internet connection. Several CD-ROMs can be combined in a set, and because the disks are small, a large library can be accommodated in a reasonable physical space.

The main limitation of CD-ROM is the fact that updating cannot be done as frequently as on the Internet. In addition, producing and distributing CD-ROMs involves overhead costs that are largely nonexistent in Internet-based libraries. Some institutions have begun the task of converting classic books to electronic format for distribution on the Internet. Some files can be viewed directly in HTML format; others can be downloaded in PDF format and printed. Some publishers keep electronic files of books and produce them one unit at a time in printed and bound form on demand. Electronic distribution of intellectual and artistic property has authors, agents, and publishers concerned about the possibility of copyright infringement. It is much easier to copy a CD-ROM, or to download an electronic book and make unauthorized copies of it, than it is to reproduce bound volumes and distribute them illegitimately.

Fundamental changes in copyright law and/or changes in the way in which the laws are enforced are likely to occur as digital libraries expand and their use becomes more widespread.

HISTORY AND DEFINITION OF DIGITAL LIBRARIES

In this unit we ask two questions:

- What is a digital library?
- What are its characteristics?

In answering these questions we will learn about digital coherence, discuss the origins of digital libraries, and discover synonyms and metaphors for digital libraries. We will also touch on assumptions about a digital library, technologies of library collections, and the act of information seeking.

Digital Coherence

The term digital library has been applied to a wide variety of offerings from collections of electronic journals to software agents that support enquiry-based education to collections of e-mail to electronic versions of a public library, to personal information collections, and even to the entire Internet. The one property these various entities have in common is their digitization or digital coherence (Daniel Atkins).

Digital coherence means all the objects in a digital library, whether sounds, images, texts, or some other media, can be treated in essentially the same way. Prior to digital coherence, libraries needed to treat various media, for example, books, journals, videos, and musical recordings, differently.

One could say that digital coherence is the mechanism which permits a form of equality among various information resources. This equality has importance for delivery and integration of information.

Envisioning a World Brain and The Memex

The concept of a digital library is not new. In fact, the concept of digital libraries pre-dates the development of the first computer. H. G. Wells was one of the first authors to write about idea of a world brain that could supplement, add functionality to, and even replace traditional libraries.

It is generally agreed that Vannevar Bush's 1945 article in the Atlantic Monthly, in which Bush conceives of a memex machine, inspired much of the early application of computers to information retrieval. The memex is a mechanical device based on microfilm technology.

The concept of the memex included [a community of scholars indexing and creating] links between pieces of information in a [microfilm-based] research library combined with [microfilmed] personal notes (and classification system) and notes of colleagues, anticipating the ideas of both hypertext and personal information retrieval systems.

Lesk assures us that by 2015 (70 years after Vannevar Bush published his memex dream) "we will have the equivalent of a major research library on each desk. And it will have searching capabilities beyond those Bush imagined".

Synonyms for the Term Digital Library

In the early 1950s computers entered library services in the form of punched card applications in technical services operations and through the development of the MARC (MAchine-Readable Cataloging) standard for digitizing and communicating library catalog information.

The vision of a fully computer-based library began to emerge in terminology in the mid-60s with J. C. R. Licklider's the library of the future.

Over the years, other terms have been coined to refer to the concept of a digitized library, including electronic library, virtual library, library without walls, and bionic library. Library science professor Winfred Lancaster extended this concept beyond the functions of the library, using the term paperless society.

The use of the term digital library can be traced to the Digital Libraries Initiative, established through funding in 1994, by the National Science Foundation, the Advanced Research Projects Agency, and the National Aeronautics and Space Admini-stration in the United States. Under this funding, six U.S. universities were granted a total of $24.4 million for digital library research. Two events motivated this funding: the sudden explosive growth of the Internet and the development of graphical Web browsers. These two developments significantly increased the viability of extending library resources and services beyond their current walls and communities, facilitating the sharing of scarce resources and the reaching of under-served populations.

Metaphors for Digital Libraries

There is little discussion or agreement in the literature about what constitutes a digital library. Harter juxtaposes two extreme views: the most inclusive view, which takes a digital library to be essentially what the Internet is today, and the metaphor of the traditional library.

The essential differences between these two metaphors deal with their [presumed] properties of location, content, selection criteria, organization, authority control*, authorship, stability, access, and user groups, services and fees. The Internet has no physical or logical location; no quality control and no entry barriers; no organization scheme, authority control, or surrogates; no concept of author; and is fluid and transient. Everyone has access to the

Internet, but access may require payment and purchase of equipment by the individual user. The traditional library is perceived to have their properties and no entry fee for the individual. Names of authors, variants of works (editions), and subject headings or descriptors are all controlled and common variants are cross-listed to the designated official form.

CHARACTERISTICS OF A DIGITAL LIBRARY

ASSUMPTIONS ABOUT A DIGITAL LIBRARY

There are certain assumptions in discussions of a digital library. Levy and Marshall summarize these as: digital libraries are collections containing fixed, permanent documents which are based on digital technologies and are used by individuals working alone.

Fixity of Content

The concept of a fixed and permanent document is based on the printed book: While a title may be reissued in a revised version, once a specific volume is printed and bound, it remains unchanged. Fixity creates a comfortable environment in which to perform certain library functions.

Cataloguing practices have evolved around the largely fixed and permanent document. Fluid or transient documents, such as pamphlets and news clippings have been largely uncatalogued and stored in unclassified areas, such as the vertical file [cabinet].

The perception of lack-of-fixity in fluid digital documents, especially internet-based documents, leads to the assumption that digital items are ill-equipped for cataloguing and other library functions.

This concept of the fixity and permanence of a volume is, itself, flawed. For example, marginalia entered by the reader gives a book some degree of fluidity. Marginalia can contribute error-correction, critique, and even new content to the volume.

Marginalia is viewed as an important addition to certain texts. In addition to marginalia, vandalism— such as removal of pictures or pages from a book— makes it difficult to predict that two books, identical at binding, still contain the same contents on any library shelf.

In classifying books as fixed and permanent, the ways of altering a book after issue have been dismissed. What has, in fact, been catalogued is the pristine just-off-the-press edition. Certainly, many digital-based texts could be archived as a pristine edition, with many fluid copies existing at other sites, and perhaps even linked to and from the archived edition. While the range of variation from a digital pristine copy would certainly have the potential to facilitate and exceed the variation from a print pristine copy, the practice of cataloging and archiving documents at certain points of development can extend to digital media. Fluid copies on the internet could be considered manuscripts in progress (just as some authors circulate paper-based working drafts of manuscripts to colleagues for reading, comment and use) and at some point a revised version could be catalogued and archived, not unlike revised editions of print-based texts.

This is a simplistic discussion of fixity in print and digital media, however, it does illustrate the point that fixity is a relative concept and does not necessarily belong exclusively to the print medium.

Technologies of Library Collections

The develop of the concept of a library based on digital technologies has revolved around the concept of a library based on the book. As Levy and Marshall point out, the book is not the only material contained in library collections.

In addition to holdings of books, photographs, unbound and handwritten manuscripts and correspondents, and other ephemera which are adaptable to digital representation, libraries also contain three-dimensional artifacts, such as models, dioramas, toys and games, and realia—for example, a chameleon (for a borrow-a-pet service) or a wooden crate marked with 'Papers of [author].

Do not open until [date]. [Name of custodian or executor].' Realia and certain other three-dimensional items in a library's collection do not easily convert to digital format. Therefore, even if all currently convertible library materials were digitized, not all materials in the library would be in digital form.

The current concept of a digital library, then, is a subset of the larger concept of library, just as a video or a film library is a subset of the concept of library and not a substitute for it. While it is possible that certain libraries will collect only digital materials, it is more likely that libraries in general will make use of digital material where it best serves their patrons' needs and their libraries' budgets, much like libraries have used microforms and paperback editions. While some materials will not be suitable for digitalization, representations of these materials, such as the products of indexing and abstracting, will be. At some point in the future when applications such as virtual reality develop sufficiently, we may be able to satisfactorily convert much of the informational content of librariesU 3-D holdings to digital format.

At least for now, a comprehensive library will of necessity be a multiple format collection.

The Act of Information Seeking

The perception seems to be that the work in which the user engages in seeking information and the work in which the practitioner engages in supporting his or her patrons is a solitary act.

Contrary to this impression, research finds that the library is a meeting place where collaborative work takes place among patrons, among practitioners, and between practitioners and patrons. For digital libraries to pattern the work capabilities of the traditional library, and to pattern the work habits of the library's patrons and practitioners, collaborative functionality must be included in digital library design. An exceptional example of progress towards this goal, the work of Robertson, Jitan and Reese of the US WEST Research and Information Group, is discussed later.

THE SCOPE OF THE DIGITAL LIBRARY

The term "Digital Library" has a variety of potential meanings, ranging from a digitized collection of material that one might find in a traditional library through to the collection of all digital information along with the services that make that information useful to all possible users. As the WG discussed possible scenarios and challenge problems to drive our discussion of metrics, we found the need to come to at least a loose agreement on the scope of the digital library. This document is intended to serve that purpose.

Much of the question about the scope of the term is how broad a view should be taken of the digital library. Does it encompass all of information management or is a more tightly constrained view appropriate?

In this document, and for the purposes of the deliberations of the WG, we choose to take a very broad view. This is driven by the recognition that to do otherwise would require setting boundaries that are fairly artificial.

The structure of this document is as follows. In the first section, a brief definition of the term "digital library" is given, as a set of characteristics. The remainder of the document elaborates each of those characteristics.

At the kickoff meeting of the WG (held January 7-8, 1998 at Stanford University), the following definition was proposed:

The Digital Library is:

- The collection of services
- And the collection of information objects
- That support users in dealing with information objects
- And the organization and presentation of those objects
- Available directly or indirectly
- Via electronic/digital means.

THE COLLECTION OF SERVICES

A digital library is much more than just the collection of material in its repositories. It provides a variety of services to all of its users (both humans and machines, and producers, managers, and consumers of information). Thus we start our definition with the notion of the collection of services that the digital library represents. There are a large and varied set of such services, including services to support management of collections, services to provide replicated and reliable storage, services to aid in query formulation and execution, services to assist in name resolution and location, etc.

The Collection of Information Objects

The basis for a digital library, however, must be the information objects that provide the content. A basic charact-eristic of the digital library is that the information objects are found in collections with associated management and support functions. The types of information objects vary from traditional "documents" through to live objects (*e.g.* sensor readings) or dynamic query results.

Supporting Users Deal with Information Objects

The goal of the digital library is to assist users by satisfying their needs and requirements for management, access, storage, and manipulation of the variety of information stored in the collection of material that represents the "holdings" of the library. Users may be humans or they may be automated processes acting on behalf of or in support of human needs. Users also vary and include those who are "end" users (those not involved in the management and operation of the library but rather are the customers), library operators, and information "producers" who want their material available through the library.

The Organization and Presentation of those Objects

The key to effective collections management is to implement simple structural organizations and be able to present those organizations in a way that library users find useful and can understand easily.

In traditional libraries, books are primarily stored by subject, title, author, and date, and accessed by following signs to the appropriate floor, room, bookcase, shelf, and spine-labeled book. The size and relative celebration of each portion of the collection gives patrons information about the collection and can reveal the library's collection management objectives as well.

A library is created to serve a community of users. Users who participate in the digital library should be aware of its design and be able collectively to refine that design to better serve their own information needs.

Therefore, the ongoing human usability of a digital library depends on the clear and unobtrusive exposure of the library's design, its near-term goals, and its overall objectives.

Furthermore, digital libraries should continue the ongoing tradition of coupling utility with aesthetics in the organization and presentation of materials.

Available Directly or Indirectly

These information objects may be digital objects or they may be in other media (*e.g.* paper) but represented in the library via digital means (*e.g.* metadata).

They may be available directly over the network (*e.g.*, using a query service of the library to find and then retrieve electronically the information object) or indirectly (*e.g.*, the result of the query may give instructions on how to obtain the object, but that is done outside the scope of the library itself.)

Electronic/digital Availability

Although the objects may not even be electronic, and although the objects themselves may not be available directly over the network, the objects must be represented electronically in some manner through, *e.g.*, metadata or catalogs. Otherwise, we would not consider the objects to be part of the *digital* library. The term *digital library* – denotes a collection of literature and its attendant metadata (data about data) stored electronically.

According to Herbert Samuel, a library is "thought in cold storage", and unfortunately digital libraries can be cold, isolated, impersonal places that are inaccessible to both machines and people.

Many scientists now organize their knowledge of the literature using some kind of computerized reference management system (BibTeX, EndNote, Reference Manager, RefWorks, etc.), and store their own digital libraries of full publications as PDF files.

However, getting hold of both the data (the actual publication) and the metadata for any given publication can be problematic because they are often frozen in the isolated and icy deposits of scientific publishing.

Because each library and publisher has different ways of identifying and describing their metadata, using digital libraries (either manually or automatically) is much more complicated than it needs to be, and with papers in the life sciences alone (at Medline) being published at the rate of approximately two per minute, only computerized analyses can hope to be reasonably comprehensive. What then, are these digital libraries, and what services do they provide?

As far as computational Biologists are concerned, and for the purposes of this Review, we shall define a digital library more broadly as a database of scientific and technical articles, conference publications, and books that can be searched and browsed using a Web browser. As of early 2008, there is a wide range of these digital libraries, but no single source covering all information (in part because of the cost, given that there are some 25,000 peer-reviewed journals publishing some 2.5 million articles per year). Each library is isolated, balkanized, and has only partial coverage of the entire literature.

This contrasts with the historically pre-eminent library of Alexandria whose great strength was that it brought together all the useful literature then available to a single location. Like Alexandria, most digital libraries are currently *read-only*, allowing users to search and browse information, but not to *write* new information nor add personal knowledge. Other digital libraries are in danger of becoming *write-only* "data-tombs", where data are deposited but will probably never be accessed again. Indeed, the literature itself is now so vast that most scientists 1choose to access only a fraction of it, at potentially considerable intellectual loss. Digital libraries provide electronic access to documents, sometimes just to their abstracts and sometimes to the full text of the publication. Presently, the number of abstracts considerably exceeds the number of full-text papers, but with the emergence of Open Access initiatives (*e.g.*, –), Institutional Repositories (*e.g.*, –), and the like, this is set to change considerably.

This is very important, as much additional information exists in full papers that is not seen in abstracts, and, in addition, full papers that are available electronically are likely to be much more widely read and cited –. The format of the full text of such documents can vary significantly among publishers.

Such formats can be described using a Document Type Definition (DTD), *e.g.*, that provided by the (U.S.) National Library of Medicine and, since not all publishers (especially those of non-biomedical material) conform to the NLM DTD, this can considerably affect the types of analysis that can be done on such documents. In a similar vein, there is not yet a recognized (universal) standard for describing the metadata, although some such as the Dublin Core are becoming widely used. Since all of these libraries are available on the Web, increasing numbers of tools for managing digital libraries are also Web-based.

They rely on Uniform Resource Identifiers (URIs or "links") to identify, name, and locate resources such as publications and their authors. By using simple URIs, standard Web browser technology, and the emerging methods of the next generation Web or "Web 2.0", it has become possible for digital libraries to become not just *read-only* or *write-only*, but both *read–write*.

These applications allow users to add personal metadata, notes, and keywords (simple labels or "tags",) to help manage, navigate, and share their personal collections. This small but significant change is helping to improve digital libraries in three main ways: personalization, socialization, and integration. The focus of this Review is largely about searching and organizing literature data together with their metadata. For reasons of space, we do not consider in any detail issues surrounding Open Access, nor structured digital abstracts, (note the recent initiative in FEBS Letters – and the RSC's Project Prospect for whole papers).

Neither do we discuss the many sophisticated tools for text mining and natural language processing, for joining disparate concepts for literature-based discovery, and for studies of bibliometrics literature dynamics, knowledge domains, detecting republication, and so on, all of which become considerably easier to implement only when all the necessary data are digitized and linked together with their relevant metadata. This Review is structured as follows: the section Digital Libraries, DOIs, and URIs starts by looking at the range of information in digital libraries, and how resources are identified using URIs on the Web. In the section Problems with Digital Libraries, we consider a fairly standard workflow that serves to highlight some problems with using these libraries. The following section, Some Tools for Defrosting Libraries, examines what Web-based tools are currently available to defrost the digital library and how they are making libraries more personal, sociable, and integrated places. Finally, the section A Future with Warmer Libraries looks at the obstacles to future progress, recommends some best practices for digital publishing, and draws conclusions.

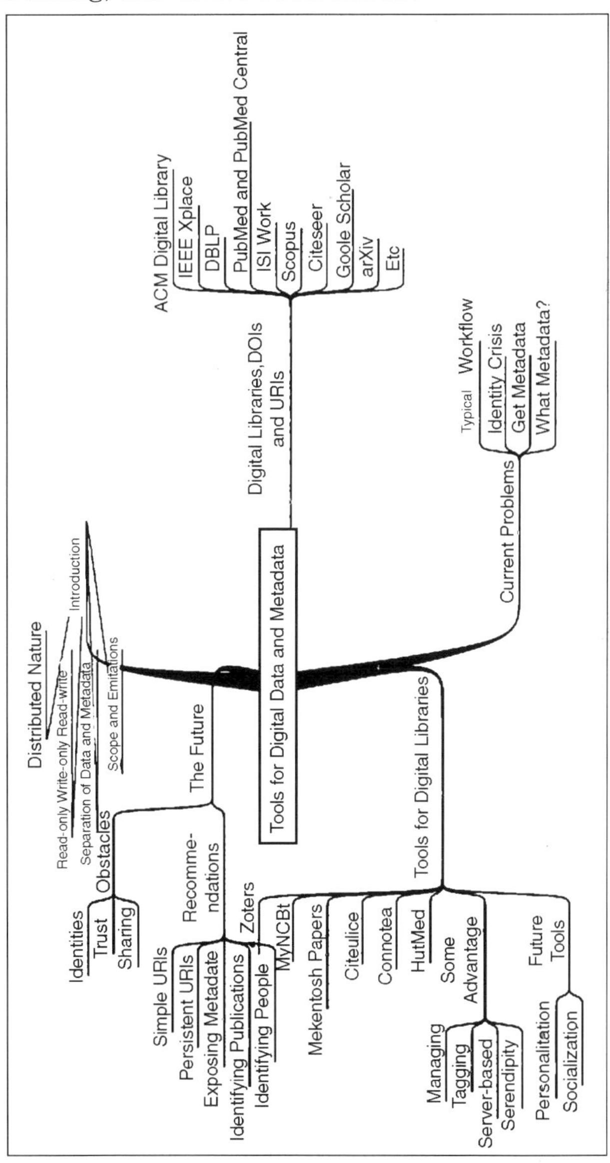

Fig. A Mind Map Summarizing the Contents of this Article in a Convenient Manner.

Digital Libraries, DOIs, and URIs

Because computational biology is an interdisciplinary science, it draws on many different sources of data, information, and knowledge. Consequently, there exists a range of digital libraries on the Web identified by URIs and/or DOIs, that a typical user requires, each with its own speciality, classification, and culture, from computer science through to biomedical science.

DOIs are a specific type of URI and similar to the International Standard Book Numbers (ISBN), allowing persistent and unique identification of a publication (or indeed part of a publication), independently of its location. The range of libraries currently available on the Web is described below, starting with those that focus on specific disciplines (such as ACM, IEEE, and PubMed) through to libraries covering a broader range of scientific disciplines, such as ISI WOK and Google Scholar.

For each library, we describe the size, coverage, and style of metadata used. Where available, DOIs can be used to retrieve metadata for a given publication using a DOI resolver such as CrossRef, a linking system developed by a consortium of publishers. We illustrate with specific examples how URIs and DOIs are used by each library to identify, name, and locate resources, particularly individual publications and their author(s).

We often take URIs for granted, but these humble strings are fundamental to the way the Web works and how libraries can exploit it, so they are a crucial part of the cyberinfra-structure required for e-science on the Web. It is easy to underestimate the value of simple URIs, which can be cited in publications, bookmarked, cut-and-pasted, e-mailed, posted in blogs, added to Web pages and 1wikis –, and indexed by search engines.

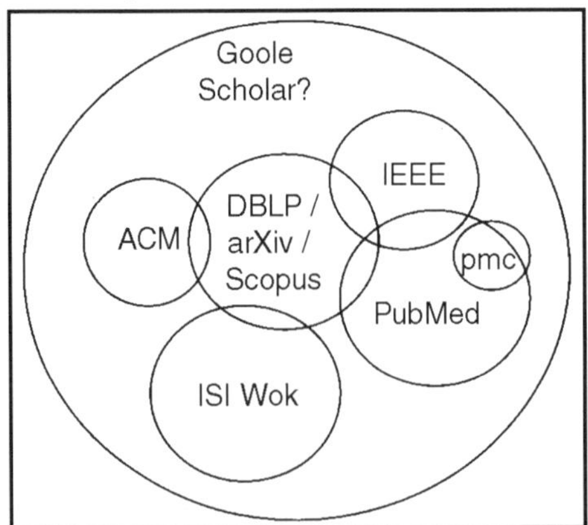

Fig. The Approximate Relative Coverage and Size of Selected Digital Libraries Described in the section Digital Libraries, DOIs, and URIs.

Simple URIs are a key part of the current Web (version 1.0) and one of the reasons for the Web's phenomenal success since appearing in 1990. As we shall demonstrate with examples, each digital library has its own style of URI for being linked to (inbound links) and alternative styles of URI for linking out (outbound links) to publisher sites. Some of these links are simple, others more complex, and this has important consequences for both human and programmatic access to the resources these URIs identify.

Of all the libraries described, Google Scholar probably has the widest coverage. However, it is currently not clear exactly how much information Google indexes, what the criteria are for inclusion in the index, and whether it subsumes other digital libraries in the way shown in the figure. Note: the size of sets (circles) in this diagram is NOT proportional to their size, and DBLP, Scopus, and arXiv are shown as a single set for clarity rather than correctness.

The ACM Digital Library

The Association for Computing Machinery (ACM), probably best known for the Turing award, makes their digital library available on the Web. The library currently contains more than 54,000 articles from 30 journals and 900 conference proceedings dating back to 1947, focusing primarily on computer science. Like many other large publishers, the ACM uses Digital Object Identifiers (DOI) to identify publications.

So, for example, a publication on scientific workflows from the 16th International World Wide Web Conference (WWW2007) is identified by the Digital Object Identifier DOI:10.1145/1242572.1242705. The last part of the DOI can be used in ACM-style URIs as follows: http://portal.acm.org/citation.cfmdoid12 42572.1242705. Metadata for publications in the ACM digital library are available from URIs in the style above as EndNote and BibTeX formats; the latter is used in the LaTeX document preparation system.

IEEE Xplore

The Institute of Electrical and Electronics Engineers (IEEE) provides access to its technical literature in electrical engineering, computer science, and electronics, through a service called Xplore. The exact size of the Xplore archive is not currently described anywhere on the IEEE Web site.

Xplore identifies publications using Digital Object Identifiers that are supplemented with a proprietary IEEE scheme for identifying publications.

So, for example, a publication on text-mining in *IEEE/ACM Transactions on Computational Biology and Bioinformatics* is identified by both the Digital Object Identifier DOI:10.1109/TBME.2007.906494 and an internal IEEE identifier 1416852. These identifiers can be used in URIs as follows: http://dx.doi.org/10.1109/TBME.2007.9064 94 and http://ieeexplore.ieee.org/search/wrappe r.jsparnumber 1416852.

Metadata for publications in IEEE Xplore are available from URIs in the style above in EndNote, Procite, and Refman. Alternatively, publication metadata are available by using a DOI resolver such as CrossRef. Currently, the IEEE offers limited facilities for its registered members to build a personal library and to share this with other users.

DBLP

The Digital Bibliography and Library Project (DBLP) created by Michael Ley, provides an index of peer-reviewed publications in computer science. Recently, DBLP has started to index many popular journals with significant computational biology content such as *Bioinformatics* and *Nucleic Acids Research*, and currently indexes about 900,000 articles, with links out to full text, labeled EE for electronic edition.

Thus an article by Russ Altman on building biological databases is identified by the URI http://dblp.uni-trier.de/rec/bibtex/jour nals/bib/Altman04. Metadata for publications in DBLP are available in BibTeX format only. Unlike some libraries that we describe later, DBLP is built largely by hand, rather than by bots and crawlers indexing Web pages without human intervention.

One of the consequences of this is that authors are disambiguated more accurately, *e.g.*, where an author's middle initial(s) is not used or alternative first names appear in metadata. This kind of author disambiguation is particularly relevant to the naming conventions in some countries.

PubMed gov and PubMed Central

PubMed is a service provided by the National Centre for Biotechnology Information (NCBI). The PubMed database includes more than 17 million citations from more than 19,600 life science journals. The primary mechanism for identifying publications in PubMed is the PubMed identifier (PMID); so, for example, an article describing NCBI resources is identified by the URI http:/ /pubmed.gov/18045790.

Publication metadata for articles in PubMed are available in a wide variety of formats including MEDLINE flat-file format and XML, conforming to the NCBI Document Type Definition, a template for creating XML documents. PubMed can be personalized using the MyNCBI application, described later in the section Some Tools for Defrosting Libraries.

PubMed Central, a subset of PubMed, provides free full-text of articles, but has lower coverage as shown in Figure. Related sites are also emerging in other countries, such as that in the UK. A URI identifying the NCBI resources article in the US PubMed Central is: http://www.pubmedce-ntral.nih.gov/article render.fcgiartid1781113. Metadata are available from URIs in PubMed Central as either XML, Dublin Core, and/or RDF by using the Open Archives Initiative (OAI) Protocol for Metadata Harvesting (PMH), a standard protocol for harvesting metadata. For example, embedded in the page identified by the URI above, there are Dublin Core terms such as DC.Contributor, DC.Date, and DC.title, which are standard predefined terms for describing publication metadata. In addition to such standard metadata, PubMed papers are tagged or indexed according to their MeSH (Medical Subject Heading) terms, curated manually.

ISI Web of Knowledge (WoK)

ISI WoK is The Institute for Scientific Information's Web of Knowledge, a service provided by The Thomson Reuters Corporation, covering a broad range of scientific disciplines (not just computer science or biomedical science). The size of the library is somewhere in the region of 15,000,000 "objects" according to the footer displayed in pages of search results.

Unfortunately, ISI WoK does not currently provide short, simple links to its content; so, for example, the URI for an NCBI publication in ISI WoK is hidden behind a script interface called cgi; this is usually displayed in the address bar of a Web browser, regardless of which publication is being viewed, as in this example: http://isiknowledge.com It is possible to extract individual URIs for publications, but regrettably they are usually too long and complicated and contain "session identifiers," which make them expire after a set period of time (usually 24 hours).

Temporary and long URIs of this kind cannot be easily used by humans, and prevent inbound links to the content. ISI WoK also provides various citation tracking and analytical features such as Journal Citation Reports, which measures the impact factor, of individual journals. Metadata for publications in ISI WoK are provided in BibTeX, Procite, Refman, and EndNote. WoK provides citation tracking features, particularly calculating the H-index for a given author, as well as "citation alerts" that can automatically send e-mail when a given paper is newly cited.

Scopus.com

Scopus is a service provided by Reed Elsevier and seems to be the Digital Library with individually the most comprehensive coverage, claiming (June 2008) >33,000,000 records (leaving aside Web pages). As far as linking is concerned, Scopus allows links <1?show=[to]?>to its content using OpenURL, which provides a standard syntax for creating URIs. For example, the URI http:/ /www.scopus.com/scopus/openurl/doc ument. urlissn 03029743 volume 3298s page 350 identifes a publication from the Semantic Web conference, with the ISSN, volume, and page as part of the URI. The Scopus OpenURL link shown above is the simplest kind that can exist; many get much more complicated as more information is included in the URI, doubling the length of the one shown. The longer and more complicated URIs become, the less likely they are to be useful for humans. Scopus also links out to content using OpenURL and provides citation tracking. Metadata can be exported in RefWorks, RIS format (EndNote, ProCite, RefMan), and plain text, etc.

Citeseer

Citeseer is a service currently funded by Microsoft Research, NASA, and the National Science Foundation (NSF), covering a broad range of scientific disciplines and more than 760,000 documents, according to Citeseer. The URI http://citeseer.ist.psu.edu/apweiler04un iprot.html identifies a paper about UniProt.

Publication metadata are available from Citeseer in BibTeX format, and citation tracking is performed annually in the Most Cited Authors feature.

Google Scholar

Google Scholar is a service provided by Google which indexes traditional scientific literature, as well as preprints and "grey" self-archived publications from selected institutional Web sites. A typical page from Google Scholar is shown in Figure. The size and coverage of Google Scholar does not seem to have been published, and the exact method for finding and ranking citations has not yet been made completely public.

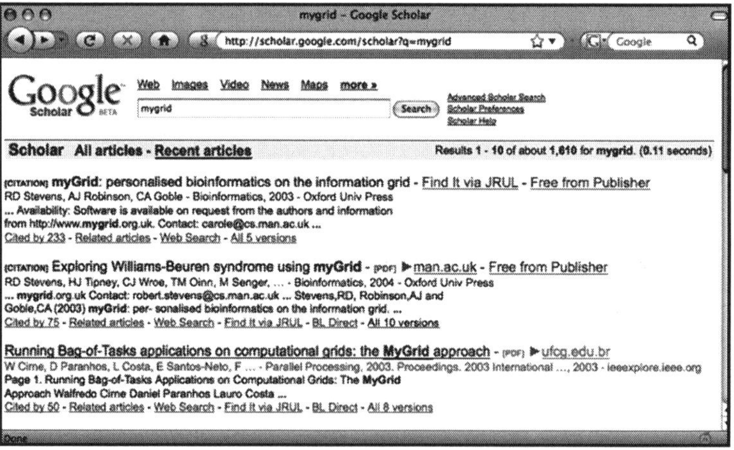

Fig. Google Scholar Search Results, Identified by http://Scholar.google.com/scholar?q = mygrid.

Google Scholar links out to external content using a number of methods including OpenURL, shown here by the "Find it via JRUL" (JRUL is a local library) links. Unlike, *e.g.*, WoK, it is relatively easy to create inbound links to individual authors and publications in Google Scholar.

In contrast to some other digital libraries, Google Scholar provides simple URIs that link to different resources.

For example, http://scholar.google.com/scholarcites 98 56542662207029505 identifies citations of a publication by Tom Oinn. At the time of writing, Google Scholar does not currently offer any specific facilities for creating a personal collection of documents or sharing these collections with other users, other than using simple links such as the one above. Publication metadata can be obtained from Google Scholar where OpenURL links are found in its search results; otherwise, metadata can be obtained by clicking through the links to their original sources.

ArXiv.org

ArXiv provides open access to more than 44,000 e-prints in physics, mathematics, computer science, quantitative biology, and statistics, and was created by Paul Ginsparg. It is a leading example of what *can* be done, although it is presently little used by biologists. The arXiv has a different publishing model from that of the other digital libraries described in this paper, because publications are peer-reviewed *after* publication in the arXiv, rather than before publication. (A related but non-identical strategy is pursued with PLoS ONE, where papers are peer reviewed before being made accessible, but if they do not pass peer review they do not appear.) The arXiv is owned, operated, and funded by Cornell University and is also partially funded by the National Science Foundation. arXiv uses simple URIs to identify publications that incorporate the arXiv identifier. Because arXiv acts as a preprint server, some of its content eventually becomes available elsewhere in more traditional peer-reviewed journals. For example, an article on social networks published in *Science* is also available from http://arxiv.org/abs/cond-mat/0205383. Metadata for publications in arXiv are available in BibTeX format, with various citation-tracking features provided by the experimental citebase project.

This alternative approach to manual citation counts works by calculating the number of times an individual paper has been downloaded, as with the Highly-accessed feature on BioMedCentral journals. In a short review such as this one, it is not possible to describe every single library a computational biologist might use, because there are so many. Also, it is surprisingly hard to define exactly what a specific digital library is because the distinction between publishers, libraries, and professional societies is not always a clean one.

Thus, we have not described the digital libraries provided by Highwire, WorldCat, JSTOR, the British Library, the Association for the Advancement of Artificial Intelligence (AAAI), the Physical Review Online Archive (PROLA), and the American Chemical Society (ACS) (*e.g.*, SciFinder).

Neither do we discuss commercial publisher-only sites such as SpringerLink, Oxford University Press, ScienceDirect, Wiley-Blackwell, Academic Press, and so on here, since *most* of this content is accessible, typically via abstracts, via the other libraries and databases described in the section on digital libraries with links out to the publishers' sites.

Summary of Libraries

Although they differ in size and coverage, all of these digital libraries provide similar basic facilities for searching and browsing publications. These features are well-documented elsewhere, so we will not describe them in detail here. With the exception of arXiv and PubMed Central, which provide full free access to entire articles, all other libraries described here provide free access to metadata (author, year, title, journal, abstract, etc.) and link to data (the full-text of a given article), which the user may or may not be licensed to view. The approximate relationship between the different libraries, as far as coverage is concerned, is shown in Figure.

Where these libraries differ is in the subscription, personalization, and citation-tracking features. So, for example, ISI WoK is a subscription-only service, not freely accessible, but which offers more extensive citation tracking features (such as ranking papers by citation counts, the impact factor and h-index) than other libraries.

Other services, such as the NCBI, are available freely, and provide additional features using custom tools to freely registered users. Other services such as Google Scholar and Citeseer are free, but currently offer no personalized view. Both ISI and Google Scholar provide services for counting and tracking citations of a given paper, which are not provided by most other libraries.

These libraries also differ considerably in the nature and power of their indexing by which users can search them on specific topics of metadata. Most permit Boolean searches on the basis of authors, keywords, words in a title or abstract, and so on, though none does this in real-time, and comparatively few allow sophisticated combinations.

All of this reflects the fact that these libraries and the means of searching them evolved independently and largely in isolation.

Consequently, it is generally difficult for a user to build their own personalized view of *all* the digital libraries combined into one place, although tools described in the section Some Tools for Defrosting Libraries are now beginning to make this more feasible.

Before we describe these further, we shall look at some of the current issues with using these digital libraries, as it is exactly these kinds of problems that have motivated the development of new tools.

These tools, and the digital libraries they are built on, have to manage two inescapable facts:

- *Redundancy*: any given publication or author can be identified by many different URIs;
- *Representing metadata*: there are many different ways of identifying and describing

INFORMATION MANAGEMENT IN DIGITAL LIBRARIES

The Self-Organising Map (SOM) has been proposed as an alternative interface for exploring Digital Libraries (DL), in addition to conventional search and browsing. With advanced visualisations assisting the user in understanding the contents of the map and its structure, as well as advanced interaction modes as zooming, panning and area selection, the SOM becomes a feasible alternative to classical search and browse interfaces.

Several applications show the SOMs utility for this task. However, there are still shortcomings in helping the user understanding the map there are insufficient methods developed for describing the map to support the user in the analysis of the map contents.

In this paper, we give an overview of existing techniques and applications of SOMs in Digital Libraries, and present recent work in assisting the user in exploring the map by automatically describing maps using advanced labelling and summarisation of map regions. Therewith, the SOM becomes an attractive tool for Information Management.

The Self-Organising Map (SOM):

- Is a popular unsupervised neural network model that provides a mapping from a high-dimensional input space (for example text documents described in a vector space model) to a low, often two-dimensional, output space. The mapping of the SOM is topology preserving – elements close in the input space will also be close in the output space. Due to its interesting properties, the SOM has been used in several applications to automatically organise documents in a Digital Library by their content. Examples are text, as in the SOMLib Digital Library system.
- Or in a map of news texts.
- Or music in the SOMeJB system.
- As a recent example also the Digital Library Management System (DLMS) developed by the DELOS Network of Excellence.
- Reckons the possibilities of using the SOM as an interface to a Digital Library's content, as it offers the user support in analysing and exploring the content. With advanced visualisations and interaction possibilities, the user can exploit the full potential of the SOM. However, we still lack techniques to adequately help the user in analysing the contents of the map. For large maps, containing several tens of thousands documents describing various different topics, it becomes increasingly difficult to quickly analyse the map.

In this paper, we give an overview of existing applications of the Self-Organising Map in Digital Libraries and techniques to explore and interact with the map. Furthermore, we present recent work in making the SOM more usable for Information Management by automatically describing regions in the map through adding semantic labels to the SOM, using clustering methods to identify topical areas and selecting representative labels for those regions. Moreover, we present work on automatically summarising the content of those regions on the SOM.

The remainder of this paper is organised as follows: Section II gives a brief overview of the Self-Organising Map and its application in the context of Digital Libraries. Section III describes our work in labelling and summarising regions, while Section IV presents the experiments conducted. Section V presents conclusions and future work.

SELF-ORGANISING MAP

The Self-Organising Map (SOM) has been successfully used for clustering various kinds of data. It provides a mapping from a high-dimensional input space to a lower-dimensional output space.

In the context of Digital Libraries, the input space is mostly a vector-space model representation of the documents the Digital Library holds, may it be text, images, audio, video, or any other media that can be represented in vectorial form. Although many different architectures exist, the output space is in many applications organised as a two-dimensional rectangular grid of units, a representation that is easily understandable for users due to its analogy to 2-D maps. Each of the units on the map is assigned a weight vector, which is of the same dimensionality as the vectors in the input space.

During the training process, vectors from the input space are presented to the Self-Organising Map, and the unit with the most similar weight vector to this input vector is determined. The weight vector of this unit, and, to a lesser extent, of the neighbouring units, are adapted towards the input vector, *i.e.* their distance in the input space is reduced.

At the end of the training process, the output space will be arranged in a way to represent the input space as closely as possible.

For more details on the SOM training process, please refer *e.g.* to. An important property of the SOM is that the mapping is topology preserving – elements which are located close to each other in the input space will also be closely located in the output space, while dissimilar patterns will be mapped on opposite regions of the map.

The SOM therefore provides a sort of clustering of the data, however, without explicitly assigning data items to clusters. It neither identifies cluster boundaries as opposed to, e.g, the k-Means method. The generated map can help the user in getting a quick overview of the patterns in the input space. With fitting visualisations highlighting boundaries, it also allows an easier interpretation of the cluster structures and correlations in the content.

A. Self-Organising Maps in Digital Libraries

The Self-Organising Map as an interface to digital document collections has already been proposed in the WEBSOM project., where the contents of a newsgroup collection containing a million of articles was clustered on the map. The application provides the user with a map of the document collection which she can zoom into by pre-defined levels and navigate in.

- On the most detailed zooming level, a list of the documents mapped onto that region of the map is provided. The map itself, and the exact position of the documents on the map, is not available anymore. To add semantic meaning, the map gets automatically labelled by the names of the most dominant corresponding newsgroups, which is a feasible approach when some kind of categorisation is available for the documents. The labels are however not determined by topical clusters, but rather on a unit basis. The SOM as an interface to Digital Libraries has further been demonstrated in the SOMLib Digital Library System
- The SOMLib system utilises the SOM and other techniques to support the user by employing as many concepts as possible which she already knows from a conventional library. Similar to a map of a conventional library, depicting the arrangement of the shelves where books on certain topics are located, the SOM gives the overview over the contents of the Digital Library. Similar to finding related books in the same shelf, once the user has found a specific document of interest, she can find documents that are related in content in the neighbourhood of that document. A symbolic visualisation of bookshelves using the LIBViewer method further supports this metaphor. The SOMLib system utilises a labelling algorithm to automatically add semantic descriptors to the single map units, without having the need for any category information being available.
- The SOM is used to create a web-based knowledge map of news articles. The application supports hierarchical zooming into the map in pre-defined levels of zoom. However, the map layout changes on different levels of zooming. Besides the map, also a hierarchical list of topics is displayed as an alternative for users who prefer a onedimensional visualisation. uses clustering on the map to apply labels to regions, which are generated based on term and document frequencies, using a tf $\times$ idf-based approach.

The focus in this work is on the visualisation, which tries to resemble geographical maps as closely as possible. This is achieved using a separate GIS software system.

The interaction possibilities for the user are limitedzooming is in predefined levels, the labels cannot be changed interactively, and only one type of visualisation is available. Based on the concept of the SOMLib system, a sophisticated desktop client software has been developed, which allows for various ways of user interaction with the Digital Library content.. With zooming and panning functionalities, the user can analyse the content at any desired detail level, from viewing the whole map at once down to viewing single documents.

Tools for selecting rectangular regions or units along a path allow the user to select several documents at once, and open them for example in a text viewer or in an audio application for playlist generation. One important aspect of SOMs as interfaces to Digital Libraries is that they should not be meant to replace traditional query and retrieval techniques, but rather be complementary to it. This approach is presented in., where a Self-Organising Map is integrated into the popular open-source system Greenstone as a new service, based on the existing query services such as search or list browsing. That way, the user can still use all the basic functionalities provided by Greenstone, but she will also be able to use the wealth of additional information the SOM mapping provides about the documents matching the query results and the whole collection itself.

A screenshot of the system is depicted in Figure, where the left side figures the traditional Greenstone search interface, the lower part the document result listing, and the right part holds the map. The map can be used in two different ways. First, results of the Greenstone search will be highlighted on the map by markers. The user can immediately see which documents have a topical similarity, as these documents will usually all be located close to each other and form a cluster on the map. This way, distinguishing between different topics found on an ambiguous word as *e.g.* 'jaguar' becomes easily – the documents referring to the sports car will be clearly separated from those talking about the animal because they appear in a different context together with other words.

Additionally, outliers found via the search become visible as isolated spots on the map. Secondly, the user can explore the map – she can select nodes, upon which the documents lying on that nodes will be added to the result list of the Greenstone search.

This allows the user to retrieve potentially relevant documents for a specific information need, even if they were not initially retrieved by the (usually rather short) query issued. Documents that have been matched both by the map selection and the search result will be marked especially, as they may be of higher importance. The user can get additional information on the content of the collection by mouse-over popups displaying terms that best describe the documents on a certain node. A small user study suggested that this interface is suitable for Digital Libraries once the user has become a bit familiar with the map. The SOM has also been used for other types of media besides text. In the SOMeJB project, the concept of the SOMLib system has been extended to audio and music documents.

Similar to the SOMLib system, the SOMeJB arranges musical pieces, described by a set of feature vectors extracted solely from the audio content, into topical clusters by the sound characteristics, as the user is familiar with from a traditional record store. In the PicSOM project., the SOM has been used for Information Retrieval in image databases, incorporating methods of relevance feedback.

III. DESCRIBING THE SELF-ORGANISING MAP REGIONS

In this section we present our work on identifying and describing regions in the mapping generated by the Self- Organising Map. As the SOM does not generate a partition of the map into separate clusters, we utilise another clustering algorithm on the weight vectors of the units to identify the regions.

Applying the LabelSOM method, we create semantic labels for those regions that assist the user in getting a first glance overview of the contents of the map. To further support the analysis phase, we additionally provide summarisation of documents of the regions using Automatic Text Summarisation methods.

Clustering

Clustering is an unsupervised process of finding natural groupings amongst unlabelled objects. The members of a cluster are similar in some way, and are dissimilar to members of other clusters.

To identify topical regions, we are clustering the units of a SOM applying an agglomerative, hierarchical clustering algorithm on the units' weight vectors. In the beginning of an agglomerative clustering process, every unit lies in its own cluster. In each subsequent step, the two nearest clusters are merged, until finally only one cluster remains. Specifically, we use Ward's linkage (also known as minimum variance clustering) as one of the most performant within the linkage clustering families.

In this algorithm, the distance of each pair of clusters is defined by the increase in the "error sum of squares" (ESS) if the two clusters are to be combined. The ESS of a cluster X of |X| values is defined as:

$$\mathrm{ESS}(X) = \sum_{i=1}^{|X|} \left| x_i - \frac{1}{|X|} \sum_{j=1}^{|X|} x_j \right|^2$$

and the distance D between two clucters X and Y is defind by

$$D(X,Y) = \mathrm{ESS}(X,Y) - [\mathrm{ESS}(X) + \mathrm{ESS}(Y)]$$

where XY is the union of clusters X and Y. The result of the Ward's algorithm is a hierarchy of clusters which the user can browse through. Increasing the number of displayed clusters means splitting existing clusters into two new ones, while reducing the number of clusters is achieved by merging two clusters into one.

This is advantageous over a non-hierarchical clustering algorithm, where changing the number of clusters might completely change the layout of clusters, which obviously is not a desired behaviour when we want to allow the user to interactively analyse the map contents by changing the number of clusters.

Moreover, hierarchical clustering allows us to at the same time display multiple layers with a different number of clusters. In contrast to other clustering algorithms, the clusters of a layer with more clusters can never be cut by clusters of a layer with less clusters.

Labelling Units with LabelSOM

To assist the user in interpreting the regions of the SOM, we automatically generate labels for the clusters we identified previously.

The cluster labels are based on the units labels generated by the LabelSOM method, which assigns labels to the units of the SOM describing the features of the data points mapped onto the respective unit.

This is done by utilising the quantisation error qik of the vector elements, which is the sum of the distances for a feature between the unit's weight vector mi and all the input vectors xj 2 Ci, *i.e.* the vectors mapped onto the unit i.

$$q_{i_k} = \sum_{x_j \in C_i} \sqrt{\left(m_{i_k} - x_{j_k}\right)^2} \quad k = 1...n$$

This means that a low quantisation error characterises a feature that is similar in all input vectors to the weight vector. Thus the assumption is made that this feature describes the unit well. If the input vector however contains features which are non existent and therefore have the value of 0, those attributes often also have a quantisation error of almost 0 for a unit.

Such features are in most cases not appropriate for labelling the unit, since this would describe what the unit does not contain. Therefore, we require a feature to also have a minimum average value, calculated from all the input vectors mapped to the unit.

Labelling Regions

To choose a label for a region, we consider only the unit labels present in that cluster, as the unit labels are already a selection of features describing the contents of each unit. This method is faster in computation than checking all possible features. Depending on the data, it is preferable to choose the region label based upon a low average quantisation error, a high mean value, or a combination of both.

Therefore we offer the user the possibility to interactively assign priority weights for those two measures, to achieve more meaningful labels.

Making use of the properties of the hierarchical clustering as described in Section III-A, we can also display two or more different levels of labels, some being more global, some being more local. In the visualisation of the SOM, the labels are placed in the centroid of the cluster, which may result in some overlapping labels. To achieve a clear arrangement, the labels can be manually moved on the map, or adjusted in their size and rotation. For some labels, it might also be useful to edit their text, for example if the label text is only a word stem as in our experiment described later in this paper.

Region Summarisation

Even though labelling the map regions assists the user in quickly getting a coarse overview of the topics, labels can still be ambiguous or not conveying enough information. Therefore, we also employ methods from the Automatic Text Summarisation field. Based on the regions identified from the clustering process, we automatically provide a short summary of the contents of the documents mapped onto those regions, allowing the user to get a deeper insight into the contents. Automatic Text Summarisation tries to automatically generate a summary of one or more texts to present the main ideas of the contents in a short and compact form. It can in principle be divided into two areas: single and multidocument summarisation.

Single document summarisation deals with providing a summary of a single document, may it be by extraction of the most relevant sentences, or the more sophisticated approach of generating an abstract of the text. Multi-Document summarisation, on the other hand, deals with generating summaries of a whole collection of documents. Simple approaches would just treat each single document separately, generate the summary of it, and then present all the summaries to the user. This approach of course does not consider redundancy in the extracted sentences. More advanced techniques would treat the whole document collection at once, and extract the sentences which are most important concerning all documents. Redundant sentences are eliminated first by applying a measure for overlapping words, and remove sentences with too high similarity.

Although we also provide summaries of single documents in our application, the main focus is to assist the user in analysing the contents of the Digital Library by providing summaries of the previously identified regions using multidocument summarisation. The application allows the user to select whole regions, or manually any other rectangular shape or units a long a path.

For the chosen documents, the user can choose from several different summarisation algorithms using different weighting schemes to determine the importance of sentences for the summaries, and can also specify the desired length of the summary, measured in per cent of the original sentences.

PROBLEMS USING DIGITAL LIBRARIES

The digital libraries outlined in the previous section all differ in their coverage, access, and features, but the abstract process of using them is more standard.

Figure shows an abstract workflow for using any given digital library.

We do not propose this as a universal model, which every user will follow, but provide it to illustrate some of the problems with managing data and metadata in the libraries described in the previous section on digital libraries.

Tasks represented by white nodes are normally performed exclusively by humans, while tasks shown in blue nodes can be performed wholly or partly by machines of some kind. The main problematic tasks that make digital libraries difficult to use for both machines and humans are "GET" (publication) and "GET METADATA". These are shown in bold and discussed further in the Identity Crisis section of this paper.

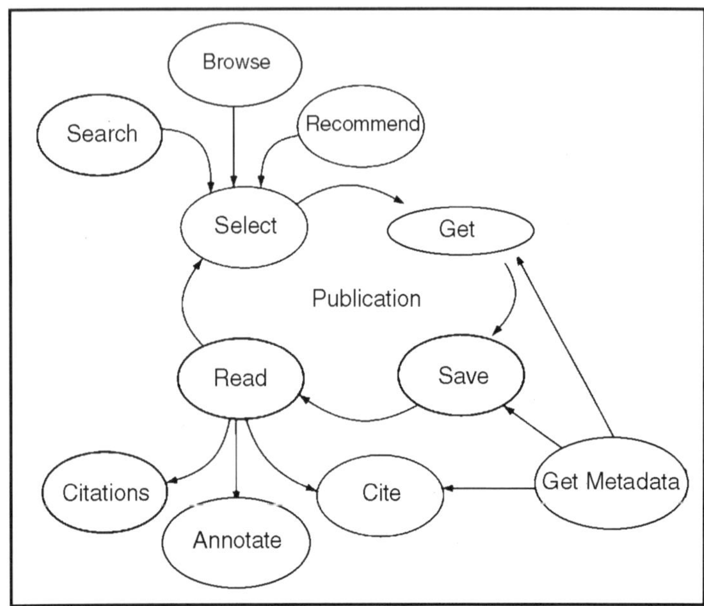

Fig. A Typical Workflow for Using a Digital Library Representing a Subset of the Literature.

To begin with, a user selects a paper, which will have come proximately from one of four sources:

- Searching some digital library, "SEARCH" in Figure;
- Browsing some digital library ("BROWSE");
- A personal recommendation, word-of-mouth from colleague, etc., ("RECOMMEND");
- Referred to by reading another paper, and thus cited in its reference list ("READ").

Once a paper of interest is selected, the user:

- Retrieves the abstract and then the paper (*i.e.*, the actual paper itself as a file), "GET" in Figure)
- They save the paper, for example by bookmarking it, storing on a hard-drive, printing off, etc., ("SAVE"). Saving often involves getting the metadata, too, ("GET METADATA"). By metadata, we again mean the basic metadata about a publication, such as the author, date, journal, volume, page number, publisher, etc. In practice, this means any information typically found in an EndNote or BibTeX entry;
- They read the paper, "READ" in Figure;

- They may annotate the paper, ("ANNOTATE");
- Finally, they may cite the paper ("CITE"). Citing requires retrieving the metadata, if these have not been retrieved already.

This abstract workflow is idealized, but highlights some problems with using current digital libraries, for both humans and machines.

- *Identity Crisis*: There is no universal method to retrieve a given paper, because there is no single way of identifying publications across all digital libraries on the Web. Although various identification schemes such as the PubMed identifier (PMID), Digital Object Identifier (DOI), ISBN, and many others, exist, there is not yet one identity system to "rule them all."
- *Get Metadata*: Publication metadata often gets "divorced" from the data it is about, and this forces users to manage each independently, a cumbersome and error-prone process. Most PDF files, for example, do not contain embedded metadata that can be easily extracted. Likewise, for publications on the Web there is no universal method to retrieve metadata. For any given publication, it is not possible for a machine or human to retrieve metadata using a standard method. Instead there are many inadequate options to choose from, which add unnecessary complexity to obtaining accurate metadata.
- *Which metadata*? There is no single way of representing metadata, and without adherence to common standards (which largely already exist, but in a plurality) there never will be. EndNote (RIS) and BibTeX are common, but again, neither format is used universally across all libraries.

We describe each of these issues more fully in the following sections.

Identity Crisis

We are suffering from an acute identity crisis in the life sciences. Just as sequence databases have trouble managing the multiple identities of sequences, digital libraries also suffer from being unable to identify individual publications and their authors.

These are essential pieces of information that make libraries easy to use, and also help to track citations, but in the present implementation they create considerable barriers to users and machines. Any single publication or author is identified by numerous different URIs.

An important task for managing these disparate collections involves reconciling and normalizing these different identity schemes, that is, calculating if two different URIs identify the same resource or not.

For example, a human can fairly easily determine that each of these URIs identify the same publication, but writing a generic programme to automate this for arbitrary URIs is more challenging: http://nar.oxfordjournals.org/cgi/conten t/full/36/suppl_1/D13; http://www.ncbi.nlm.nih.gov/pubmed/18045 790;

http://www.pubmedcentral.nih.gov/article render.fcgiartid1781113; and http://dx.doi.org/10.1093/nar/gkm1000.

Where DOIs exist, they are supposed to be the definitive URI. This kind of automated disambiguation, of publications and authors, is a common requirement for building better digital libraries. Unlike the traditional paper library, machines play a much more important role in managing information.

They come in many forms, typically search-engine bots and spiders such as Googlebot, but also screen-scrapers, feed-readers workflows programmes, Web services,, and ad hoc scripts, as well as semantic Web agents and reasoners.

They are obviously of great importance for text-mining, –, where computer algorithms plus immense computing power can outperform human intelligence on at least some tasks. Publication metadata are essential for machines and humans in many tasks, not just the disambiguation described above. Despite their importance, metadata can be frustratingly difficult to obtain.

Metadata: You can't Always GET What you Want.

As well as the problem of extracting metadata from PDFs, getting metadata for any given URI which identifies a publication is also problematic. Although the semantic Web has been proposed as a general solution to this –, it is currently a largely unrealised vision of the future.

The Open Archives Initiative mentioned previously provides a solution to this problem, though it is not adopted by all publishers. So, given an arbitrary URI, there are only two guaranteed options for getting any metadata associated with it. Using http, it is possible to for a human (or machine) to do the following.

- *Http GET the URI*: Getting any URIs described in the previous section Digital Libraries, URIs, and DOIs will usually return the entire HTML representation of the resource. This then has to be scraped or parsed for metadata, which could appear anywhere in the file and in any format. This technique works, but is not particularly robust or scalable because every time the style of a particular Web site changes, the screen-scraper will probably break as well. Some Web sites such as PubMed Central make this easier, by clearly identifying metadata in files, so they can easily be parsed by tools and machines.
- *Http HEAD the URI:* This returns metadata only, not the whole resource. These metadata will not include the author, journal, title, date, etc., of the publication but basic information such as the MIME type which indicates what the resource is (text, image, video, etc.), Last-Modified date, and so on.

The lack of an adequate method for retrieving metadata has led to proposals such as the Life Sciences Identifier (LSID), and BioGUID (Biological Globally Unique IDentifier). These may be useful in the future if they become more widely adopted, but do not change the current state of the digital library.

As it stands, it is not possible to perform mundane and seemingly simple tasks such as, "get me all publications that fulfill some criteria and for which I have licensed access as PDF" to save locally, or "get me a specific publication and all those it immediately references".

Metadata for Publications

Even if there were a standard way to retrieve metadata for publications, there is still the problem of how to represent and describe them. In addition to EndNote (RIS) and BibTeX, there are also various XML schemas such as the U.S. Library of Congress Metadata Object Description Schema (MODS) format and RDF vocabularies, such as the Dublin Core mentioned earlier.

Having all these different metadata standards would not be a problem if they could easily be converted to and from each other, a process known as "round-tripping". However, some conversions gain or lose information along the way. Lossy and irreversible conversions create dead-ends for metadata, and many of these mappings are non-trivial, *e.g.*, XML to RDF and back again.

In addition to basic metadata found in EndNote and BibTeX, there are also more complex metadata such as the inbound and outbound citations, related articles, and "supplementary" information.

The identity crisis, inability to get metadata easily, and proliferation of metadata standards are three of the main reasons that libraries are particularly difficult to use and search as automatically as one would wish. These are challenging problems to overcome, and the tools we describe in the next section tackle these problems in different ways.

Some Tools for Defrosting Libraries

Although libraries can be cold, the tools described in this section could potentially make them much warmer. They do this in two main ways. Personalization allows users to say this is my library, the sources I am interested in, my collection of references, as well as literature I have authored or co-authored. Socialization allows users to share their personal collections and see who else is reading the same publications, including added information such as related papers with the same keyword (or "tag") and what notes other people have written about a given publication.

The ability to share data and metadata in this way is becoming increasingly important as more and more science is done by larger and more distributed teams rather than by individuals.

Such social bookmarking is already available on the Web site of publications such as the Proceedings of the National Academy of Sciences (http://www.pnas.org) and the journals published by Oxford University Press.

The result of personalization and socialization is integration of a kind that cannot be achieved by machines alone. First, we look at personalization-only style tools, then we examine tools that also allow socialization of the library through sharing.

Zotero.org and Mendeley

Zotero is an extension for the Firefox browser that enables users to manage references directly from the Web browser. As with most Web-based tools, Zotero can recognise and extract data and metadata from a range of different digital libraries. Users can bookmark publications, and then add their own personal tags and notes.

Currently, Zotero does not allow users to share their tags in the same way that more "sociable" tools such as CiteULike and Connotea do, although enhancements to the current 1.0 version of Zotero may include this feature. Zotero bookmarks cannot be identified using URIs, so it is not possible to link in from external sources to these personal collections.

Mendeley is a similar application that helps to manage and share research papers, although as well as having a Web-based browser version it is possible to store bibliographies using a more powerful desktop-based client that automatically extracts metadata from PDF files, but it can only do this where metadata is available in an amenable format.

MyNCBI

MyNCBI allows users to save PubMed searches and to customise search results. It also features an option to update and e-mail search results automatically from saved searches. MyNCBI includes extra features for highlighting search terms, filtering search results, and setting LinkOut, document delivery, and external tool preferences.

Like Zotero, MyNCBI currently allows personalization only, with no socialization features. It is also limited to publications in PubMed. As we have previously seen, computational biologists frequently require access to many publications outside PubMed, so they cannot capture their entire library in MyNCBI alone. Like Zotero, it is currently not possible to link to personal collections created in MyNCBI.

Mekentosj Papers

Papers, is an application for managing electronic publications, originally designed by Alexander Griekspoor and Tom Groothuis. Although it is not a typical browser-based Web application, it can be closely integrated with several services on the Web-like Google Scholar, PubMed, ISI Web of Knowledge, and Scopus mentioned in the Digital Libraries section of this paper.

The Papers application demonstrates how large collections of PDF files can be managed more easily. Papers provides a simple and intuitive interface shown in Figure to a collection of PDF files stored on a personal hard drive.

It looks and behaves much like Apple's iTunes, an application for managing music files, because the user does not have to know where the data (PDF file) is stored on their hard drive. Unfortunately, Papers is only available for Apple Macintosh users, and there is no version for Windows, which limits its uptake by scientists. It looks and feels much like the popular iTunes application, allowing users to manage their digital libraries by categories shown at the top. It is presently available only under Mac OS/X.

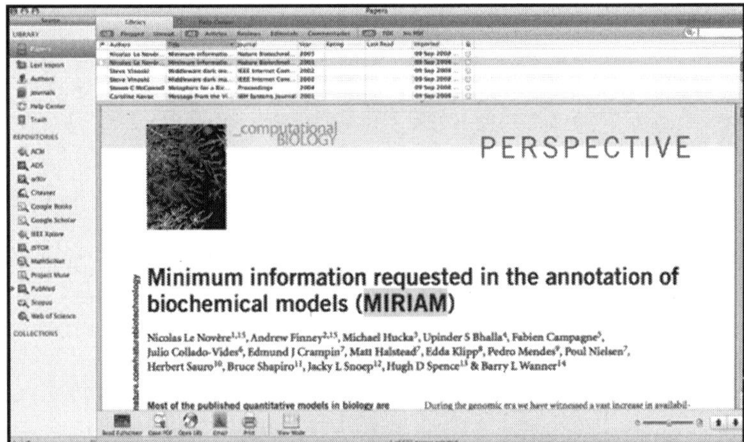

Fig. Mekentosj Papers can Organize Large Collections of Locally Stored PDF files, with their Metadata.

The personalization of libraries is nothing especially new or groundbreaking, and scientists have been creating personal libraries for years, for example by having their own EndNote library or BibTeX file. Tools such as Zotero, MyNCBI, and Papers just make the process of personalization simpler.

However, socialization of digital libraries *is* relatively new, in particular the ability of *multiple* users to associate arbitrary tags with URIs that represent scientific publications. This is what CiteULike, Connotea, and HubMed all allow, thereby capturing some of the supposed "wisdom of crowds" in classifying information.

CiteULike.org

CiteULike is a free online service to organize academic publications, now run by Oversity. It has been on the Web since October 2004 when its originator was attached to the University of Manchester, and was the first Web-based social bookmarking tool designed specifically for the needs of scientists and scholars.

In the style of other popular social bookmarking sites such as delicious.com it allows users to bookmark or "tag" URIs with personal metadata using a Web browser; these bookmarks can then be shared using simple links such as those shown below.

The number of articles bookmarked in CiteULike is approaching 2 million, indicated by the roughly incremental numbering used. While the CiteULike software is not open source, part of the dataset it collects is currently in the public domain. Publication URIs are simple: http://www.citeulike.org/article/1708098.

CiteULike normalizes bookmarks before adding them to its database, which means it calculates whether each URI bookmarked identifies an identical publication added by another user, with an equivalent URI. This is important for social tagging applications, because part of their value is the ability to see how many people (and who) have bookmarked a given publication.

CiteULike also captures another important bibliometric, viz how many users have potentially *read* a publication, not just cited it. It seems likely that the number of readers considerably exceeds the number of citers and this can be valuable information. Time lags matter, too.

This is particularly the case with Open Access, where the "most-accessed" *Journal of Biology* paper of 2007 had in June 2008 been accessed in excess of 12,000 times, but has been cited just nine times (note that early access statistics can provide good predictors for later citations).

CiteULike provides metadata for all publications in RIS (EndNote) and BibTeX, providing a solution to the "Get Metadata" problem described in the previous section Metadata: You Can't Always GET What You Want, because every CiteULike URI for a publication has metadata associated with it in exactly the same way.

Connotea.org

Connotea is run by Nature Publishing Group and provides a similar set of features to CiteULike with some differences. It has been available on the Web since November 2004. Connotea uses MD5 hashes to store URIs that users bookmark, and normalizes them after adding them to its database, rather than before.

This post-normalization means Connotea does not always currently recognize when different URIs (such as the examples in the section Identity Crisis) identify the same publication, a bug known as "buggotea", which also affects CiteULike to a lesser extent. Like CiteULike, URIs in Connotea are simple. A publication about Connotea, for example, is identified by the URI http://www.connotea.org/uri/685b90ae66cf bc3fc8ebeed0a5def571. Metadata are available from Connotea in a wider variety of formats than from CiteULike, including RIS, BibTeX, MODS, Word 2007 bibliography, and RDF, but these have to be downloaded in bulk only, rather than individually per publication URI. The source code for Connotea is available, and there is an API that allows software engineers to build extra functionality around Connnotea, for example the Entity Describer.

HubMed.org

HubMed is a "rewired" version of PubMed, and provides an alternative interface with extra features, such as standard metadata and Web feeds which can be subscribed to using a feed reader. This allows users to subscribe to a particular journal and receive updates when new content (*e.g.*, a new issue) becomes available.

An example URI for a publication on HubMed is http://www.hubmed.org/display.cgiuids168 45111. Like CiteULike, HubMed also solves the "Get Metadata" problem because metadata are available from each HubMed URI in a wide variety of formats not offered by NCBI.

This is one of HubMed's most useful features. At the time of writing, HubMed provides metadata in RIS (for EndNote), BibTeX, RDF, and MODS style XML. Users can also log in to HubMed to use various personalized features such as tagging.

Advantages of using CiteULike and Connotea

Both CiteULike and Connotea require users to invest time and effort learning how to use them, and importing or entering bibliographic information. Why should they bother? Managing bibliographic metadata using these tools has several advantages over the common scenario of storing un-indexed PDF files locally on a personal computer.

Both CiteULike and Connotea provide a single place (a Web server) where data (PDFs) and metadata can both be shared and more tightly coupled; this has the following benefits.

Searching

Easier and more sophisticated searching is possible. Conversely, given a collection of PDFs on a hard drive, it is typically difficult (or impossible) to make simple queries such as "retrieve all papers by [a given author]".

Managing

When authoring manuscripts, managing references in a Web-based repository can save some of the pain of re-typing metadata (*e.g.*, author names) for a given publication. Provided the publication has a URI that is recognized by these tools, metadata are automatically harvested on behalf of the user, saving them time.

Tagging

Tags are just keywords, but these allow both persona-lisation and socialisation of bibliographic data, see for papers cited in this Review as an example. Tagging of papers by other users allows non-expert users to explore related papers in ways that may not be possible through traditional reference lists, since exploring a subject of research in which you are not expert is made easier by following links added by other potentially more expert users.

Server-based

Hosting a bibliography on a Web server means that, if and when the user moves computer, the library is still accessible. However, keeping local and remote versions requires appropriate synchronisation, which can be problematic.

Serendipity

Many serendipitous discoveries or intellectual linkages that may be determined via co-occurrences (*e.g.*, –) exist in science, and these can be assisted by browsing links provided via social tagging.

Future Tools

The tools described here are the first wave of Web 2.0, Library 2.0, or even Science 2.0 style tools that are helping to defrost the digital library. There will certainly be plenty more in the future; for example, the Research Information Centre from the British Library is investgating innovative new tools in this area, backed by Microsoft.

Some are calling it "Web 3.0", but, whatever the name, it seems likely that we will see many digital library applications that will exploit the novel social features of platforms such as Facebook, and OpenSocial. Here they can exploit the identity mechanisms already built into those systems.

Personalization and socialization of information will increasingly blur the distinction between databases and journals, and this is especially true in computational biology where contributions are particularly of a digital nature. Scientific contributions to digital knowledge on the Web often do not fit into traditional scientific publishing models.

This is usually because they are either too "small" or too "big" to fit into journals. Web logs or "blogs" are beginning to fill the "too small" gap and can be used for communicating preliminary results, discussion, opinion, supplementary material, and short technical reports – in the style of a traditional laboratory notebook. Biological databases, such as those listed in the annual NAR database review, have long filled the "too big" gap in scientific publishing.

They are clearly more significant than their publications alone. As we move in biology from a focus on hypothesis-driven to data-driven science, it is increasingly recognized that databases, software models, and instrumentation are the scientific output, rather than the conventional and more discursive descriptions of experiments and their results. In the digital library, these size differences are becoming increasingly meaningless as data, information, and knowledge become more integrated, socialized, personalized, and accessible. Take Postgenomic, for example, which aggregates scientific blog posts from a wide variety of sources. These posts can contain commentary on peer-reviewed literature and links into primary database sources. Ultimately, this means that the boundaries between the different types of information and knowledge are continually blurring, and future tools seem likely to continue this trend.

A Future with Warmer Libraries

The software described in the section Some Tools for Defrosting Libraries are a promising start to improving the digital library. They make data and metadata more integrated, personal, and sometimes more sociable. While they are a promising start, they face considerable obstacles to further success.

Obstacles to Warmer Libraries

We suggest that the main obstacles to warmer libraries are primarily social rather than technical in nature. Identity, trust, and privacy are all potential stumbling blocks to better libraries in the future.

One Identity to Rule them all?

The basic ability to identify publications and their authors uniquely is currently a huge barrier to making digital libraries more personal, sociable, and integrated. The identity of people is a twofold problem because applications need to identify people as *users* in a system and as *authors* of publications.

The lack of identity currently prevents answering very simple questions such as, 'show me all person *x* publications', unless the authors concerned are lucky enough to have unique names. Both the NCBI and CrossRef have initiatives to identify authors uniquely in digital libraries, but these have yet to be implemented successfully. The use of Single Sign-On (SSO) schemes such as Shibboleth and OpenID (the latter is used in projects such as myExperiment.org and Connotea) could have a huge impact, enabling identity and personalization, without the need for hundreds of different usernames and password combinations. It remains to be seen what their impact on scientific literature will be. Technically, there are also tough challenges for creating unique author names such as synonymy, name changes, and variable use of initials and first names, which are ongoing legacy issues.

Passing valuable data and metadata

Passing valuable data and metadata onto a third party requires that users trust the organization providing the service. For large publishers such as Nature Publishing Group, responsible for Connotea, this is not necessarily a problem. That said, many users are liable to distrust commercial publishers when their business models may unilaterally change their data model, making the tools for accessing their data backwards incompatible, a common occurrence in bioinformatics. Smaller startup companies, who are often responsible for innovative new tools, may struggle to gain the trust of larger institutions and libraries. Most of the software described in the section Tools for Defrosting Libraries require a considerable initial investment from users to import their libraries into the system. Users have to trust service providers that this investment has a good chance of paying off in the longer term.

Scientists also have to decide how much to trust and rely on commercial for-profit companies to build and maintain the cyberinfrastructure they require for managing digital libraries. Not all commercial companies provide the best value-for-money services, and this is often true in scientific publishing.

Paul Ginsparg, for example, has estimated that arXiv operates with a cost that is 100 to 1,000 times lower than a conventional peer-reviewed publishing system. If the market will not provide scientists with the services they require, at a price they are willing to pay, they need to build and fund them themselves.

The danger is that too much electronic infrastructure will be owned and run by private companies, and science will then be no better served than it was with paper-based publishing.

data Scientists want to Share

Although the practice of sharing raw data immediately, as with Open Notebook Science, is gaining ground, many users are understandably cautious about sharing information online before peer-reviewed publication.

Scientists can be highly secretive and reticent at times, selfishly not wanting to share their data and metadata freely with everyone and anyone, for fear of being "scooped" or copied without proper credit and attribution. Some tools provide security features, *e.g.*, both CiteULike and Connotea allow users to hide references. However, this requires users to trust external providers to respect and protect their privacy, since the information is on a public server, and out of users' control.

Recommendations

Warmer digital libraries cannot be achieved by software tools alone. The digital libraries themselves can take simple steps to make data and metadata more amenable to human and automated use, making their content more useful and useable. Only with proper and better access to linked data and metadata can the tools that computational biologists require be built. We make the following recommendations to achieve this goal.

Simple URIs

URIs for human use should be as simple as possible, to allow easy linking to individual publications and their authors. Short URIs are much more likely to be used and cited than longer, more complicated URIs.

Persistent URIs

It has been noted many times before but it is worth repeatedly restating: persistent URIs make digital libraries a much more useful and usable place. Although URIs will inevitably decay many (but not all) will be preserved by the Internet Archive and every effort should be made to keep them persistent where possible.

Exposing Metadata

Publication metadata, in whatever style (EndNote, BibTeX, XML, RDF, etc.), should be transparently exposed and readily available, programmatically and manually, from URIs, HTML, and PDF files of publications.

Identifying Publications

URNs (such as Digital Object Identifiers) should be used to identify publications wherever possible. Most large publishers already do this, although there are still many confounding exceptions.

Identifying People

This problem is twofold: people need to be identified as users of a system and as authors of publications. To tackle the first issue, tools and libraries should use Single Sign On (SSO) schemes, such as OpenID to provide access to personalized features where possible, as this prevents the endless and frustrating proliferation of username/passwords to identify users in Web applications. The second requires unique author identification, an ongoing and as yet unsolved issue for digital libraries.

By following these recommendations, publishers, scientists, and libraries of all kinds can add significant value to the information they manage for the digital library.

Conclusions

The future of digital libraries and the scientific publications they contain is uncertain. Rumours of the death of printed books and the death of the journal have (so far) been greatly exaggerated. In scientific publishing, we are beginning to see books and electronic journals becoming more integrated with databases, blogs, and other digital media on the Web.

These and other changes could lead to a resurgence in the role of nonprofit professional societies and institutional libraries in the scientific enterprise as the cost of publishing falls. But the outcome is still far from certain.

What is certain is the fact that we can look forward to a digital library that is more integrated, sociable, personalized, and accessible, although it may never be completely "frost-free". Ultimately, better libraries will be a massive benefit to science. The current breed of Web-based tools we have described are facilitating this change, and future tools look set to continue this trend. Ultimately, data and metadata will become less isolated and rigid, moving more fluidly between applications on the Web. There are still issues with trust, privacy, and identity that may hinder the next generation of Web-based digital libraries, and these social problems will need addressing.

It has frequently been observed that scientists lag behind other communities in their use of the Web to communicate research, and that this is ironic given that the Web was invented in a scientific laboratory for use primarily by scientists.

Most scientists are painfully familiar with the shortcomings of the databases and software described in this Review, because these tools are at the very heart of science. Digital libraries are, and always will be, fundamental components of e-science, and of the "cyber-infrastructure", –, necessary for both computational and experimental biology in the 21st century.

5

Application of Data Mining Techniques for Library System

INTRODUCTION

At the beginning of each adjustment in a library, librarians or library managers need to think about which kind of books are going to purchase or what kind of magazines have to be ordered in the coming renewal period of the year. The purpose of project is to provide statistics and analysis software. It will offer librarians or managers sufficient information to make right decisions. The statistical data or chart produced by the programme will easily make librarians sense what changes need to be made. We are going to research the reader's behaviour from these statistical data or charts and then improve or modify our library service.

The library professionals do not know which books a patron wants, which is offered for their studying, or which patron prefers what class of book. The library may offer a book that no patron wants to borrow, or the offered books may not have enough readers. Librarians should make a decision so that this kind of book may never be or seldom ordered in the future. On the other hand, librarians have to use a lot of their budget for much used books to provide the reader more services. Librarians will be helped by this programme. This kind of feedback can be researched and can present some trends. This will be important information for further improvement of the library. Data Mining in a Library System will be a product after we digitalize the library. Librarians may get a lot of worthwhile information immediately such as the students' studying trend, the top 10 of circulation in the library, the hottest field of studying by using this system. Not only librarians want this but also patrons need it. This is also a knowledge management strategy system for the current library. Actually, the system will enhance the librarian's efficiency in controlling library resources. Librarians could imagine the future library from it.

The uncertainties of the Internet challenge the modern workplace but also promise unexpected opportunities. Converting uncertainties to opportunities requires human efforts to enhance the capabilities of technology to benefit professional endeavour. In the library profession, practices of unstructured and unrestricted information dissemination and retrieval from the World Wide Web (WWW) not only create an information explosion but make uncertain the future of the profession as well. Facing the need to adapt to the new climate of the information world, academic librarians are charged to extend their services from the reference desk to the virtual environment on the WWW.

To meet the challenge, new information technologies that can assist in organizing and retrieving information are constantly being investigated by academic libraries. Web mining is one of these new technologies that deserves special attention because of its capability to discover and analyse useful information from the Web.

ELEMENTS OF DATABASE DESIGN

As discussed earlier, spatial data are representations of real-world phenomena. The digital representation of the real world is often referred to as a digital landscape model (DLM). With the flexibility to represent different characteristics of the features of data at different levels of scale, the DLM is a central component in the processing of spatial data and for analysis. Model generalisation, or conceptual generalisation, refers to the process that uses a geometric component in the model. Generalisation means the reduction in the complexity of information.

Unlike in cartography, which means suppressing unnecessary detail, in database development, generalisation means information abstraction, or the suppression of detail in order to widen the meaning of the information. Utilising the digital landscape model, the user can derive graphic representations of different aspects of spatial data in either digital form or traditional cartographic processes. A common model is the ANSI/SPARC layered model of database architecture.

Three schema, a physical schema, a conceptual schema, and user views, comprise this model. For example, using this model in the building of a spatial database provides organisation to a data set. A schema adds order to the variables in a database. An overall framework (or logical structure that defines the database) is identified and defined as the physical schema. Database variables are mapped and their attribute relationships identified. Concepts can be mapped as well and their relationships are also identified. The first step in organising a spatial database is defining a logical schema for a set of variables. This initial step recognises data categories that outline the parameters of groups of data.

The framework allows for inserting attribute information, which further describes the attributes of the variables. Populating data categories creates a DLM. Since, the DLM is an object-orientated topographic database, its data structure facilitates spatial analysis and linkage of geographic objects to external data. A DLM uses the vector as its primary geometric form, and often contains explicit or implicit topological information.

Table. ANSI/SPARC Architecture Data Models and Schemas

Schemas	Models
Schema	Models used to derive the schema
Extermal views	Based on diffirent n user perspectives, a spatial model is created by defining and de scribing a sub set of the real world.
Conceptual schema	External views synthe sized to create conceptual schema using semantic data modeling techniques, for example, the entify-relationship approach.
Logical schema	Conceptual schema transformed into a logical schema using the ralational model. Emphasis is on redundancy removal.
Physical schema	Logical shema mapped into data stuctures and algorithms. A 'hidden' process not accessible or seen by user.

The objects, their attributes, and the relations between the objects are referred to in terms of real-world entities. Entities are comprised of type classification, attributes, and relationships.

An entity may have one or more attributes, such as a building's (entity) attributes may be its characterising material, such as block, brick, or frame. Attributes describe quantitative data ranked by three levels of accuracy: ordinal, interval, and ratio.

Ordinal (ranked) may rank an entity from 'worst to bad to good to better to best,' interval (numeric) may address an entity's age or income, and ratio (scale) may address the length or area of an entity. Another aspect of designing a database is in evaluating user perceptions of the data.

Since, a database generally serves multiple users or user groups, users may have very different perceptions of the attribute data collected. Each user (or group) receives his or her external view of the database to create a personalised conceptual database schema.

Database designers then merge the external views of the data into a single conceptual schema of the database. In designing a database, a conceptual schema is not determined by the parameters of a measurement tool, technique, or paradigm, but by its flexibility, which allows it to deal with the vagueness and uncertainty of defining different aspects of humancentered phenomena in the real world.

After the phenomena types are defined, the conceptual schema is transformed into a logical schema using one of the logical data models, such as a relational data model. Since, each fact should be stored only once in a database, the logical schema allows the development of a redundancy-free dataset. A physical schema is the result of the implementation of the logical schema with particular database management software.

Table. Data Modeling

Physical Reality	Real World Model	Data Model	Database	Language
Phenomena	Entity	Object	Object	Symbols Lines
Properties	Type	Type	Type	Text
Connections	Attributes	Attributes	Attributes	Images
	Relationship	Relationship Geometry Quality	Relationship Geometry Quality	Tables Charts

The structure of spatial databases provides a method for libraries with digital geospatial data collections and services to create a system for the discovery and querying of geographic information across the online environment of the Internet. Many of the sources of digital geospatial data, such as private corporations and government agencies, reside in locations across the United States and the globe. Besides spatial databases, building a digital geospatial collection in an online environment will use a variety of software applications and hardware tools that will assist in the administration of information as it passes from host to user. Next is a brief discussion of the development of some of the applications and protocols utilised in data transfer in the online environment of the Internet.

EMERGENCE OF A TELECOMMUNICATIONS NETWORK

The contemporary information economy emerged as industries in established economic sectors, such as manufacturing and production services, incorporated computer technologies to their daily operations. The concentration of industrial, technological, and social capital of such industries in urban areas enabled the building of advanced telecommunication services.

Firms were able to take advantage of existing telephone lines and exchanges to build new information networks that were quickly using new communication software applications. In 1961, a researcher at RAND for the U.S., Department of Defence, working on how the U.S., telecommunications infrastructure could survive a "first strike, published a proposed digital data communica-tions system based on a distributed network concept".

He introduced the concept of redundancy and the use of message-block (packet-switching) networks with no single outage point as a method of building communications systems to withstand outages. This became the underlying data communications technology for the Internet. The development of ARPANET, created by the Advanced Projects Agency of the U.S., Department of Defence in 1969, was an early catalyst in the integration of computer and telephone technologies, and enabled the exchange of information related to scientific study occurring in advanced computing centers.

In the beginning, ARPANET's architecture consisted of 4 nodes (sites) located at the University of California at Los Angeles, the University of California at Santa Barbara, the University of Utah, and Stanford Research Institute. Early experimentation with the system resulted in the creation of Telnet, an openly accessible public packet data service that allowed a computer operator at a terminal or PC to log onto a remote computer, run a Programme, and initiate FTP, an early file transfer protocol (FTP). The CCITT (International Consultative Committee on Telephony and Telegraphy) approved the first guidelines for X.25, a network protocol using virtual circuits that became the backbone of the TCP/IP (Transmission control protocol/Internet protocol) protocol.

Table. 10.3. TCP/IP Protocol

Layer	Function	Protocols Used
Process (Application) Layer	'Higher level' protocols, such as SMTP,FTP,SSH, HTTP, and so forth operate in this layer. TELET, TLS/SSL,	SMTP, FTP, SSH HTTP, DHCP, IMAP4, IRC, MIME, POP3, SIP, SNMP, RPC, RTP,SDP, SOAP.
Host to Host (Transport) Level	Flow control and connection protocols live here, Opens and maintains connections. Ensures packets are actually received.	TCP, UDP, RSVP DCCP, SCTP.
Internet (Internet) working Layer	Defines IP addresses and routing schemes for navigating packets from one IP address to another Performs network Segmentation/desegmentation desegmentation and error control functions.	IP, UDP, BGP, ICMP, IGMP IGP, RARP.
Data Link Layer	Responsible for node to node (hop to hop) packet delivery	ATM, Bluetooth, DTM, Ethernet, FDDI, Frame relay, GPRS, PPP Modems, Wi-Fi
Physical Layer	Describes the physical equipment necessary for communication, such as twisted pair cables, the signaling used on level protocols using that signaling.	Bluetooth RF, Ethernet physical layer, ISDN, Modem, ₹232 SONET/SDH, USB, Wi-Fi, Power line communication

Why is a communication protocol important? Communication between computers means sending messages from one machine to another. There are three types of communication. Simplex communication is message travel in only one direction. Half-duplex communication is asynchronous message travel in both directions.

Halfduplex communication is not simultaneous, for example, much like using ham radio, the first person must say 'over' at the end of his communication so the person at the other end knows that it is his turn to talk. Full-duplex communication is simultaneously sending and receiving messages in both directions simultaneously, with no lags or gaps in the transmission or receipt.

Obviously, addressing mechanisms that allow unique identification of senders and receivers are very important. Other critical mechanisms are rules on how data travels, error-detection and error-correction, disassembling and reassembling long messages, avoiding data overflow due to fast transmitters and slow receivers, and routing of messages.

32 Bits				
Version	IHL	Type-of-Service	Total Length	
Identification			Flags	Fragment offset
Time-to-Live		Protocol	Header Checksum	
Source Address				
Destination Address				
Options (+ Padding)				
Data (Variable)				

Fig . The 14 Fields that Comprise an IP Packet

TCP/IP is the basic communication language, or protocol, of the Internet and for private networks (*e.g.*, intranets or extranets). TCP/IP communication is primarily a point-to-point protocol (PPP), meaning each communication is from one point (or host computer) in the network to another point (or host computer). There are five layers to the TCP/IP protocol. The higher layer, the transmission control protocol, disassembles a message or file into smaller packets that are transmitted over the Internet and received by a TCP layer that reassembles the packets into the original message.

The third layer, the Internet protocol, handles the address part of each packet so that it gets to the right destination. TCP/IP and the higher-level applications that use it are collectively said to be 'stateless' Since, every client request is considered a new request and unrelated to any previous request. Being stateless frees network paths so that everyone can use them continuously, unlike 'dedicated' lines, such as plain old telephone service (POTS) or fax lines. By the late 1980s and early 1990s, the Web was accelerating away from a dedicated mainframe environment to a distributed client-server system. This distributed system challenged the development of new protocols. Considering the variety of personal computers, simple terminals, servers as well as platforms, and operating systems, requirements for new protocols had to be simple, cross-platform, and Non-computer specific.

Based upon the idea of HyperCard, Berners-Lee of the Conseil Européen pour la Recherche Nucléaire (CERN; European Council for Nuclear Research) developed hypertext transfer protocol (HTTP) and its accompanying text format, hypertext mark-up language (HTML).

HTML was based on SGML (standard generalised mark-up language), an internationally agreed upon method for marking up text into structural units, such as paragraphs, headings, and so forth, that was Non-machine, Non-platform specific. Two significant components of HTTP and HTML are the use of hypertext links to 'anchor' items to each other inside and outside the 'page' and the 'www' naming protocol (URL) used for addressing Web sites.

A uniform resource locator (URL) consists of three parts: the name of the protocol (http), the host name where the page resides, and the name of the hypertext document (home.htm). HTTP, TCP/IP, FTP, Telnet, and SMTP form a 'suite' of protocols that Internet users use as a matter of course. Building on a basic design of a document-sharing protocol, the Web eventually developed into a medium for the creation of a variety of Web sites that met myriad individual and organisational demands and needs. Although many of the top-level domains of the net were still educational, much of the early development of the Internet occurred in the private sector, with Internet service providers (ISPs), such as America Online (AOL).

From its beginning as a specialised dial-up service for Apple Macintosh users in 1989, within 6 years AOL had a million subscribers. This was a substantial inroad in an environment where there were about 20 to 30 million users. The success of these early Internet service providers triggered tremendous growth in the number of Web sites during the second half of the 1990s. The availability of inexpensive access through local land telephone lines and relatively cheap cost of transmitting data. The number of commercial (.com or dot com) domains increased from around 1 million in 1994 to nearly 25 million at the beginning of 2000, while other categories of users (.net,.mil,.org, and.gov) added another 19 million domains, of which 15 million were cable-based net service providers. The development of HTTP and HTML spawned thousands of new sites and inspired new information services, such as 'browsers,' 'search engines,' and 'portals' to enable net users to find information of interest. More specialised and powerful search engines continue to emerge, including the current leader, Google. Additional Web-based services, and continued growth depended on the established telecoms or cable TV systems and their telephone wire infrastructure. Rapid development of the Internet in the 1990s was accompanied by a simultaneous investment in construction of new telephone access lines in the United States.

Investment in new lines by major carriers in the United States increased 32 per cent between 1990 and 2000 from 119.8 million to 157.6 million lines. The number of the new lines that incorporated ISDN (integrated services digital network) technology was 129.6 million, an increase of over 850 per cent from the previous number of 13.6 million.

Transmitting data at speeds ranging from 128 kilobits per second to over 150 megabits per second, ISDN networks support a wide of range of simple to complex voice and Non-voice services, and allow for the transmission of multiple channels of information, such as voice, data, fax, and video, over a single wire.

The spatial distribution of ISDN-technology-enabled networks across the United States is uneven, with a concentration of high-speed data lines in areas that have the necessary infrastructure for its development. Broadband, defined as 200 megabits per second of data output, is about fourtimes faster than a 56 Kbps dial-up modem and about eight-times faster than most people's actual download speeds, Since, many IPS's modems offer a maximum of 28.8 Kbps. Since, many contemporary computer applications, for example, music clips, video clips, and streaming video, use considerable amounts of bandwidth, broadband access is growing as an essential Internet service expectation. These graphics intensive applications have many business and entertainment functions, and are not possible at lower dial up Internet connections.

Broadband Internet access is usually provided through digital subscriber line (DSL) technology. Data on the Regional Bell Operating Companies indicate that more than 56 per cent of all cities with populations above 100,000 had DSL available, but less than 5 per cent of cities with populations less than 10,000 had DSL service. A number of ISPs have been building data lines in predominately rural areas. These ISPs tend to be small businesses that fill in gaps in data line access where no larger telecommunication firms are present. Since, the costs of establishing Internet service warrant a subscriber base of at least 200 households, some small telephone exchanges are too small to sustain an ISP of that size. The rural ISPs offer dial-up access in low bandwidth transmission formats. Most of the Internet services in rural areas tend to be related to e-mail and e-commerce transactions. If access to more services or larger bandwidth is required, costs are significantly higher for the user as well as the ISP, Hence,, Internet use in rural areas is held down by higher costs.

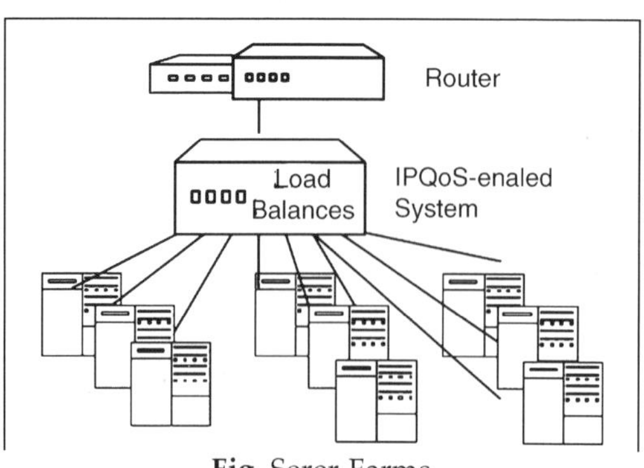

Fig .Serer Farms

The economics of Fibre optics can be expensive for urban connections as well. In situations where new trenches must be dug for the cable, installing Fibre in metro areas can run in the hundreds of thousands of dollars per mile.

Although installation cost can often be reduced by intensive use of existing infrastructure, it is difficult to justify the investment when existing phone lines can deliver adequate bandwidth via ADSL (Asymmetric Digital Subscriber Line) technology. ADSL is a modem technology that transforms POTS (plain old telephone service) lines into high-speed digital lines. By splitting an existing telephone line signal into two, one for voice and the other for data, ADSL technology can work at up to 8-Mbps download. Since, the baseband is occupied by POTS, should ADSL fail, POTS service is guaranteed. Similar to telephone switching centers, the Internet requires specialised host computers called servers and routers. Servers are typically clustered in so-called 'server farms' around the world, located in urban areas where most of the traffic originates. Server farm capacity is currently increasing at an annual rate of 50 per cent.

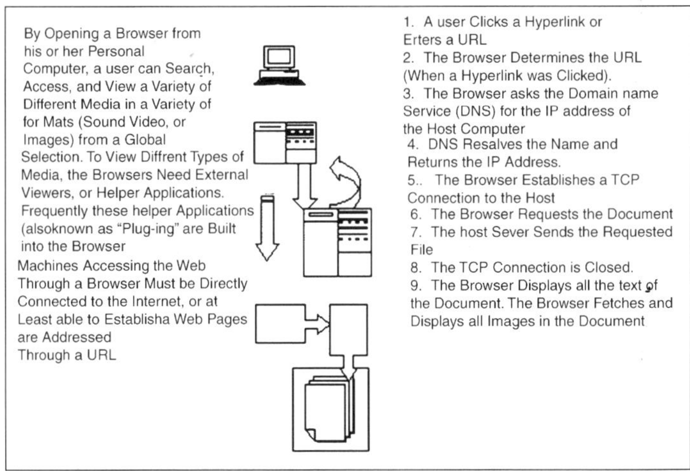

Fig . Putting it all together Retrieving Data from the Web

One of the biggest providers is Exodus Communications, with 9 server farms in Silicon Valley alone and 35 more in big cities around the world. Think of server farms as 'wholesalers' in the Internet and the 'data caches' as retailers, located around the world near consumers of content. Technically, the function of the data caches is to recombine the individual packets of data, dispatched by the routers by different routes (because of changing conditions from moment to moment), into coherent streams designated for final customers. The leader in this field is Akamai, with 11,000 caching servers in 62 countries. Akamai's customers are the content providers (including CNN and Yahoo!).

The net result of all this investment was to create an oversupply of long-distance Fibre-based carrier capacity, without a matching growth in local broadband access capacity for which the established telecoms retained their monopoly (except where cable TV was also available). As of early 2002, long-distance optical Fibre channel capacity is said to be only 2 per cent–5 per cent utilised, whereas local access in many places outside the biggest cities, still dependent on copper wires, is badly congested. The limiting factor is electric power consumption, especially as the farms get larger (one new server farm, being built by iXguardian near London, will have its own gas-fired power plant). By opening a browser from his or her personal computer, a user can search, access, and view a variety of different media in a variety of formats (sound, video, or images) from a global selection.

To view different types of media, the browsers need external viewers, or helper applications. Frequently these helper applications (also known as 'plug-ins') are built into the browser. Machines accessing the Web through a browser must be directly connected to the Internet, or at least able to establish a PPP connection with an ISP. Web pages are addressed through a URL.

- A user clicks a hyperlink or enters a URL.
- The browser determines the URL (when a hyperlink was clicked).
- The browser asks the domain name service (DNS) for the IP address of the host computer.
- DNS resolves the name and returns the IP address.
- The browser establishes a TCP connection to the host.
- The browser requests the document.
- The host server sends the requested file.
- The TCP connection is closed.
- The browser displays all the text of the document. The browser fetches and displays all images in the document.

Building on the data transfer capabilities of the Internet, also known as the World Wide Web, and its accompanying telecommunication infrastructure, the online environment of the Internet is rapidly becoming a standard platform for GIS as government agencies and private companies begin to exploit the data exchange capabilities of the Internet.

CHARACTERISTICS OF DISTRIBUTED SPATIAL DATABASES

Spatial data infrastructures are based on large amounts of spatial data distributed over many agencies. The survey of the information economy indicates that industries in the information sector rely on efficient data transfer between organisations and users for their operations. Even though spatial databases may have useful socioeconomic purposes, a system linking many spatial databases would have far greater applications in the distributed environment of the information sector. What is the structure of a distributed spatial database system? First, two components, a database and a database management system, comprise a database system. The database (DB) is an organised collection of stored data; the database management system (DBMS) is software for building and maintaining a database. The strength of a database system is in its design. It contains a number of features, such as 'persistency, storage management, recovery, concurrency control, ad hoc queries, and data security,' that allow for the efficient processing of data. A persistent storage capability allows data to exist independently of the application of a Programme.

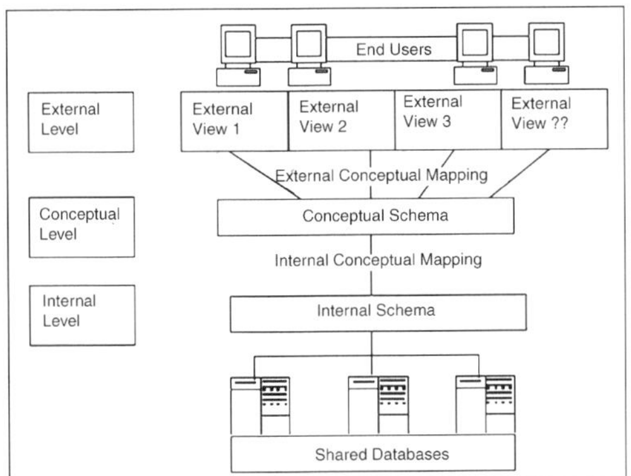

Fig . Visual Representation of the ANSI/SPARC Architechure

The ability to recover data is important in the workings of a spatial database system. If in the execution of a Programme is not successful, the database management system can return the database to its former state before the attempted software application or to its former uncorrupted state. A concurrency control mechanism is also part of the normal operations of a distributed spatial database system. Its purpose is to avoid inconsistencies caused by concurrent read and write operations to the database and security access to the server on which the database is located.

The ability of the database system to offer access to multiple users is also based on having data access security delineations. The architecture of most databases is based on the standards of the ANSI/SPARC Study Group on Data Base Management Systems. These databases have three levels: internal, conceptual, and external level.

The external level is closest to the user, the internal level is closest to the physical storage, and the conceptual 'exists in the middle.' Although individual users may have different external views on the database, there is only one conceptual view and one internal view. A data definition language (DDL) defines the views.

A data manipulation language (DML) describes the processing of the database objects. Databases store models of conceptualised real-world phenomena. In the design process of a database, several data models are used to describe the various feature attributes of the variables in the database. A data model describes the contents and organisation of the data. As discussed earlier, they can be classified into conceptual, logical, and physical data models.

Proceeding with the variable feature descriptions as defined by the various data models, the data are then organised as conceptual model.

The next step would be to construct a logical data model. A database management system can then implement the logical data model. An example of a logical data model is the relational data model, which is in widespread use among desktop GIS users using commercial software. A relational data model is characterised by a clear distinction between the graphical and descriptive data of features representing real-world elements.

Graphical elements are stored in layers of the digital map file and attribute data is stored in the form of a relational database table. Spatial features on the digital map are linked through the identifier with the record of the relational database table containing further descriptive data of the feature. A commonly used language for the relational database model is structured query language (SQL). Supported by all major relational DBMS vendors, SQL is both a data definition and data manipulation language.

In a spatial data infrastructure, many databases are distributed over many organisations across a network, and are interconnected through a communication network. Every site runs a unique database management system. Local applications operate on local hardware, while distributed or global applications can involve multiple sites on the data infrastructure. The design process for distributed databases builds on the design process for most database design, that is, it has a conceptual step, logical step, and physical design phase step.

An additional design dimension is the distribution design step. The integration into a network introduces a number of design ideas to the building of distributed databases, such as distribution transparency, fragmentation, and replication. Distribution transparency indicates that most users do not know where the data in a database is actually located. Replication, where duplicate datasets may be stored in different locations, and fragmentation, when different parts of a dataset may be stored on different servers, are frequently performed for security and practical reasons.

In both cases, the user always perceives a centrally located database. Kainz notes that 'there are two possible approaches to the design of distributed databases: top down and bottom up. The top-down design is applied to new databases that are designed from scratch'.

Many GIS data producers and providers participate in the United States Federal Geographic Data Committee (FGDC) data infrastructure initiative. A system of distributed spatial databases that provide users with access to myriad federal, state, and local datasets, the central component of the data infrastructure is the 'clearinghouse.' Originally defined as a 'system of software and institutions to facilitate the discovery, evaluation, and downloading of digital geospatial data,' today the FGDC defines a clearinghouse as "a community of distributed data providers who publish collections of metadata that describe their map and data resources within their areas of responsibility, documenting data quality, characteristics, and accessibility. The FGDC clearinghouse(s) also address the descriptive component of the data through the use of metadata. The clearinghouse computer systems integrate many interoperating metadata servers, using a distributed, client-server architecture.

On the client side, the most common software application is usually browser-based, such as Internet Explorer or Netscape Navigator. A client residing on computer X can interact with server Y, located at another location, using a set of instructions called protocols. Since, most traffic on the Internet uses the TCP/IP (transmission control protocol/Internet protocol), the TCP/IP software suite is frequently embedded in a computer's operating system (OS) software, such as in Microsoft Windows, MAC OS X, Unix, and Linux free ware. One protocol selected to provide search interoperability among different servers is the ISO 10163-1995 search and retrieve protocol. The Z39.50, initially developed for the library community, contains client and server software that establishes a connection, relays a query, returns the query result, and presents retrieved documents in various formats.

DATABASES, WEB SERVICES, AND INTERNET GIS

There are a number of advantages to a GIS that is available from the Internet including world wide accessibility, use of a standard interface, and cost-effective maintenance. The traditional model of GIS is a system that consists of a single software package, and accompanying data on a single machine. With the advent of distributed producers and consumers of digital geospatial data, this model is no longer valid. As Green and Bossomaier note "many GIS projects are often multi-agency, multi-disciplinary, multi-platform, and multi-software. Large numbers of contributors may be involved, and there may be a large pool of potential users". Further, "a central practical issue is how to provide widespread, device-independent access to GIS for large numbers of contributors and users". The essential differences between a traditional GIS and an online GIS are the 'separation of user interface, data storage, and processing'. In stand-alone GIS, all of the elements are within a single machine; in an online environment, the elements are distributed across many computers. During the 1980s, GIS was conceptualised strictly as a software application: A computer based system that provides the following four sets of capabilities to handle georeferenced data:

- Input;
- Data management;
- Manipulation and analysis; and
- Output.

This definition is accurate when conceptualising GIS as an application; however, it does not address GIS as an interactive system where hardware, software, data, methods, and people come to create geographic knowledge for distribution. In the early 1990s, the concept of a GIS system evolved.

ESRI, a privately held consulting firm, defined GIS as an "organised collection of computer hardware, software, geographic data, and personnel designed to efficiently capture, store, update, manipulate, analyse, and display all forms of geographically referenced information".

Reid, Higgins, Medyckyj-Scott, and Robson observed, "The exploitation of geospatial data within diverse policy environments, allied with the increasing attention being afforded to cross-discipline social and environmental issues, has led to the demand for infrastructures to assist in the discovery, dissemination, and exploitation of geospatial data". The authors also note that the structures are often referred to as spatial data infrastructures (SDIs). " Most SDIs will integrate geospatial data and metadata, which can provide the means to access the data and also establishes the needed licensing agreements between users to make use of the data". The diverse information services of SDIs mirror information services of digital libraries, the latter defined as a collection of services and the collection of information objects that support users in dealing with the information objects and the organisation and presentation of those objects through electronic means.

Three significant factors of SDIs are the provision, organisation, and presentation of information and services to a specific group of users. By integrating with the digital library environment, the process of mining through digital geospatial data becomes more varied with additional data added to the original projection datum. In delivering digital geospatial data over the Internet, the identification, retrieval, and delivery of information in a virtual environment is described as a "URL-addressable resource that performs functions and provides answers". Web services are described as an "encapsulation of existing software functionality in a common form that allows the services it performs to be visible and accessible to other software applications".

The single Web services-based application can request services from other Web services, and can expect to receive the results or responses from those requests in an expected form. One advantage of Web services technology is its ability to interoperate in a loosely coupled manner, an 'ask and wait' approach. The user can request a certain type of service across the network, and wait for responses. Web services can also be found and used by other applications, agents, and clients on the Internet.

In a digital geospatial data retrieval system, a Web service can be published inside or outside the host's firewall by providing a document describing its operation and function. Using the Web services definition language (WSDL) markup language, the core of the document may illustrate a service when interpreted on a national grid reference responds with relevant coordinates on the host's mapping system. The document then described how the service is prompted and what the executables are.

The document can also be published to a node, a clearinghouse, or other Internet site using the Universal Discovery, Description, and Integration (UDDI) registry. Parson also notes that communication between Web services pass "XML messages wrapped in an interoperable framework to allow the messages to cross different networks, use different application architectures and systems". The widespread use of digital geospatial data by a number of different individuals and agencies in both the public and private sectors will continue to create large amounts of archived data.

To make such data sets searchable across the environment of the Internet, librarians must be willing to take a varied approach in determining the appropriate metadata scheme to enable effective mining across the World Wide Web. A significant factor in the development of Web GIS services and in online services in digital libraries has been the National Spatial Data Infrastructure initiative by the Federal Geographic Data Committee.

ORGANISING A NATIONAL DATA INFRASTRUCTURE

In 1994 the Federal Geographic Data Committee (FGDC) recommended that a National Spatial Data Infrastructure (NSDI) be organised. The NSDI would be an "umbrella of policies, standards, and procedures under which organisations and technologies interact to foster more efficient use, management, and production of geospatial data". The NSDI was conceptualised as fostering more cooperation and interaction between different organisations from the public and private sector. The recommendation was a response to alterations in the traditional flows of data across the government based on new convergences of information, computer technology, and communication. A significant component of the data being used in government transactions and commercial transactions was digital geospatial data.

The FGDC considered digital geospatial data as being critical to solving many 'environmental, economic, and social problems.' The FGDC had also recognised that 'the use of GIS technologies for the digital analysis of spatial problems had become pervasive'. With the integration of GIS and increased use of geospatial data into problem-solving operations, a major goal of the NSDI was to make 'an environment to respond to the current need of digital geospatial data.'

The FGDC envisioned building the framework around the procedures, technology, and guidelines that enhance integration, sharing, and use of these data, and the institutional relationships and business practices that encourage the maintenance and use of data. The framework would represent the best available data for an area, and be certified, standardised, and described according to a common standard. Today, the FGDC standards provide a foundation on which organisations can build by adding their own detail and compiling other data sets.

MEETING DIGITAL GEOSPATIAL DATA NEEDS

The FGDC reported that many billions of dollars are spent by organisations on an annual basis in both the public and private sector in attempts to manage digital geospatial data. With digital geospatial data becoming a valuable asset within the business practices of many public and private sector organisations, most organisations can only afford to collect or purchase only a small portion of information they require. Often only the most basic digital geospatial data is acquired by organisations, usually a dataset that pertains to a specific geographic area or that has some unique attribute characteristics.

The datasets are often incompatible with other datasets, due to differences in software platforms. Researchers at the FGDC found that data collected by differing organisations may be similar in geographic extent use different geographic bases and standards. Hence,, "many of the resources organisations spend on geographic information systems (GIS) go Towards duplicating other organisations' data collection efforts.

The same geographic data themes for an area are collected again and again, at great expense." A data framework would improve the ability for organisations to share data. The framework would provide a "basic geographic data in a common format and an accessible environment that anyone can use and to which anyone can contribute.

In this environment, users can perform cross-jurisdictional and cross-organisational analyses and operations, and organisations can funnel their resources into applications, rather than duplicating data production efforts". Researchers at the FGDC further noted in their findings that "geographic data users from many disciplines have a recurring need for a few themes of basic data: geodetic control, orthoimagery, elevation, transportation, hydrography, governmental units, and cadastral information".

Many organisations produce and use such data every day. The framework provides basic information for these data themes. By attaching their own geographic data, which can cover innumerable subjects and themes, to the common data in the framework, users can build their applications more easily and at less cost. The seven data themes provide basic data that can be used in applications, a base to which users can add or attach geographic details and attributes, a reference source for accurately registering and compiling participants' own data sets, and a reference map for displaying the locations and the results of an analysis of other data. Researchers at the FGDC envision the information framework to be an evolving data resource to which geographic data producers can contribute. Integral components of the information network incorporate "procedures, guidelines, and technology to enable participants to build, integrate, maintain, distribute, and use framework data. These elements ensure that users can depend on accurate, detailed data that can be certified and integrated into the framework to create a trustworthy data source; users can update their data holdings from the framework data; and users can attach additional information to the framework". These procedures would ensure the standardisation of datasets and enable the efficient transfer of digital geospatial data across the Internet.

The FGDC envisions the information framework integrating data from all types of organisations in both the public and private sector. The framework environment is designed to be responsive to the needs of the geographic data community in terms of 'data creation and maintenance, and provides unrestricted access to data'.

A COOPERATIVE INFORMATION NETWORK

The FGDC also envisions organisations building the information framework by coordinating data development activities. Organisations can coordinate framework data along two dimensions. "The first dimension emphasises opportunities for organisations with similar needs. An example is a metropolitan area in which local governments, their customers, state and federal agencies with facilities in the area, utilities, and others require high-resolution spatial data for their operations.

In this case the framework provides a starting point for sharing the commonly needed geographic base information and allows each organisation to add the unique information it requires to meet its business needs". The second dimension emphasises opportunities for organisations needing different amounts of detail for an area. For example, a local government, a regional transportation planning organisation, and a state transportation agency may require road data for an area, but at different levels of geography.

For efficient data sharing the organisations would have to share the results of their individual efforts and would benefit from using a common geographic base and generalised data created from this base. The framework provides a starting point for a base and the data generalised from it, "providing the organisations with contemporary and consistent data for decision making and helping them avoid confusion caused by differences in the vintages, common attributes, and other characteristics of the base data". The framework is being developed by this entire community, with organisations from all areas playing roles. For some, the framework will supply the data they need to build applications. Others will contribute data, and some may provide services to maintain and distribute data. Some organisations will play several roles in framework development, operation, and use. An essential community partner in the information network can be libraries. Librarians have the skills and experience needed to help the information network to facilitate digital geospatial data and to aid in its search and mining procedures. Some researchers have advocated the 'geolibrary' as a possible model for a library to facilitate digital geospatial data.

DIGITAL GEO-LIBRARIES AND DIGITAL COLLECTIONS

One approach used by librarians in making digital geospatial data available to their users is to incorporate Web-based mapping functions with their library geospatial information holdings. Such efforts combine the locational aspects of the metadata descriptions of the geospatial data in the catalog with the mapping capabilities of GIS software. In building Web-based functions into their geospatial collections, some libraries have termed their collection a 'digital geolibrary.'

Different perspectives about geolibraries have been discussed in the scholarly geography and information science literature such as from Boxall and Goodchild. Goodchild refers to a geolibrary as being comprised of georeferenced information that can be accessed by a geographic footprint. Likewise, in his discussion of geolibraries, Boxall notes that their scope extends beyond the traditional map library if the construct of a geolibrary is based upon the idea that information has a geographic footprint. His discussion references earlier research that explains georeferenced information as including such things as photographs, videos, music, and literature that can be given a locational variable that defines a footprint. The collection areas of geolibraries extend beyond the traditional scope of map libraries and archives to include almost all information contained within libraries.

He later mentions that it can include information outside of libraries as well. This is the theoretical basis for what we now view as geolibraries. Boxall discusses that a significant focus of geolibraries is on digital information and metadata, as well as the distributed nature of the libraries and 'collections.'

He adds that "...Distributed geolibraries provide a useful framework for discussion of the issues of dissemination associated with the National Spatial Data Infrastructure (NSDI)". The vision is readily extendible to a global context. Boxall feels any discussion of 'Digital Earth' (DE), the 'Global Spatial Data Infrastructure' (GSDI), and 'Distributed Geolibraries' should be framed around the broadest definitions of information and infrastructures; namely to include and focus upon the people, technology and organisations which give rise to and sustain such infrastructures'.

An early significant effort at establishing a digital spatial library was the Alexandria Digital Library at the University of California Santa Barbara. The Alexandria Digital Library was one of six federally funded library projects. The U.S., National Science Foundation founded it in early 1994.

The Library's collection and services focus on georeferenced information: maps, images, data sets, and other information sources with links to geographic locations. Much of the information in the collection was primarily of the University's service area, or Southern California. A key aspect of the collection is the ability to perform data queries and retrieve results by geography location. The basic means of describing and finding information is with a geographic footprint. A footprint depicts the location on the surface of the earth associated with either an object in the collection such as a map, remote sensed image, or aerial photograph, or with a user's query.

The footprint may be represented as a point or polygon, with latitude and longitude coordinates. As a user queries the collection through a user interface, the user creates a footprint or an interactive map to indicate the area of interest. The query area is matched with the object footprints in the metadata to retrieve relevant objects about the query area. This approach to query structure allows the user to choose arbitrary query areas and is not limited to geographic areas with place names. The objects in the collection that fall within a particular query area do not have to have the names associated with them that the user enters for a text based query.

By translating a user's textbased query into a footprint query for a certain geographic area, the user can retrieve all types of information about a location such as remote sensed images, data sets, aerial photographs, and textual information. The catalog for the Alexandria Digital Library is configured for searches that will retrieve objects that are either in an online format or physical location as a map. Using the Alexandria Digital Library as a model, the Idaho Geospatial Data Center was started in 1996 by a team of geographers, geologists, and librarians. The aim of the team was the establishment of digital library of public domain geographic data for the state of Idaho. As a theoretical and practical foundation for their digital spatial collection, which they termed a 'geolibrary,' the team used a set of parameters as defined by Goodchild.

Goodchild defined a geolibrary's components as including a browser or specialised software application running on the user's computer and providing access to the geolibrary through a computer network. A geolibrary also includes a 'basemap' or geographic frame of reference for the browser's queries. A basemap would provide an image of an area corresponding to the geographical extent of geolibrary collection. The basemap would depend on the scale of the search being performed from a large geographic area, such as a state, or a smaller location, as a city block.

A gazetteer or index that would link place names to a map would also be included. A large collection of collection catalogs would be maintained on distributed computer servers. The servers would be accessed over a network with the browser, using basic server-client architecture. A geolibrary would ideally provide open access to many types of information with geographic referenced queries regardless of the storage media. Using a grant from the Idaho Board of Education's Technology Incentive Programme, the team built a geographic digital data repository or the Idaho GeoSpatial Data Center (IGDC).

The library contained a number of digital geospatial datasets that was searchable through a flexible browsing tool. The collection contained a number of public domain information such as Digital Line Graphs and Digital Raster Graphics from the United States Geological Survey and U.S., Bureau of the Census TIGER boundary files for the state of Idaho. The site provided an interactive visual analysis of selected demographic/economic data for Idaho counties.

The site also contained interactive links to other Idaho and national spatial data repositories. A key aspect of the IGDC's collection was the development of the GeoLibrary's browser, which was implemented using MicroSoft Visual Basic 5.0 and ESRI MapObjects technology. The interface of the browser consisted of three panels resembling the Microsoft Outlook user interface.

A first panel, a map panel, would be used to explore the geographic coverage of the geolibrary and to select an area of interest. A second panel in the interface was where the query would be performed. The final panel is where the query results would be displayed for analysis and to download spatial data. In many ways, librarians are well aware of the ideas outlined in the discussion on the concepts and components for digital data infrastructure. Library collections and services in electronic form, such as a digital library, integrate many aspects of the client-server architecture in providing access to materials in an online distributed environment.

Digital libraries have in them collections of digital information objects of various formats in an ordered database defined by descriptive data standards. Organised in a regular manner, the database is searchable using query applications via a user interface, usually through an online catalog. Information is compartmentalised in short descriptions using metadata tags to ease search and retrieval applications. The overall structure is guided by administrative oversight that takes into account the needs of the various users involved in the community.

Researchers, such as Goodchild, envision an intersection of the concepts of the digital library and that of the spatial data infrastructure in a sort of 'geolibrary'. Goodchild envisions a geolibrary as a library filled with 'georeferenced information that can have a geographic footprint.' Including multimedia, images, and music that could be assigned a location attribute, geolibraries would thus extend beyond the scope of a traditional map library, and provide new services and resources for users to discover.

The survey of the characteristics of spatial data databases and related infrastructure indicate the involvement of many different factors in assembling a data infrastructure. However, in addition to data providers, databases, metadata, data networks, technology, and institutional arrangements, there is also a significant in organisational and human resource factors. Nogueras-Iso et al. offer six talking points that are essential to consider in building a spatial data infrastructure. These include technology, policies and standards, human resources, institutional arrangements, spatial data and metadata, and data networks. They suggest that spatial data infrastructure should not recreate the wheel in its technology development. It would be prudent to look at what information technology has accomplished to date, and then integrate that knowledge with GIS expertise, regardless of the difficulties involved. Integration of existing technology also applies to standards and policies. Standards enhance communication and development with a common language and concepts, leading to guidelines that affect architecture, processes, methods, or policies. There should be a common consensus of minimal guidelines that can accommodate those working with geospatial data, retrieval, and discovery.

User-guided development is also critical when examining the human resources side of GIS information and technology. Further, the use of qualified researchers and developers is essential. To create institutional frameworks, agreements have to be certified to establish national, regional, and global spatial data infrastructure. These spatial data infrastructures should be created over the geographic data, stored in the spatial databases, and their description in rich, descriptive metadata. Finally, open systems and ease of access is of strategic importance to ensure quality and accuracy from remote systems.

The need for data description standards for digital geospatial data is especially apparent in the proliferation of WebGis applications in the wake of spatial data distribution enabling initiatives, such as the NSDI. WebGIS describes a type of geographic information system. WebGIS basically consists of client, server, and network model, wherein the client is integrated in a Web browser. While creating many opportunities for librarians in making available unique geospatial datasets, the tremendous growth in WebGIS has created many challenges for libraries in trying to incorporate digital geospatial data in their services and legal considerations in the use of distributed data.

WEB GIS AND LIBRARIES

In recent years the number and scope of WebGIS applications has grown tremendously. In their survey of WebGIS applications, Yang *et al.,* discuss a wide number of interactive mapping sites available on the Internet. They note that many users of the Internet have already experienced using WebGIS software tools through interactive mapping tools available on the Internet. Such sites include: Yahoo Maps, National Map, and GoogleEarth.

Other WebGIS applications that are available on the Internet give access to a varying amount of specialised geospatial data. Many local government Web sites for city and county governments across the United States offer interactive mapping sites such as the City of Albuquerque and City of Durham for users to access technical data about their municipalities. These mapping sites give access to socioeconomic, demographic, and planning data.

Many government sites use ESRI software products such as ArcGIS and ArcWEB services to facilitate data searches for information. Other WebGIS applicatiosn include environ-mental planning, agricultural planning wetlands management, archaeological research, health planning research, transportation planning, citisen political participation, and education planning. Other developments in WebGIS include different data visualisations to offer unique perspectives on information for analytical purposes, such as three-dimensional modeling and combinations of software such as multimedia and WebGIS to offer comprehensive views of geospatial data A net effect of the increasingly popularity of WebGIS.

The popularity of WebGIS applications among the public has led to unequal data distribution across the Internet, Since, bandwidth is constrained. In their study of WebGIS, Yang identify two issues related to improving access to digital geospatial data on the Interent. The first issue concerns the sharing of and interoperability for heterogeneous data among different systems, different communities, and different users. The second issue is a quality of service issue, that of how to improve the system performance so data are delivered to the users within a reasonable time span. In regards to the first issue, the authors identify international organisational efforts at creating accepted conventions in data descriptive standards in regards to interoperability and data access, such as the OpenGIS Consortium (OGC) and the Technical Committee 211 of the International Organisation of Standards. The strides being made by the aforementioned organisations and agreement between international geospatial data producers and providers is creating an environment wherein libraries have access to geospatial Web Services, such as ESRI's Geography Network and Geosptatial One Stop. Web service Internet sites essentially provide access to GIS data, software, educational and mapping, or related services.

For libraries, the services can give access to current and large amounts of geospatial data are usually available in a timely manner. In his study of how academic libraries can integrate digital geospatial data into their collections and services, Morris provides a good overview of the issues involved in trying to facilitate Web Service data in an academic library. Some drawbacks of attempting to integrate Web services into a library environment can include lingering technical issues like linking data resources, developing sustainable licensing models, and negotiating access rights to digital geospatial data.

DATA MINING AND WEB MINING

Data mining is one of the hottest topics and buzz word in information technology. It automatically and exhaustively explores very large datasets, consequently uncovering otherwise hidden relationships among data.This technology has been successfully applied in science, health, marketing and finance to aid new discoveries and strengthen markets. In addition, data mining techniques are being applied to discover and organize information from the Web.Data mining itself is in the second generation of artificial intelligence; the core concept of data mining is focused on machine learning.This machine-learning ability allows modification of search criteria automatically before the next execution, once particular patterns or trends have been discovered in the data searched.It is important to understand that data mining is a discovery-oriented data analysis technology and not a single product or a system. It is a highly focused data transformation framework.

This transformation process uses a series of analytical techniques, such as clustering, association and classification.These techniques are taken from the field of mathematics, cybernetics and genetics, and can be used independently or cooperatively. The function is to extract high quality information to identify facts and draw conclusions based on relationships or patterns among the data. Most important, data mining can ask a processing engine to "show answers to questions we do not know how to ask".For example, bank customers' data are kept in different databases, thus, they are isolated from each other.

Data mining technology can search all the different databases together, and provide a better customer view so that the bank can concentrate more on potentially good customers.The rationale is that when asking for specific relationships, more important relationships might be missed. Asking to find relationships that we do not know exist will yield more meaningful data or business knowledge.The combination of these two areas, data mining and the WWW, is known as Web mining.

When data mining is applied to the Web, it can perform several functions including:

- Resource discovery the discovery of locations of unfamiliar files on the network;
- Information extraction the acquisition of useful information from the WWW;
- Generalization the discovery of information patterns from said resources

There are two primary dimensions of Web mining: Web content mining and Web usage mining.

WEB CONTENT MINING

Web content mining is the "process of information or resource discovery from millions of sources across the World Wide Web ".There are two approaches in Web content mining: the agent-based and database approaches. The agent-based approach involves artificial intelligence systems that can "act autonomously or semi-autonomously on behalf of a particular user, to discover and organize Web-based information ".Some intelligent Web agents can use a user profile to search for relevant information, then organize and interpret the discovered information. Some use various information retrieval techniques and the characteristics of open hypertext documents to organize and filter retrieved information.

Another kind of agent is programmed to learn user preferences and use those preferences to discover information sources for those particular users. The database approach focuses on "integrating and organizing the heterogeneous and semi-structured data on the Web into more structured and high-level collections of resources." These organized resources can then be accessed and analysed. These "metadata, or generalizations, are then organized into structured collections and can be analysed".

WEB USAGE MINING

The other dimension of data mining is Web usage mining. This is the process of discovering user access patterns, as data are automatically collected in daily access logs. Recently, referrer logs, which collect information about referring pages for each reference and user registration, also have been included. Web usage mining is crucial in establishing user profiles for a better structured Web site. "As the manner in which the Web is used continues to expand, there is a continual need to figure out new kinds of knowledge about user behaviour that needs to be mined for".

TEN STEPS OF DATA MINING

The following are ten steps of Data Mining for extracting hidden knowledge from data:

IDENTIFY THE OBJECTIVE

The purpose of Step 1 is creating a list of analyses to perform, questions to investigate, and hypotheses to test. The first of thing is to be clear on what you hope to achieve with your analysis. It includes some advanced planning about what type and level of information you intend to capture from the database. Make sure whether or not the objective is measurable. This advance planning can save you time and money in your data mining efforts.

SELECT THE DATA

The next step is to select the data to meet this objective. In this step, the data is organized for analysis and to produce an effective representation.

The following are some examples for a quick checklist:

- Is the data adequate to describe the phenomena, the data mining analysis is attempting to model?

- Is there a common field in your data that can be used for linking it to other database?
- Are internal and external information available for the analysis?
- Is the data stable—will the data being mined be the same and available after the analysis?
- Is there redundancy in the data sets when they are merged?
- How current and relevant are the data to the business objective?
- Is there lifestyle or demographic data available?

PREPARE THE DATA

Once you've organized the data, you must decide which features to convert into usable formats. The purpose of this step is to produce a "data mining-ready" data set.

- Establish strategies for handling missing data, extraneous noise, and outliers
- Identify redundant variables in the dataset and decide which fields to exclude
- Determine the distribution frequencies of the data

For example, it may be efficient to have an account establish date in the format of YY-MM-DD, but it may be necessary to transform this field to one total account number days like NNNN. You can postpone some of these decisions until you select a data mining tool. For example, if you need a neural network or polynomial network you may have to transform some of your fields.

EVALUATE THE DATA

"Evaluate the structure of your data in order to choose the appropriate tools:

- What is the ratio of categorical/binary attributes in the database?
- What is the nature and structure of the database?
- What is the overall condition of the dataset?
- What is the distribution of the data set?

Balance the objective evaluation of the structure of your data against your users' need to understand the findings." For example, neural networks generally work best on data sets with a vast number of numeric attributes.

FORMAT THE SOLUTION

In conjunction with the evaluation of data and business objective determine the format of the solution.

You may think about:

- What is the optimum format of the solution—decision tree, rules, C code, graph, or SQL syntax?
- What are the available format options from the data mining process?
- What is the goal of the solution, classification, and segmentation?
- What does the end-client need—graphs, reports, code?

SELECT THE TOOLS

This step is to select an appropriate data mining tool for the business objectives and data structure.

While selecting a data mining tool, we may consider:

- Is the data set heavily categorical?
- What platforms do your tools support?
- Are the tools ODBC-compliant and incorporated with an end-user interface?

A data mining tool should help you understand the results of its analysis and the kind of solutions the tool generates. No single tool is able to provide the answer to your data mining project. Some tools integrate several technologies into a suite of statistical analysis programmes, a neural network, and a symbolic classifier.

CONSTRUCT THE MODEL

At this stage the data mining process begins. "This is the process of searching for patterns in a data set and the generation of classification rules, decision trees, clustering, scores, weight, and evaluation and comparison of error rates. Usually the first step is to use a random number seed to split the data into a training set and a test set and construct and evaluate a model."

Resolve these issues:

- What are the model error rates? Are they at acceptable levels? Can they be improved?
- What extraneous attributes did you find? Can those noisy and redundant be purged?
- Is additional data or a different methodology necessary to improve model performance?
- Will you have to train and test a new data set?

VALIDATE THE FINDINGS

This step involves testing a model. It is important after achieving your data mining analysis that you share and discuss the results of the analysis with the administrator, designer, analysts, managers, and engineers.

Ensure that the findings are correct and appropriate to the objectives:

- Are the findings available and do they make sense?
- Does the process have to return to any previous steps to improve results?
- Can other data mining tools be used to produce the same findings?

DELIVER THE FINDINGS

This step provides a final report to the business unit or client. The report should document the entire data mining process such as data preparation, tools used, test results, source code, and rules. Thus, you will know if the findings meet the objective, if additional data can improve the analysis, what strategic insight you dig out and how it is applicable, and what proposals can result from the data mining analysis.

INTEGRATE THE SOLUTIONS

Finally, you share the findings with all interested end-users in the appropriate business units. This process involves incorporating the results of the analysis into the company's business procedures. Although data mining tools automatically invoke database analysis, they can make some mistaken findings and erroneous conclusions if you're not careful.

ADVANTAGES OF DATA MINING

Data mining uses advanced technology for gleaning valuable insights from database that enable the business user to make the right business decisions. It turns up data that gives business companies just a little edge, but the payoff for this small edge is large. One obtains the competitive advantages required to grow in today's competitive environment. Data mining is simple in theory, but it can get quite involved in practice. That means that users will probably need some help getting set up. Many data mining software solutions are available for small and large businesses in most industries and these tools are constantly improving. The accuracy of mining will make a difference in the bottom line of business. "A recent META Group survey revealed that Fortune 500 firms were using data mining for three general purposes: 64 per cent for strategic planning, 49 per cent for competitive intelligence, and 46 per cent to increase their market share."

So far, the following have been the traditional applications of data mining technology by industry sectors:

- Retailers Database marketing, advertising effectiveness, inventory and category management.
- Banking and Insurance Financial modeling, fraud detection, market and industry profiling, database marketing, customer segmentation.
- Brokerage/Stock Exchange
- Telecommunication call detail record analysis, optimal use of capital equipment, targeted marketing.
- Government Collections, workload selection, logistics, and intelligence gathering.
- Manufacturing Production quality control, supply-chain and inventory control

Data mining provides companies extremely valuable insight that has, to date, been closely guarded as corporate stealth technology to protect competitive advantage. However, there is sometimes a breakthrough when trying something new. Some mistakes will be made. Mistakes can be remedied with statistical expertise, but the technology is becoming more useful for more users.

Data mining is also not designed to fix all business problems or tell you what the real problem is, but it gives a company a sense which can be used to help make intelligent business decisions.

"Most of all, data mining is an ongoing process that involves a lot of analysis and refining along the way, so think of it as a worthy investment. And like any investment, even if your data-mining portfolio only uncovers small golden nuggets at first, those nuggets properly managed yield a lot of value."

DATA MINING TECHNIQUES ENHANCE LIBRARY SYSTEM

Suppose a library system has the following goals:

- Increase books borrowing rate.
- Attract more users to borrow books.
- Assist library professionals in making policy on the acquisition of duplicate copies and new publications.

The relationship between Data Mining and Library Management can be shown as in figure

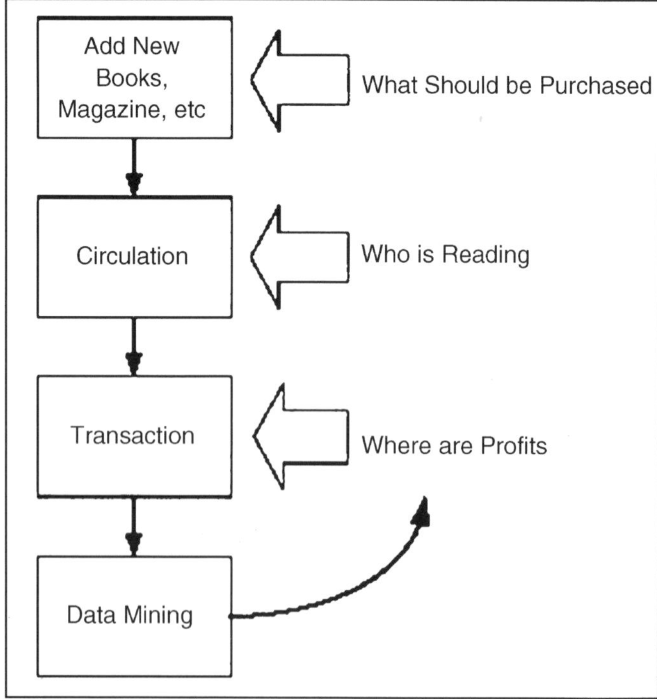

Fig. The Cyclical Relationship between Data Mining and Library Management

EXAMPLE

Consider a library whose books database includes the data of 2000 volumes of books, and the borrowing history of 5000 users who have borrowed books from library. From this database, we have developed a report system to represent the relationship between books and students. And then we use the data mining association rule to analyse the books of the same cluster borrowed by the students. A report chart of books will be produced, so that the library professionals will find references to the books for making a decision. Additionally, the library collection may be used more effectively.

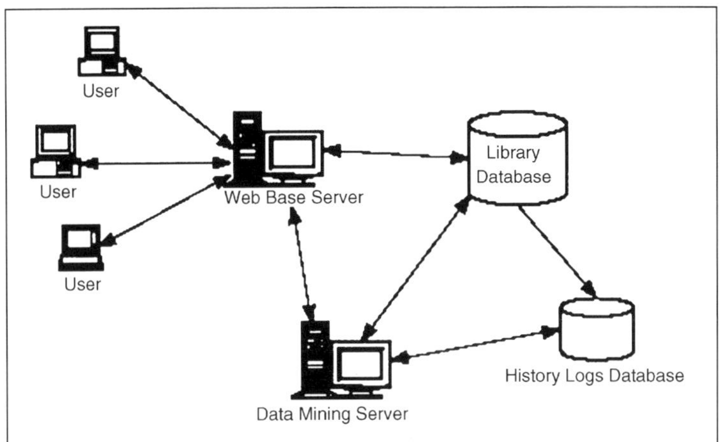

Fig. The Prototype of a Library Architecture

The library database includes seven tables. The first of them is *BOOKS* which contains each of the books' basic information. The table *BOOKS* was improved from *MARCBOOKS* which comes from the previous library system. It kept most of the columns from MARCBOOKS. Machine-readable Cataloguing (MARC) is a kind of metadata to describe a book. *USERS* has part of a student's basic information from the registration system and coordinates with the library system. *COPY* describes the actual volumes in the library. *LOCATION* reports the real location of each book. *CIRCUL* records each circulation of a book. *RESERVATION* has the information that is stored when a user holds a book. Figure shows the schema of these tables. Between each table, there is a key column that sometimes is a primary key in one of them. For instance, the relation key between *BOOKS* and *COPY* is ISBN.

The data mining system is under statistics in a library system. It is an advantageous part of the library system. The process between the main page of data mining and its four functions is shown in figure. On the main page of data mining, the administrator has four functions to execute. The first function is backup the *CIRCUL*. The second one is the list of top ten books. The third one is to execute rule. The final one is rule manager. The following paragraphs are describing them.

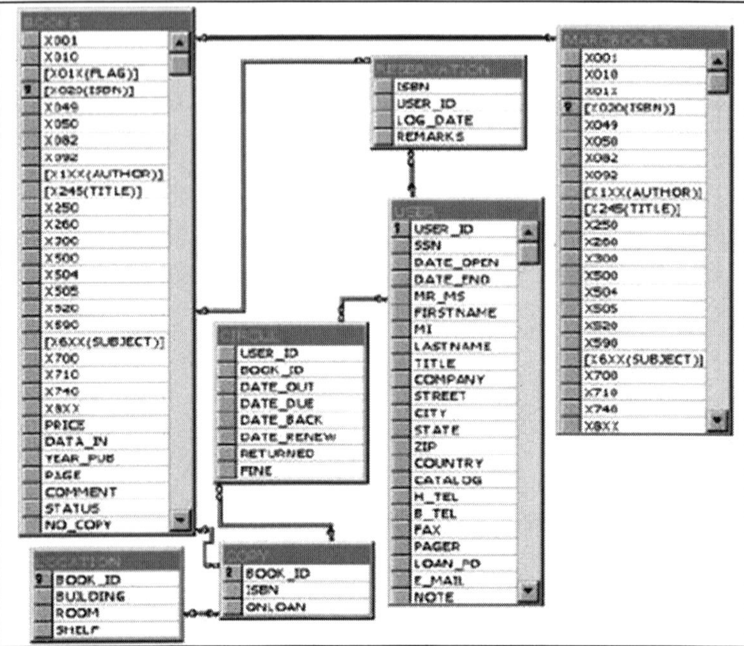

Fig. The Schema of the Library Database

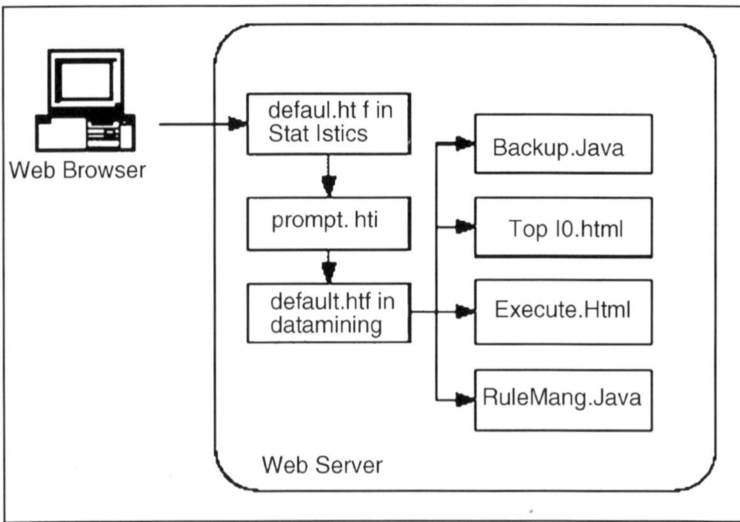

Fig. The Main Process of the Data Mining System

CONCLUSION

It is unlikely that libraries will continue to satisfy users' information needs using the traditional catalogs as the primary access mechanisms. To be certain, online catalogs provide good access to books, films, microfiche, audio tapes, and other materials traditionally kept in libraries. However, few, if any, libraries have succeeded in using their online catalogs to provide adequate access to a significant number of digital materials. In an era where information costs rapidly increase while budgets remain flat, libraries must find alternatives to slow, awkward, and expensive manual cataloguing. The Artificial Intelligence methods such as genetic algorithms and machine learning, or statistics method support data mining tools to accomplish tasks. These methods are fast and thorough and exploit the tremendous power of computers to find nuggets of useful information embedded in mountains of data. In the future, advanced data mining technology will depend on computer architecture and database technology.

6

Library Planning in Twenty-first Century

ROLE OF INFORMATION IN PLANNING

WHAT IS PLANNING

Planning is a simple process used every day. In the process, one decides where he is, where he wants to be, and how he gets there. Getting to work every day, grocery shopping, preparing for a vacation or trip, and saving for retirement are examples of events that require planning. More formally, planning is an organizational process of envisioning a desired future and developing the necessary infrastructure to achieve it.

WHY PLAN

Overall, the purpose of planning is to achieve excellence in public library service.

Some specific benefits:

- Planning provides information to use in decision-making.
- Planning provides a blueprint for future library development.
- Planning guides decision-makers in setting necessary priorities about who receives what service with what efficiency.
- Planning provides information to use in the allocation of resources, particularly when they are scarce.
- Planning leads to structured positive change resulting in improved library service.
- Planning makes crises less critical.
- Planning encourages staff creativity and cooperation.
- Planning encourages accountability.
- Planning provides a basis for evaluating the library's performance.
- Planning can improve communication and give everyone who works with the library a sense of common purpose.
- Planning pays off—organizations that plan out-perform those that do not.

WHAT ARE THE STEPS IN THE PROCESS

There are many approaches to planning. Significantly, the Public Library Association published a new approach to public library planning; *Planning and Role Setting for Public Libraries: A Manual of Options and Procedures* is designed to meet the special needs of this community. The following is a summary of the eight major steps recommended.

PLANNING TO PLAN

- Organizes the planning process,
- Shapes the planning process to the library's needs and resources,
- Coordinates planning with other management activities,
- Defines the responsibilities of major planning participants, and
- Organizes and trains the Planning Committee.

LOOKING-AROUND

- Identifies information needed for planning,
- Collects information about the library and the comm-unity it serves, and
- Analyses information gathered for planning decisions.

DEVELOPING ROLES AND MISSION

- Describes eight distinct roles, or service profiles, that public libraries may emphasize in providing services to their comm-unities;
- Describes a method of determining which roles are to receive a major commitment in the library and which are to be supported only minimally;
- Guides planners in writing a mission statement as a concise expression of the roles chosen for emphasis;
- Helps the library communicate its service focus to the public, elected officials, and staff.

WRITING GOALS AND OBJECTIVES

- Translates the library's role choices and mission into statements of desired ends or targets,
- Defines goals as long-range and representing a vision of excellence in library service,
- Defines objectives as specific, time limited, and measurable or verifiable, and
- Provides a framework for implementation and evaluation.

TAKING ACTION

- Produces tangible evidence of the library's planning,
- Identifies possible activities to implement the goals and objectives,

- Selects activities best suited to the library's circum-stances and resources, and
- Leads to cycle of annual objective setting and updating of five-year plan.

WRITING THE PLANNING DOCUMENT

- Describes creation of a formal report of the library's planning activities, and
- Provides an opportunity for communication with the public, the library staff, and governing officials.

REVIEWING RESULTS

- Reviews the plan and its implementation activities after a period of time,
- Reviews extent to which objectives were accom-plished, and

"LEVELS OF EFFORT" AS A PLANNING TOOL

Planning and Role Setting for Public Libraries introduces the concept of "levels of effort," an approach that allows library planners to adapt the process to a particular library's needs, purposes, and resources. There are three levels of effort — basic, moderate, and extensive. Any of these will result in acceptable plans. Each library's level-of-effort choice reflects the interplay of several different factors.

- *Participants:* The more individuals and groups represented, the higher the library's level of effort for planning will be.
- *Resources:* Higher levels of effort call for a propor-tionally greater commitment of the library staff's time and larger expenditures from the library's budget.
- *Library Context:* Libraries serving a community with rapid growth or change, a complex and diverse population, shifting economic conditions, or libraries facing a major change in funding may need to plan at a higher level of effort.
- *Planning Purposes:* What the library expects the planning process to accomplish may affect the level of effort chosen for some planning phases.
- *Planning Structure:* Libraries planning at a basic level of effort may approach many planning activities informally; but as library complexity increases, the planning structure becomes more formal, thus increasing the level of effort.
- *Planning Schedule:* Some libraries may complete their first objectives cycle over a very short time period; higher levels of effort may require twelve to eighteen months to complete.

ROLE SETTING AS A PLANNING TOOL

Another unique feature of the planning process developed by the Public Library Association and introduced in *Planning and Role Setting for Public Libraries* is the concept of public library roles.

Public library roles are library service profiles that describe a combination of factors in planning and include:

- What the library is trying to do?
- Whom the library is trying to serve? and
- What resources the library needs to achieve these ends?

PLANNING FOR LIBRARY AUTOMATION

Library Automation refers to the use of computers to serve the needs of library users. The operations of a library get a quantum jump with the introductions of computers. The computers help to provide fast and reliable access to the resources available in the library as well as elsewhere. The application of computers in the library operations avoids repetitive jobs and saves lot of labour, time, speeds up operations, increases use of library resources. Computers are not only used as a tool for processing the data, but also for data storage and accessing. Planning for an automated system, no matter how big or small, should be part of an overall long-range plan for the library. Automation should always be used as a means to achieve overall better patron service. Careful planning for technology will assure that your automation project is 'sustainable', *i.e.*, enhances the organisation's ability to meet its service mission without disrupting the organisational stability of the institution.

The present scenario of library worldwide is:

- Vastly expanded storage of indexes, statistical data bases, and document databases within the library.
- Full-text storage of documents, complete with full-text keyword searching and on-demand printing.
- Access by users to library databases from home or office, with direct downloading of information and text on demand.
- The ability to access remote databases across the country and the world, and to download information and text on demand.
- Storage of pictorial and graphic material.
- Availability of 'intelligent systems' providing transparent, one-step searching and access to various library in-house and remote databases.

These capabilities and far more have become reality. Accordingly, today's integrated system must not only provide access to the traditional cataloguing, circulation, public catalogue (OPAC) and acquisitions modules, but must be capable of connecting through the local system into the systems of other vendors, remote bibliographic databases, CD-ROM drives on a local area network (LAN), and the Internet.

Users are expecting that their library systems be capable of, among other things:

- Providing seamless integration between system gateway and OPAC modules.
- Providing access for external users on the Internet to the library's OPAC.
- Monitoring the usage of remote databases that have been accessed through the gateway.
- Accessing the Internet using a variety of graphical interfaces.

Essentially, what this means is that libraries must plan to use a local library system as a vehicle for achieving access to resources outside that system. Stimulated by the Internet, which has created universal connectivity to information resources heretofore unknown and/or inaccessible, and by Z39.50 interoperability standards and 'gateways,' users of individual local systems are expecting to access the resources of other systems—anywhere and anytime. Moreover, the traditional definition of 'publishing' has been stretched by the creation and instant availability of informational home pages and Web sites worldwide.

Given such increased complexities and heightened levels of expectation, libraries must learn all the more how to plan for the introduction of automation in an organised and systematic fashion. There is little mystery involved here: It is entirely a matter of building upon what you already know about your library, using tools that are readily at hand and, most importantly of all, involving the people—staff and users—who must live with the consequences of any automation decisions.

WHAT IS LIBRARY AUTOMATION

Traditional library work consisting of acquisitions, technical processing, serials control, circulation and reference services all entail time consuming manual work. Though these activities are essential to proper functioning of a library, they consume professional staff time that might otherwise go towards user services and library development. Library computerisation is now gaining importance necessitating the establishment of profession-wide standards. Comprehensive studies of library computer systems world over include discussions of machine-managed acquisitions, cataloguing, serials control, circulation and bibliographic service modules. The litreature in this area highlights major aspects of computer's role in the library environment. Similar to several aspects of library management, the demand for more and faster information services and the decline in library resources are compelling librarians to appreciate the role of computers within their operations.

In general, librarians are looking to maximize the benefits of automation by spreading computer use to as many aspects of library activities as possible by taking advantage of developments in computer hardware and software and telecommunications.

NEED FOR LIBRARY AUTOMATION

Even though this question seems to be very fundamental it is essential to emphasise this aspect, as the library automation is yet to take off in majority of the Indian libraries. Secondly, while justifying need for library automation more than cost-effectiveness the benefits derived by the library users become the major consideration. To appreciate the advantages it becomes necessary to highlight the different levels of library automation.

Following are considered as important factors for Library Automation:

- Information explosion.
- Increase in the collection of libraries.
- Inability of users to explore the unlimited litreature and information of their interest.
- Advances in the computer and communication technology.
- Wastage of user/ staff time in locating the information.
- Provide wide access to resources within the libraries and elsewhere.
- Better access.
- Quality in service.
- Cooperative efforts (Resource Sharing).

Out of all libraries an academic library has a difficult task of defining its mission and operating objectives. The automation programme will have to mange a wide range of litreature associated with numerous departments and educational programmes of the academic institution. Furthermore, in an academic library the collections will be diverse unlike a special research library where the collection is relatively homogeneous.

The user group will also range widely, including faculty, staff, students, scholars, administrators and the general public. The position of an academic library funded largely by the government further complicates the process of identifying and prioritising objectives.

As difficult as the task might at first appear, it is nevertheless essential to the process of establishing automated systems of any type. In addition the overall health of ones library operation will benefit from a modicum of intellectual rigour in this area.

AREAS OF LIBRARY AUTOMATION

As a first step in a planning process, it is desirable to formulate a model for computerisation listing all itemised and prioritised information systems being maintained on a manual basis by the library. For this exercise it is necessary to break down these procedures into their constituent parts. When further subdividing these activities, each item is to be considered of its functional elements. The systems and subsystems listed below are only indicative and may vary with differing library system environments.

These are:

- Acquisitions:
  - Selection
  - Ordering
  - Claiming/cancellation
  - Receiving/invoice processing
  - Extended procurements
  - Gift tracking
  - Fund Control
  - Maintains information about all library related funds
  - Ability to group funds (nesting)
  - Track fund allocations and adjustments
  - Fund encumbrance
  - Fund expenditure
  - Cash Balance
  - Free Balance
  - Automatic updating of fiscal information through recording of specific transactions
  - Track year-to-date expenditures
  - Create Purchase Orders
- Technical Services:
  - Books
  - Serials
  - Special Collections
- Cataloguing:
  - Books
  - Serials
  - Special Collections
- Circulation:
  - Charge/Renewal
  - Discharge
  - Loan Periods
  - Processing schedules
  - Holds
  - Messages
  - Blocks
  - Notices
  - Transaction Recording Devices for off-line processing
  - Member control
  - Inventory control

- Serials Control:
  - Receipt (check-in)
  - Claiming
  - Bindery control
  - Replacements
  - Monographic serials
  - Invoice processing
- Reference Services:
  - Desk services
- User tools
- Bibliographic utilisation
- Reprography
- Inter-library communications
- General Administration
- Grants Administratiuon
- Library Publications
- Bindery
- Periodical Citation Searching
- OPAC
- Bibliographic Database

PLANNING OF LIBRARY AUTOMATION

Planning for library automation has been defined as planning for 'integrated systems' that computerise an array of traditional library functions using a common database. While this is still generally true, rapid technological change is forcing a re-examination of what it means to 'automate the library.' As physical, spatial and temporal barriers to acquiring information are crumbling, libraries must plan for a broader and more comprehensive approach to providing automated services.

DEVELOPING A LIBRARY 'PROFILE'

One of the most important planning tools involves collecting basic statistical information on the library and its operations. You will find that the same basic data will be needed again and again—whether for vendors from whom you are requesting cost estimates, or for other libraries with whom you may be seeking to cooperate in implementing automation.

The following are examples of commonly needed data:

- Number of titles and volumes in the collection, current and projected.
- Number of borrowers, current and projected.
- Number of materials circulated, current and projected.
- Number of new materials acquired, current and projected.
- Interlibrary loans, lent to and borrowed from other libraries.

- Description of any cooperative arrangements involving the library.
- Library address and hours of operation.

In addition, it is important to take stock of any existing automation in the library by compiling the following data:

- Percentage of collection that has catalogue records in machine-readable form.
- Description of collection without machine-readable records, by category, (, monographs, audiovisuals).
- Description of currently-automated library functions (if any).
- Estimates of the location and number of workstations (to show where you intend to have equipment in any future system).
- Specifications for any existing equipment to be re-used with any future system (if any).

At the same time that this data is being assembled, it is important to assess user needs and set service priorities. This can be accomplished by undertaking a focused, strategic planning process designed to involve the library's 'stakeholders.'

DEVELOPING A STRATEGIC PLAN

A library planning to automate should undertake a process by which representative staff and users can identify service needs and objectives. The purpose of such an effort is to allow participants to articulate their interests and concerns, share perspectives and learn about possibilities in a collaborative setting. Group interaction is an important contributing factor in the success of the goal, which is to develop and sustain library automation in the years ahead.

Here are the basic steps involved in this process:

- Plan on a two-day, intensive planning effort.
- Ask participants to identify strengths, weaknesses, opportunities and threats in the library's environment (known as 'SWOT' factors in strategic planning) that are characteristic of or that confront the library.
- Group these factors into critical issue areas that are likely to have an impact on the libraries' future in developing and sustaining automation.
- *Ask participants to identify ideas and perceptions in relation to the question*: "How do you see the library providing user-friendly, cost-effective automated services in five years?
- Through a method of your own devising, ask participants to prioritise all of the ideas that come out of the above two 'brainstorming' exercises.
- Ask participants to shape these priorities into the draft of a strategic 'vision' for automation development consisting of a statement of purpose, goals and objectives for the library.

SETTING SERVICE PRIORITIES

Your strategic vision must now provide the framework or context for the next step in the automation process, which is to determine which library functions should be automated and in what order of priority. For example, processes that are repetitive, occupy large amounts of staff time, require retrieving information from large, unwieldy files, or are high-profile functions of the library (such as the public catalogue) are prime candidates for automation. Determining the functions that you wish to automate and their priorities relative to each other is important for all sorts of reasons.

If needs and priorities are clear, functions can be automated in phases, allowing for more effective use of frequently scarce funding. Moreover, it is a way to develop credibility with funding agencies and be able to take advantage of 'sudden' funding opportunities. Finally, evaluations of systems and options will be easier and more productive if you are able to match your highest functional priorities against the corresponding modules available in the marketplace.

A WORD ABOUT COSTS

Speaking of funding, planners need to be aware that there are certain cost elements involved in the installation and operation of any automated system.

These may be summarised as follows:

- Planning and consulting costs include direct, out-of-pocket costs, (*e.g.*, hiring a consultant) and indirect costs, (*e.g.*, training staff) associated with getting started.
- Purchase of the system includes the cost of acquiring the initial system hardware and software, as well as the cost of preparing a site for the computer system.
- Telecommunication costs are those fees paid to telephone companies for connecting remote terminals or workstations to a central computer system.
- Conversion costs are those associated with the creation of machine-readable bibliographic and, for circulation systems, patron, records.
- On-Going Operating costs include:
  - Maintenance fees
  - Utility costs
  - Bar code labels
  - Miscellaneous supply costs
  - Telecommunications costs
  - Salaries and benefits (if extra staff are hired).
- Additions to the existing system may be required to maintain performance specifications, to accommodate new users, or to allow for additional automated functions.

SYSTEM SPECIFICATIONS

At some point, you will need to re-formulate your functional priorities into 'functional specifications,' which may be defined as what you want an automated system to do for you, including things that your current manual system cannot do.

'Technical specifications' must also be established. These include standards that must be adhered to, system performance, operation, and maintenance, as well as infrastructure requirements, such as stable sources of electricity and telecommunications, and sufficient bandwidth. Developing clear and accurate functional and technical specifications that are specific to your library is one of the most important, if not THE most important, activity that you will engage in as you plan for your automated system.

These specifications will carry you through the entire procurement process, and will ensure that the system which most closely matches them will be the most useful and the most responsive to your needs.

DEVELOPING A FORMAL SPECIFICATIONS DOCUMENT

It is very difficult to compare systems sensibly and pragmatically solely by randomly looking at systems, talking to sales representatives, reading litreature or comparing broad cost quotations. For this reason, libraries use a formal document—often known as a 'Request for Proposal,' or RFP—that organises and standardises the information provided to and requested from the various system vendors.

Utilising an RFP to solicit written responses from vendors makes it possible for you to systematically compare functionality, cost, maintenance, support, and all the other issues that are involved in system procurements. The process can save you money and will result in a wiser decision.

An RFP document should include these essential elements, among others:

- Background information on the library.
- A description of how the proposals should be arranged and submitted.
- Instructions on receiving vendor business and financial information.
- Criteria the library will use to evaluate vendor proposals.
- Questions regarding vendor training and documentation.
- Your functional and technical specifications.

Also, vendors should be asked to describe:

- How they will create bibliographic, item and borrower databases.
- Their system maintenance programmes and services.
- Their site preparation requirements.
- Their delivery and installation methodologies.
- Their system performance guarantees.
- Their pricing and cost strategies, in detail.

EVALUATING VENDOR PROPOSALS

Upon the receipt of vendor proposals, it will be time to begin the process of system evaluation and selection.

This process involves a number of key steps:

- If possible, form a project team of persons to assist with the evaluations and the selection who have some knowledge of automation or who work in the area(s) being automated. People involved in the strategic planning process would be a good choice.
- Try to weed out proposals that are 'fatally flawed,' *e.g.*, where the vendor fails to reply to any of the functional specifications or the system is missing a module for a high-priority function.
- Begin in-depth reading of the 'surviving' proposals, carefully noting both deviations from the requirements as defined by the RFP and any aspect that is handled unusually well. Make a list of any parts of the response that are not clear and require further clarification.
- Schedule system demonstrations. They are an important component of the evaluation process. Allow the vendors to show off the vendor's system in the most attractive light; however, be prepared with a list of what you want to see along with questions you would like answered. Use the same list with each vendor. This permits more effective cross-comparisons.
- Consider using computerised spreadsheet software in order to compare and evaluate vendor cost proposals. Costs may not be what they seem at first glance.
- Contact some of each vendor's current clients—sites of the same library type, and of similar size, where the hardware and software modules that have been proposed to you are currently in use.
- Assign point values to the criteria listed in the RFP and assign scores to the different proposals. The system with the highest score becomes the number one finalist, the system with the second highest score number two and so on. To maintain a negotiating edge, it is better to cut to two vendors rather than one. If that is impossible, maintain the illusion anyway. Remember: The selection process is not over until the contract is signed. Until that point, never let any vendors know that they have been eliminated, including those with fatal flaws.

PUTTING SYSTEMS INTO PLACE

After the system selection process is complete, there are several important steps which must occur. You and your vendor will have to negotiate and sign a contract. You will want to test the system and make sure it suits your needs. You will want to make provisions for system maintenance. Finally, you will want to train both your staff and your users as much as possible to prepare them for when the system is up and running. With regard to training, the following must be considered: In thinking of automation planning, there is often a tendency to focus on the hardware and software aspects of planning, and to ignore the human aspects of automation—training and public relations. Without these, however, even the most carefully designed system may not be accepted by library staff or library users. To assure the success of your hard planning work, a training and public relations plan should be part of any automation project.

Fortunately, training can begin long before the system is installed. By involving staff at all levels in the analysis of operations, the identification of needs, the setting of priorities, the development of specifications, and the evaluation of systems, staff will gain much of the knowledge they need as the planning progresses. User acceptance and enthusiasm for your new automated system is certainly an important ingredient in a successful planning effort. If you are implementing a public access catalogue, it is probably the most important measure of success.

Public relations can allow you to accomplish three things:

- Make users aware of your new system and services;
- Motivate them to use the system; and
- Train them in using the new system and services effectively.

RETROSPECTIVE CONVERSION

In the rush to acquire hardware and software, librarians often forget that their most valuable product is the library's database. The creation of a high-quality machine-readable database provides the cornerstone upon which all present and future automation efforts rest. Vendors will come and go, hardware will become obsolete, software will be replaced, but a well-constructed, well-maintained database, with its accompanying local holdings, will be the library's transportable and viable link from system to system. Moreover, as library users begin to access not only their local system but systems in other libraries as well, the quality of respective databases will influence both the outcome of search strategies and the availability of materials.

Database readiness has several important facets:

- Catalogue records must be carefully converted from manual to machine-readable formats.
- Collections must be prepared for conversion through effective and ongoing weeding and inventory programmes.
- Once converted, collections must be properly maintained as titles are added, withdrawn, transferred and recataloged.
- Standards—for bibliographic, item and patron records as well—must be adhered to. In particular, adherence to well-established and accepted standards of description for bibliographic information in a

machine-readable database is critical because: without standards, files cannot easily be transferred from one automated system to another.

- It is essential for libraries wishing to participate in resource sharing arrangements with other libraries, who will require such adherence as a condition of participation.

7

Impact of Information Technology on Libraries

LIBRARY AND INFORMATION TECHNOLOGY

The *'Information Technology'* revolution has brought about impact upon the society and economy activities. Information has become a significant component of world economy activity and being recognised as a major economic resource. Organisations have grown to view their information resources as a *strategic asset,* utilising these resources as an instrument in enhancing the country's competitiveness in industry and international trade.

Traditionally, major organisational assets were classified as human, financial, material, equipment and management resources. Khosrowpour view that during the decade of the 1980s, the technological advancements of information technology caused many organisations to regard their information technology resources as the *sixth major organisational asset.* Harker claimed that a tidal wave of *change* is headed towards the *telecommunication industry,* and it will ultimately transform the economic, and social and political environment for nearly every person in the world.

Researcher added that technological advancements in telecommunications allowed information users to exchange information more freely and globally. Living standards have been raised and the problems of everyday living eased considerably. Much of this change is being brought by *technological innovation* and the *information revolution*—the convergence of computing, communication and information. Organisations that acknowledge and prepare for this revolution will emerge as winners.

THE EVOLUTION OF INFORMATION TECHNOLOGY

Researcher provide a comprehensive remarks of the evolution of IT where he claimed that during the 1950s, computer systems were used mainly for scientific applications, with scientists the primary users and custodians of these systems. Business use of computers for mainly functional applications, such as accounting, began in the 1960s. The era of the 60s is known for the birth of

Data Processing (DP) or *Electronic Data Processing (EDP),* which created a whole new profession.

During this period:

- The computer was perceived as a number crunching tool.
- Attention was focused on the power of these modem tools to compute, with much less emphasis placed on the overall value of information as a resource.

In the 1970s, more organisations moved towards the use of computers to provide management with information. This concept soon became known as *Management Information Systems (MIS).* Although MIS concepts were considered to be a major breakthrough in the use of computer systems to process information, organisations still emphasised the computer itself rather than focusing on the data and information as major components of the systems.

Many other concepts evolved during this period, examples:

- Database Management Systems (DBMS).
- Decision Support Systems (DSS).

The domination of mainframe computer systems gave way to the introduction of *minicomputers.* This new generation of computers became instrumental in the development of *Distributed Systems (DS).* The introduction of personal computers or microcomputers was another landmark development of this period. The technological advancements of the 1970s paved the way for a new era in the 1980s, which became known as the *Information Age.*

The significant phenomena of this era include the greater recognition of information as a major organisational asset and its importance in a competitive world economy.

Another important characteristic of this era is the emphasis on the management of information and related resources utilised to maintain information resources. Furthermore, greater participation by users of information services became a major fact of this age.

The new generation of end users are more knowledgeable than their counterparts of a few decades earlier, and they created many networks of information systems sharing the vast powers of computers, data, information, and knowledge. In addition, technological advancements in telecommuni-cations allowed information users to exchange information more freely than ever. The old dream of developing computer systems that could think intelligently, learn, and make recommendations to decision makers carne closer to reality through many new applications of *Artificial Intelligent (AI)* and its component Expert Systems (ES).

New Information Technology Resources

There are several developments which have lead to a new perception and assessment of the use and management of information technology resources.

These include:

- Recognition of information as a major organisational resource.
- Greater emphasis on utilisation of information as a major driving force in achieving effective strategies.
- New integration of telecommunications and information processing systems.
- A vast array of components comprising information technology resources.

Today, information technology resources consists of all types of information, representing various *functional entities* of organisations. Organisational information now can appear in all forms, which are processed by a conglomeration of computer machinery, examples:

- Mainframe,
- Minicomputers,
- Microcomputers,
- Reprographics, and
- Video discs.

It is communicated through the use of communication systems. The information is generated through the use of many information proccssing and management systems in diverse organisational structures. In addition to mechanical, procedural, and technical components of information technology resources, one must also consider the human elements.

These human elements can be divided into three categories:

1. Those individuals who are involved in different activities of generating information.
2. Those who are the primary users of information.
3. The management team responsible for the overall management planning functions of information technology resources.

One can argue that the role of the information technology resources management team has become more important to the overall success and growth of many organisations. In addition, the task of managing these resources is far more complex and sophisticated in the information age. Information technology resources are no longer viewed by many organisations as number crunching 'black boxes,' but rather as vital resources for identifying new opportunities and developing strategies.

Information Management in the 1990s

The cost of computing has dropped drastically in the past two decades. There is considerably more advanced information and communication devices available. AB a result, organisations of all sizes and types have been employing this technology to increase their competitive advantages. With the rapid evolution in information technology, the effectiveness of the traditional management techniques to the management of this technology has been the subject of much speculation by both researchers and practicing managers.

Clearly, this changing technology is in need of an evolution in its management as well:

- A management approach that is as dynamic as the technology itself,
- Keeping pace in its methods and strategies as the technology matures,
- Making drastic shifts in direction when necessary, and
- Always providing new opportunities for growth, is the essential ingredient for strategic management of information technology resources.

As information technology resources become more important to the overall success of the organisation, its management may not only be limited by technical planning and execution as was true in the past. With the current number of end users and their demands for information technology services, successful organisations will utilise the expertise of their information technology personnel to provide needed support for the end user in order to obtain the necessary competitive edge.

COMPONENTS OF INFORMATION TECHNOLOGY RESOURCES

Processing Hardware:

- Mainframe-based Systems.
- Mini-based Systems.
- Micro-based Systems.
- Word Processing.
- Micrographics.
- Reprographics.
- Video Disks Processor.
- Desktop Publishing Systems.

Telecommunications:

- Private Branch Exchange (PBX).
- Broadcasting Systems.
- Local Area Networks.
- Telecommunication Access.
- Systems.
- Facsimile Systems.
- Satellite Communications.
- On-Line Processing Systems.

Information:

- Marketing.
- Production.
- Personnel.

- Financial.
- Strategic.
- Intelligent.
- Accounting.
- Legal.
- Economy.
- Government.
- Trade.
- Publication.
- Public.

Office Automation:

- Text Management Systems.
- Electronic Mail.
- Teleconferencing.
- Computer Conferencing.
- Video Conferencing.
- Intelligent Copies.
- Intelligent Printers.
- Dictating Systems.

Systems Professionals:

- Chief Information Officer (ClO).
- Systems Managers.
- Systems Security.
- Administrators.
- System Analysts.
- Database Designers.
- Programmers.
- Computer Operators.
- Data Entry Personnel.
- User Support Personnel.

Processing Software:

- Operating Systems.
- Database Management Systems.
- Procedural Programming Languages.
- Fourth Generation Languages.
- Word Processing Software.
- Electronic Spreadsheet Software.
- Communications Software.
- Graphics and Desktop Publishing Systems.
- Project Management Software.
- Miscellaneous Software.

Management Structures:

- Centralised vs. Decentralised Structures.
- Departmental Computing Structure.
- Information Center Structure.
- End-User Computing Structure.
- Chargeback Processing Structure.

Information Systems:

- Data Processing Systems.
- Management Information Systems.
- Decision Support Systems.
- Transaction Processing Systems.
- Expert and Knowledge-Based Systems.
- Database Processing Systems.
- Executive Information Systems.
- Distributed Processing Systems.

End Users:

- Strategic Planners.
- Financial Managers.
- Marketing Managers.
- Inventory Managers.
- Production Managers.
- Personnel Managers.
- General Managers.
- Accountants.
- Legal Advisors.
- Economics.
- Publication Personnel.
- Training Personnel.
- Public Relations Personnel.
- Clerical Staff.
- Technical Specialists.

NEW INFORMATION TECHNOLOGY (IT) PRODUCTS

MOST IMPORTANT PRODUCTS OF THE '90S

The 1990s was a decade of rapid technological advances. Client-server architecture evolved into a viable alternative to mainframe computing. Enterprise applications such as groupware, inventory control, supply chain, and systems management emerged as platforms for the evolution of business systems. The PC became a Ubiquitous and increasingly powerful desktop tool. And the Internet was embraced as a communication medium, consumer platform, and business conduit. Here are 10 of the most important and influential products introduced in this decade.

1. *Sun Microsystems' Java:* The brave little embedded operating system started out as a platform for write-once-run-anywhere computing and ended up as the Web's favourite tool.
2. *Nets Cape Navigator:* There's probably no greater development in the history of IT than the emergence of the Internet and World Wide Web. By the time Marc Andreessen and Jim Clark launched their graphical Web browser, Navigator 1.0, in 1994, there were more than 1 million Internet hosts. While Mosaic was the first widely distributed browser, Navigator set the standard in terms of look and functionality. And in the process, it shook Microsoft to its core—no small feat.
3. *Lotus Notes:* Lotus Development Corp. licensed Notes, the product most commonly associated with the term groupware, from Iris Associates in 1989. By the time IBM bought Lotus in 1995 for $3.5 billion—primarily to acquire the groupware technology—Notes had an installed base of almost 2 million seats. Lotus made a successful effort to integrate Notes with the Internet when it introduced Domino in 1996.
4. *Microsoft Office:* Microsoft didn't come up with the idea to bundle a spreadsheet, word processor, and graphics package into a productivity suite, but it made the most of the concept-and created a business computing standard. Microsoft has continued to enhance the bundle, including links to the Internet.
5. *Oracle's Relational Database:* The original work on relational database technology was done by Edgar Codd when he was at IBM in the early 1970s. However, Oracle took the relational model and established it as a database standard, through both rapid technological advance and aggressive marketing. In the 1990s, Oracle continued to enhance the basic architecture to incorporate symmetric multiprocessing and object extensions.
6. *Sun Microsystems' Enterprise 10000 Server:* Sun made believers out of many of those who had been skeptical about the scalability of symmetric multiprocessing servers when it shipped the 64-node E-I0000 in May 1997.
7. *SAP Rl3:* The third version of SAP's suite of enterprise applications, introduced in 1992, integrated and automated back-office systems and convinced many companies to re-engineer their business processes to accommodate the software.
8. *Computer Associates' Unicenter:* Introduced in 1993, CA's systems management software unified a disparate set of products and processes, and provided a comprehensive view of IT systems. CA continued to strengthen the product with the introduction of the graphical, object-oriented TNG version in 1997 and the three dimensional TND version in 1998.

9. *Intel's X86 Architecture:* Intel led the PC industry on a price/performance curve that mirrored Moore's Law-and then some. When Intel launched the 66-MHz Pentium processor in 1993, it set the stage for a quantum leap in desktop processing, making possible powerful personal productivity applications and eventually online commerce.
10. *Microsoft Windows:* In the spring of 1990, Microsoft CEO Bill Gates introduced the latest iteration of the company's graphical front end, Windows 3.1 and it was an instant hit with the public. Since then, billions of copies of the operating system have been sold, and, along with its siblings, Windows NT and Windows CE, Windows has proved to be one of the highest-impact products in IT.

WELCOME TO THE INFORMATION SUPERDORM

Malone regard that "we are now at the threshold of a new era, driven this time not by the technologies of production and transportation, but by the technologies of information, communication and coordination." An extraordinary array of information technologies is providing not only powerful new tools for dealing with these changes, but also a promising framework for creating entirely new opportunities. Advances in computers, software, telecommunications, networking, and electronic media are vastly increasing the quantity, quality, and accessibility of all forms of information.

Internet

Internet as a "bunch of communications protocols that enables millions of computers to talk with each other. It is already replacing overnight mail and faxes as a way to communicate quickly and over long distances.

Begun as a research project of the US Defence Department in the 1970s, it has become the:

- Technological trend in academic libraries of the '90s with dial up databases such as CompuServe, small corporate and university databases that are interconnected via the Internet.
- Thousands of companies have started to promote and sell products over the Net and at the same time, businesses are discovering that they can streamline operations and increased productivity by connecting their in-house networks to the Internet.

Almost overnight, the net grows from an academic resource into an ocean of capitalist dream.

World Wide Web

Subscribing to the Internet opens the door to many different types of information and communication possibilities. The World Wide Web, a *subset* of the

Internet and one of the Internet's most popular and employs simpler computer applications, such as Windows, and more transparent commands then the internet.

By using browser software and fast modems, a subscriber can easily:

- View individuals' and organisations' home pages.
- Graphical tables of contents to more-detailed files contained within.
- Best of all, a user need not be a computer pro or a rocket scientist to surf the Net.

With the attributes such as multimedia, hyper linked, dispersed, dynamic, versatile and multi platform, the reason for Web popularity is the ability it affords to send and receive graphics, photographs, movies, and sound along with text. Several factors have contributed to this rapid growth, "most notably, technological advances in software, hardware, and communications that have made connections more economical".

Electronic Mail (E-Mail)

A way for computer users to exchange messages in completely different offices, locations, organisations, cities, countries, even continents using the e-mail programme available through the *Internet Service Provider* (ISP) to create, read, and manage the e-mail messages. Educationally, e-mail has continue to grow more important. It has also become easier to exchange not only textual messages but a variety of files, including graphics, software programmes, spreadsheets, and databases. Ingram believe that e-mail will become part of a total distance-education system that might include elements of videoconferencing, interactive multimedia, and other learning tools.

Lotus Notes

A complete 'environment' or 'platform' for several computer applications and can be used:

- to send electronic mail,
- As an electronic calendaring system,
- As a scheduling system.
- As a bulletin board.
- As a publishing system for the web,
- As an automated workflow system and
- As a group ware system.

Intranets

James view Intranet as a network that lets people within an organisation share the kind of information one's can experience—and create—with Netscape Communicator Professional such as:

- Pages full of text, graphics, sound, and video;
- Fill-out form;

- e-mail with pictures;
- Specialised newsgroup and interactive conferences;
- Directories full of files one's can download; and
- A broad range of custom-tailored resources for research, education, or business.

Thus by using a standardised methods, or protocols for moving information from one computer to another, an entire office, or even a corporation with many physically remote sites, can communicate without worrying about specific hardware or software.

Multimedia

Multimedia tools enable us to express ideas that are more difficult to describe with words than they are to demonstrate in some way. For those who are aural or tactile learners, for example, multimedia provides a fresh new means of comprehending something.

Videoconferencing

Ingram claim that videoconferencing is increasingly used for individual and group meetings as well as to deliver education and training at a distance. Brown University Computing and Information Services view videoconferencing as an interactive audio/visual meeting channel to sites worldwide via high speed telephone lines. Thus, videoconferencing combines the benefits of face-to-face interaction with the power of telecommunications.

As claimed by Littman, the videoconferencing rationales are as follows:

- Enhance the quality and intensity of communications.
- Engender a sense of responsibility and involvement among individuals who could not otherwise meet with each other.
- Lead to the articulation of policy, goals, and objectives through consensual decision making.
- Enable academic librarians to hold interactive sessions regardless of location on such topics as Internet access and use, intellectual freedom and copyright.
- High school students can be introduced to resources in an academic library, thus saving field trip and liability insurance costs.

Virtual Reality

Virtual reality has captured most organisations. It benefits an organisation, by gathering information on customers/users, competitors, and potential markets.

Cavanaugh describes the creation of 'virtual offices' that has enable:

- Communications between employees and vendors.
- Advertise products and services globally.
- Deliver new products or packages of services.

CD-ROMs

Rogers view that the advent of CD-ROMs in libraries was the introduction to the world of high-tech ware for many librarians. CD-ROMs are found in every library today and are loaded on most business networks but are often simply presented to end users, from car mechanics to astronauts. This technology is revolutionising the way students and professionals can assemble and access information.

Being fixed systems:

- The *content* on CD-ROMs is finite, although the amount of information on a disc is still impressive.
- The *functionality* of CD-ROMs and the number of tricks they can perform is finite.

Amendments to the software, indexing, and content are done at the will of the developer and information provider. A number of business databases available on CD-ROMs has increased steadily over the past few years. At the same time, most major public libraries, colleges, and *university libraries* have made available at no cost numerous CD-ROM databases for user and customer use.

CD-ROMs Into the Future

Beiser stresses that the emergence of a high-density CD (HiCD) technology opens exciting new possibilities for all sectors of our society—not the least of which are *libraries.* CD-ROMs was a distribution and publishing medium, and not a competitor to hard disk drives. Meanwhile, HiCD can deliver text, graphics and multimedia content as well or better than a high-speed link. It is the stuff of memory cells, the repository of incredible amounts of otherwise evanescent data, a resource without which libraries will be unable to perform their designated role in an information intensive universe.

Online Databases

It offers full texts of journal and magazine articles. Tenopir claimed that academic librarians are actively looking for alternatives to print journal collections:

- As serials budgets stagnate,
- Print journals take up as much space.
- Patrons want to locate and access everything from a single workstation.

Some examples of online databases are EBSCO Elite Periodical Database, FirstSearch Online Databases, INFOTRAC Periodical and Newspaper Databases, etc.

Electronic Journals

Researcher claimed that electronic journals are mushrooming online, on the Web and in CD-ROM format. This phenomenon is due to the rapid advancement of information technologies including the Internet and digitising techniques. The quantity of e-journals is growing larger although no exact number is available.

In recent years, many more journals have been earmarked for digitising, a necessary process for turning a paper journal into an electronic one. In addition, a considerable number of journals are now published only electronically, which significantly enlarges the size of the e-journal pool. Among all the users of e-journals, academic libraries especially, are the major subscribers of e-journals.

ROLE OF INFORMATION TECHNOLOGY IN MANAGING ORGANISATIONAL

Researcher provide a comprehensive remark of the role of IT in managing organisational change and interdependence. He commented that the world is observing a strong trend of convergence of the technologies of computing and telecommunications. Changing technology economics, merging of formerly disparate technologies with different managerial traditions, and the problems of managing each of the phases of IT assimilation in different ways calls for a major reappraisal of the organisational structures designed for yesteryears. IT is becoming all pervasive and is having impact on all business—in service as well as in manufacturing. It is affecting workers at all levels of organisations—from the executives to assembly hands and clerks. IT is increasingly becoming an integral component of all types of technologies—craft, engineering, routine and non- routine.

IT'S ROLE IN MANAGING ORGANISATIONAL CHANGE

IT and Environment - Goals-Structure

Researcher defined environment as those factors which not only are outside the system's control but which determine in part how the system performs.

Uncertainty is the difference between the amount of information required to perform the task and the amount of information already possessed by the organisation:

- *Proposition* 1: Turbulent environment drives organisations to use IT for monitoring the preferences of the environment. System theorists have recognised the importance of 'feedback' for the survival of the system and for maintaining a 'steady state' or 'homeostasis'. Organisations are purposive systems that learn of the impending threats by scanning. Scanning is the process by which the organisation acquires information for decision making. The modes of scanning are primarily determined by the external environmental stimuli and are determined by the magnitude and by the direction of the discrepancy between the goal and its realisation. While surveillance is useful for information-gathering process, search is oriented towards finding a satisfactory solution to a specific problem. Complex systems require complex controllers. IT will provide the 'complex controller" to the increasingly complex organisation. The information systems of an organisation need to evolve to remain consistent with the changing organisational structure. Referring to the obscurity of causal laws of turbulence, Aldrich argued that scanning could provide the firm with the desired 'competitive edge.'

- *Proposition* 2: Turbulent environment drives organisations to use IT for translating the information on environmental preferences into goals. Continuously changing environment requires organisations to continuously reassess their goals. Effective structuring requires a consistency among the design parameters and contingency factors have demonstrated that organisations' goals can be generated by external forces, such as other groups seeking to use the organisation to further their own ends.
- *Proposition* 3: Turbulent environment drives organisations to use IT to align their structure with environmental preferences. The very efforts of the organisation to maintain a constant external environment produce changes in organisational structure. Scott argued that organisational structure and goals are driven by the preferences in the environment. The structure is determined by the information-processing capacity requirements of the organisation which in turn are governed by the IT being used. Aldrich, Perrow, Walker and Woodward have attributed structural differences to the organisation's technology. Mintzberg had suggested that the organisation's environment and technology are the independent variables that determine the structural variables of the organisation. Fowles, in his narrative on the history of organisational communications technologies contends that the phenomenal expansion of organisations can be largely attributed to advances in the technologies of organisational communication. Yates argued that in absence of technological communication organisations could have evolved differently. Preliminary econometric analyses of the overall U.S., economy for the period 1975-1985 further confirms that the increased use of IT is correlated with decreases in firm size and vertical integration.

IT and Organic Structure

- *Proposition* 4: Turbulent environment drives organisations to make more use of IT for increasing their 'organic' characteristics. 'Organic' firms are better equipped to sustain themselves in turbulent environment. A dynamic environment will drive the structure to an organic state despite other forces; the more complex the environment, the more decentralised the structure. Introduction of IT at the 'operating core' level transforms a bureaucratic administrative structure into an organic one. Effectively, automation of routine tasks eliminates the source of many of the social conflicts throughout the organisation. Law of requisite variety implies that the rate of change of organisational systems must correspond to the rate of change of environmental systems, *i.e.*, organisations with complex environmental interactions would develop complex structures like adhocracies or networks. Adhocracy is suitable for a dynamic and complex environment, when the firm has sophisticated technical systems and the focus is upon consistently offering differentiated products for retaining the customers. Future organisations would be 'networks' characterised by adhocracies with flexible systems of projects and teams brought together quickly to accomplish specific tasks. Some existing organisations have already 'farmed out' their operations by establishing them as separate organisations or contracting them out to other organisations.

- *Proposition 4a:* Turbulent environment drives organisations to use IT for empowering workers at all levels. Growing availability of telecommunications has offered technologies like distributed systems and client-server architecture that facilitate the process of empowerment of the lower levels. In the 'informated' organisation, workers would be 'empowered' by virtue of access to necessary information to perform higher-level tasks. Ramstrom has argued that tactical decisions relating to 'soft' information would be delegated to the 'grass-roots' where there is easy access to relevant information concerning the immediate environment, at the same time providing these levels with the information generated within the system by means of 'cheap' internal information systems.
- *Proposition 4b:* Turbulent environment drives organisations to use IT for increasing the spans of control. Information technologies, by facilitating the standardisation of coordination would facilitate larger spans of control or work units which would be characterised by extensive lateral communication and self- contained authority structures.
- *Proposition 4c:* Turbulent environment drives organisations to use IT for increasing lateral communications. Selective use of lateral decision processes for situations involving task uncertainty increase the information processing capacity of the organisation. Bringing the points of decision down to the points of action reduces the information overload on the managers. Since specification of 'procedures' in complex situations creates inefficiencies, organisations in turbulent environments would use more IT resource for delegating the decision-making to workers.

Increased use of groupware for lateral coordination will spell the demise of middle management.

IT and Differentiation - Integration

- *Proposition* 5: Turbulent environment drives organisations to reduce their 'dimensions' by focusing on core competencies by leveraging their use of IT.
- *Proposition 5a:* Turbulent environment drives organisations to use IT to reduce differentiation and integration to focus on increased specialisation. Organisations structure themselves to minimize coordination costs and group together similar activities to achieve the benefits of process specialisation. Environmental uncertainty or 'task predictability' is the basic independent variable influencing the design of the organisation. Faced with increased uncertainty, organisations can reduce the need for information processing by decreasing the 'diversity of outputs'. Reduced differentiation and integration of activities would decrease the coordination effort involved thus reducing the information processing requirements. Reduced coordination costs with IT would result in the substitution of IT for human coordination. Greater specialisation would be achieved by focusing on few core competencies.

IT's Role in Managing Organisational Interdependencies

- *Proposition* 6: Turbulent environment drives organisations to actively seek Inter-organisational relations to leverage their core competencies. Cooperation, especially in the international context, will be necessary to gain a competitive advantage in the future. To survive in an increasingly competitive environment, firms would form alliances that would bring together their core competencies to create the 'best of all" products.
- *Proposition 6a:* Turbulent environment drives organisations to reduce environmental complexity and uncertainty by seeking interdependencies with other organisations in the environment.
- *Proposition 6b:* Turbulent environment drives organisations to use more IT - effort to establish coordinating mechanisms with other firms.

To survive in the fast-changing environment the 'adaptive organisation" would be more like a shifting 'constellation' that has 'linkages' with independent and semi- autonomous organisations. Use of inter organisational linkages such as EDI would enable new forms of organisations and reduce the coordination costs of increasingly market-driven organisations. Increasingly, electronic linkages are becoming the necessary condition of doing businesses with larger firms. Using an analogy to the study of community chests conducted by Litwak and Hylton, we observe that in the increasingly global competition, the firms are competing for the common customers' 'fund' and the increase in one firm's revenue would come at the expense of other firm's loss. Coordination, being a function of interdependency, should grow in periods of increased competition for 'funds.'

The IT Paradox

- *Proposition* 7: Increasingly turbulent environment would feed the need for further advancements in IT which would further increase turbulence.

Business needs are incessantly driving the demands for increased capabilities of IT. In turn, increasingly advanced IT is being utilised in more and more sophisticated ways by the businesses to outdo competition. IT, which is being deployed as a solution to the increased complexity and uncertainty of the environment, has paradoxically contributed to the situation by 'compressing time and distance.' In absence of the present day advances in IT, would we be talking of globalisation or time based competition? Perhaps, not. The pace of complexity is increasing fast. Hopefully, the advances in technology would be able to keep up with the environmental changes. Turbulence refers not to chaos in the environment, but to an increasing causal interconnection that renders environments obscure to local observers. Thus how can IT help organisations in responding to the challenges of an increasingly complex and uncertain environment? How can IT help the organisations achieve the 'flexible' organisation structure? We provide academic libraries as a living educational example that has been impacted by the strong trend of convergence of the technological advancements.

THE IMPACT OF INFORMATION TECHNOLOGY ON ACADEMIC LIBRARIES

In the 1990s, academic libraries are undergoing unprecedented change deriving from a combination of accelerating prices of library materials and space, an enormous increase in the amount and types of materials available, and rapid development in electronic technologies. Whatever the local differences in academic librarianship in the countries today, there is no question that information technology is transforming research, scholarship, teaching and learning, and with it, the role of libraries and librarians. Day strongly believes we are already seeing a shift from measuring library services in terms of size and comprehensiveness of collections to one of measuring the quality of service delivery: delivery of documents irrespective of origin, increasingly in electronic form, with access to the electronic library from the users' desktop.

THE EMERGENCE OF DIGITAL LIBRARIES

A working definition of digital libraries provided by Waters are: "Organisations that provide the resources, including specialised staff, to select, structure, offer intellectual access to, distribute, preserve the integrity of, and ensure the persistence over time of collections of digital works so that they are readily and economically available for use by a defined community or set of communities."

Digital Libraries Concepts

The digital library concepts requires librarians to be information architects in order to build effective, scalable Web sites to serve the digital demands of patrons. 'Just in time", a method introduced in the early '80s to manage inventory, is now an expectation of consumers for any business providing online. 'Just in time' applied to libraries is information delivered "where you need it, when you need it, and in a format that is useful. This strategy requires libraries increasingly to adopt 24/365 service to keep up with the demands of their patrons for core services, and to offer services through what is often called the digital, electronic, or virtual library or reference desk.

Technical Requirements of a Digital Library

The United States National Information Infrastructure programme has identified a number of critical technical challenges that need to be resolved if usage of electronic networking is to be both simple and efficient.

The listing of them below illustrates that all are important for the proper running of a digital library:

- Network components that can handle voice, and text simultaneously, and can operate seamlessly
- Information appliances and services that can provide access and services in a scalable, efficient and inter-operable way
- Information access techniques that can enable efficient searches of large distributed information repositories, making the myriad of information resources understandable
- Multimedia information technologies that can, for example, synchronise and integrate real-time delivery of voice, and can support search and retrieval based on image content
- Infrastructure for application development that can provide common solutions
- Technologies that are easy to use and services that are accessible by users with widely varying skills, experiences, abilities and backgrounds
- Inter-operability among heterogeneous systems will be required on an unprecedented scale
- Security and privacy technologies that are easy to use and provide appropriate levels of security to suit the requirements, cost constraints and convenience of the end user

- Technologies and services that provide portability, mobility and ubiquity.

The Roles of Digital Libraries in the Academic Environment

Researcher provide a comprehensive remarks of the roles of digital libraries in teaching and learning. A library is fundamentally an organised set of resources, which include human services as well as the entire spectrum of media. Libraries have physical components such as space, equipment, and storage media; intellectual components such as collection policies that determine what materials will be included and organisational schemes that determine how the collection is accessed; and people who manage the physical and intellectual components and interact with users to solve information problems.

Libraries serve at least four roles in learning:

1. *First, they serve a practical role in sharing expensive resources:* Physical resources such as books and periodicals, films and videos, software and electronic databases, and specialised tools such as projectors, graphics equipment and cameras are shared by a community of users. Human resources—librarians support instructional programmes by responding to the requests of academicians and students and by initiating activities for teachers and students. Responsive services include maintaining reserve materials, answering reference questions, providing bibliographic instruction, developing media packages, recommending books or films, and teaching users how to use materials. Proactive services include selective dissemination of information to faculty and students, initiating thematic events, collaborating with instructors to plan instruction, and introducing new instructional methods and tools. In these ways, libraries serve to allow instructors and students to share expensive materials and expertise.
2. *Second, libraries serve a cultural role in preserving and organising artifacts and ideas:* Great works of literature, art, and science must be preserved and made accessible to future learners. Libraries preserve objects through careful storage procedures, policies of borrowing and use, and repair and maintenance as needed. In addition to preservation, libraries ensure access to materials through indexes, catalogs, and other finding aids that allow learners to locate items appropriate to their needs.
3. Third, libraries serve social and intellectual roles in bringing together people and ideas: This is distinct from the practical role of sharing resources in that libraries provide a physical place for academicians and learners to meet outside the structure of the classroom, thus allowing people with different perspectives to interact in a knowledge space that is both larger and more general than that shared by any

single discipline or affinity group. Browsing a catalog in a library provides a global view for people engaged in specialised study and offers opportunities for serendipitous insights or alternative views. In many respects, libraries serve as centers of inter-disciplinarily—places shared by learners from all disciplines. Digital libraries extend such inter-disciplinarity by making diverse information resources available beyond the physical space shared by groups of learners. One of the greatest benefits of digital libraries is bringing together people with formal, informal, and professional learning missions.

- Formal learning is systematic and guided by instruction. Formal learning takes place in courses offered at schools of various kinds and in training courses or programmes on the job. The important roles that libraries serve in formal learning are illustrated by their physical prominence on university campuses and the number of courses that make direct use of library services and materials. By making the broad range of information resources, digital libraries open new learning opportunities for global rather than strictly local communities.

Much learning in life is informal—opportunistic and strictly under the control of the learner. Learners take advantage of other people, mass media, and the immediate environment during informal learning. The public library system that developed in the U.S., in the late nineteenth century has been called the 'free university', since public libraries were created to provide free access to the world's knowledge. Public libraries provide classic non-fiction books, a wide range of periodicals, reference sources, and audio and video tapes so that patrons can learn about topics of their own choosing at their own pace and style. Just as computing technology and world-wide telecommunications networks are beginning to change what is possible in formal classrooms, they are changing how individuals pursue personal learning missions. Professional learning refers to the on going learning adults engage in to do their work and to improve their work-related knowledge and skills. In fact, for many professionals, learning is the central aspect of their work. Like informal learning, it is mainly self-directed, but unlike formal or informal learning, it is focused on a specific field closely linked to job performance, aims to be comprehensive, and is acquired and applied longitudinally. Since professional learning affects job performance, corporations and government agencies support libraries with information resources specific to the goals of the organisation.

The main information resources for professional learning, however, are personal collections of books, reports, and files; subscriptions to journals; and the human networks of colleagues nurtured through professional meetings and various communications. Many of the data sets and computational tools of digital libraries were originally developed to enhance professional learning. The information resources—both physical and human—that support these types of learning are customised for specific missions and have traditionally been physically separated, although common technologies such as printing, photography, and computing are found across all settings. This situation, is depicted in fig.

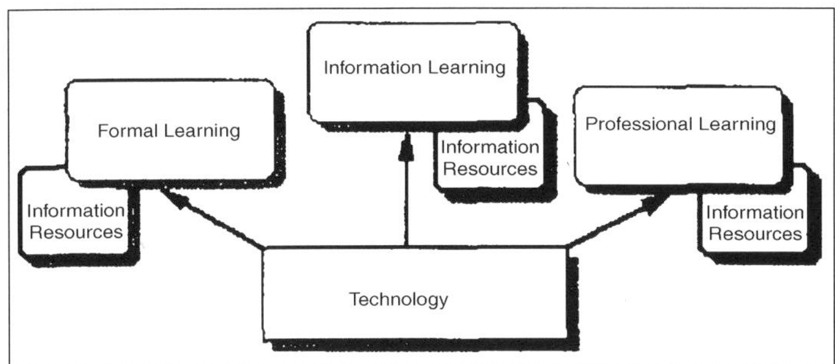

Fig .Current Models of Technological Support for Types of Learning

Digital libraries combine technology and information resources to allow remote access, breaking down the physical barriers between resources. Although these resources will remain specialised to meet the needs of specific communities of learners, digital libraries will allow teachers and students to take advantage of wider ranges of materials and communicate with people outside the formal learning environment. This will allow more integration of the different types of learning, as depicted in fig .

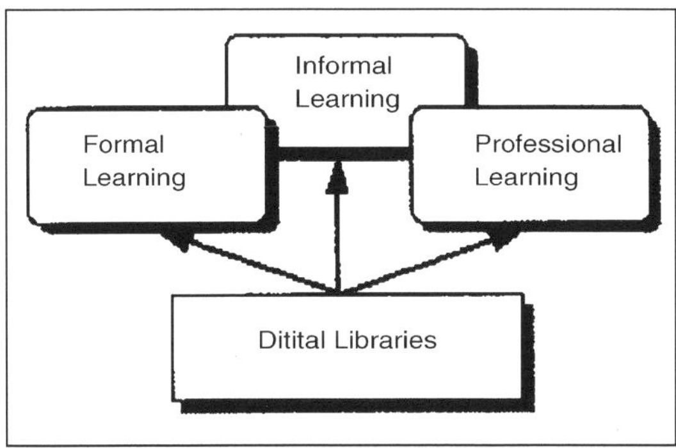

Fig. Digital Libraries Lead to Integrated Resources and Type of Learning

Although not all students or academicians in formal learning settings will use information resources beyond their circumscribed curriculum and not all professionals will want to interact even occasionally with novices, digital libraries will allow learners of all types to share resources, time and energy, and expertise to their mutual benefits.

Characteristics of Digital Libraries

A few of the now familiar characteristics that should distinguish digital libraries from traditional libraries.

The Evolving DL Faces Many Unknowns

For all of its problems and challenges, the print-on-paper environment is well known to us and largely understood. We know how to manage it; we are painfully aware of its costs; and we are familiar with its benefits and its limitations. Our digital library future, by contrast, is full of unknowns and unsolved problems. The list of these is too long and too well rehearsed to need reciting. In addition, the underlying digital technology continues to change. So, even if we could discover the unknowns and solve the problems today, we could not freeze our solutions. Consequently, we are faced with the prospect of creating organisations that are flexible and that accommodate changes, including large changes, easily and regularly.

The DL will Offer Ubiquitous Access

Digital libraries will be designed to support a great range of users at a distance rather than being limited to those on the premises. In other words, unless we create restraints, any and everyone with the necessary hardware can use our digital libraries. This characteristic means both that we should expect a larger variation in the types of users and that as suggested, be responsible to determine whether and what sort of limits will we place on access.

The DL will be more Fully Technology Based

From the creation of metadata to the provision of information services and training, digital libraries will be predominantly technology based. This stands in stark contrast to the essential character of traditional, residential libraries. This is problematical not only because librarians are reluctant to design systems that are technology as opposed to people based but also because often librarians do not possess the necessary expertise to do so. Yet we are not eager to let the process out of our hands. On the positive side, much of the cost of traditional libraries has resided in the manual processes and procedures. While no one supposes that digital libraries will be inexpensive, we should design them in so far as possible to avoid many of these costly manual procedures.

The DL will be open and Customisable and a Part of a Much Larger Information Smorgasbord

Though the qualifications of a digital library can be conveniently limited by definition, they cannot be so conveniently limited by practice. There is a debate over whether or not the Internet is a library. An approach to this question is rather more pragmatic: if growing millions of individuals use the Internet regularly as the source for information on all subjects, it is a library. For all its limitations, it may be a very poor library but it is one nevertheless. For this reason, it is unlikely that our digital libraries will monopolise the library activities of our constituencies in the same way that our traditional libraries have. Digital users today have already sampled the smorgasbord information world of the Internet and have correspondingly broadened their appetites. In addition, it is increasingly common for information users to desire to customise information retrieval, a desire that reduces patience with our more inflexible information systems.

The DL will Host Remote Users

Since digital library users will ordinarily be off the premises, anew, entirely different set of challenges will arise with regard to what we have known as reference and other help services. Our experience with help services has largely been face to face and interpersonal, and efforts to create sophisticated, remote help services are still rudimentary today.

The DL will Offer Distinctive Functions

As surely as digital libraries will discard functions common in traditional libraries, they will necessarily concern themselves with new functions. Commonly named among these are such activities as intellectual property management and database creation and management, the latter being normally associated with administrative computing and data processing. In terms of functionality, therefore, digital libraries will differ markedly from traditional libraries.

Radically Altered Job Descriptions for Information Professionals Will Evolve

To the degree that digital libraries are the business of librarians, this means the incorporation of radically changed or new functions in the librarians portfolios. Digital libraries ignore old boundaries and fall across lines currently marking divisions between libraries, computing organisations, and telephony/networking departments. Therefore, that digital libraries are not solely the province of librarians and that the new constellation of functions inherent in digital libraries will require the evolution of new information professionals with job descriptions that are as yet unspecified.

Such new job descriptions will reflect new combinations of skills represented in these currently distinct agencies along with those from other areas, such as intellectual property law and business.

As Suggested, See New Focuson Original Materials

In the rapidly passing era of traditional libraries, most of our resources and energies were expended on acquiring, organising, managing, and explaining commercially published materials. Because of the slow but steady movement of commercial publishing into the Internet environment, it is likely in the future that access to commercially published digital resources will increasingly be provided directly by publishers. The role of libraries as gateways to commercial academic materials, therefore, will diminish. At the same time, however, because of the capabilities of technology, digital libraries will increasingly focus on providing access to original materials, both those born digitally and those converted from analog formats. The effect of this will be to enrich vastly the research potential of our resources and to provide new opportunities for our institutions to benefit from the potential commercial value of such holdings. The new content paradigm for digital libraries will be raw, source materials.

The DL will have Commercial Characteristics

As a result of the shift in digital libraries to original materials, as suggested, find the means to exploit the commercial value of such materials to a degree never before possible. Digital libraries, therefore, must from the outset be designed to support commercial activities. Correspondingly, support for digital libraries will likely include business plans, replete with market assessments, commercial partnerships, and new concerns for cost-effectiveness and year-end financial performance. In other words, because of the value of their data, digital libraries will have an imperative to function in a more business-like, for-profit manner.

As Suggested, Experience New Competition

We must be increasingly aware that, as representatives of primarily traditional, not-for-profit institutions, we do not enjoy sole ownership of the future of digital libraries. Even as we gather here, a host of new competitors for the business of education and the distribution of knowledge and information resources is assembling.

For this reason, we must not presume that the digital library world will evolve to our specifications, especially if we work on digital libraries as a closed community of librarians. Just as the world-wide-web swept over us and, with unbelievable swiftness, changed the nature of our communication environment, so too may we be over-washed by some new inescapable digital library model from unanticipated sources.

Custom, User-Built Digital Libraries

Apart from large commercial interests, some user-built, highly focused information storage and retrieval services, such as the NASA Astrophysics Data System or the on-line journal of high energy physics, suggest that elements of the digital library may best be developed by the users. Creating these technically customised data and information retrieval systems requires intimate familiarity with the subject matter, jargon, and academic habits of the user communities and likely could not be accomplished by librarians. Clearly we must ponder the implications of these examples for our assumptions and methodologies.

WORKPLACE ENVIRONMENT IN THE DIGITAL ERA

What might we expect of the workplace environment in the new millennium academic library?

Libraries will take Over Campus Computer Centers

Academic libraries will pursue bolder organisational experimentation. This will include focusing on the information and services needs of users. There will be wider distribution of administrative responsibility and authority, as hierarchical structures are broken down and key activities and operations are integrated. We can expect more fluid and flexible structures, enhancement of team and small group processes, and more collegial and collaborative working relationships. Continuing a trend that is already taking root, the academic library will assume administrative control of campus academic computing services. With the expanding mandate for accountability, there will be a greater focus on data collection and analysis. This will entail a rethinking of standards and benchmarks for assessment and more creative approaches to defining output measures and quality impact.

Academic Library Funding will Remain Stable

Responsibility-center budget models will expand across higher education, embracing the library. This relatively new system of distributed financial authority places libraries into a more rigourous fiscal relationship with academic programmes. Units will be taxed to support library operations, requiting intensified communication and accountability. Library funding will remain stable. The greatest growth will continue to be in collection and information access programmes. The library budget as a percentage of total campus budget will not change substantially. Library development and fundraising activities will accelerate, as more colleges and universities pursue external funding from private, corporate, and foundation sources. This will involve a greater focus on endowments rather than on raisin funds for specified capital projects. Library budgets will increasingly fund research and development, infrastructure upgrade and replacement capabilities, and risk capital for innovation and advancement. The trend towards outsourcing of library operations and services will accelerate. We have already seen substantial success with serials jobbers, approval plans, binding, photocopy services, building maintenance, and security. This will lead to further experi-mentation in cataloging, collection maintenance, document delivery, and preservation.

Digital Acquisitions Budgets will Quadruple, and more, Eating up 40-50 Per cent of Acquisition Budgets

Print-based collections will remain dominant over the next decade. However, substantial resources will be allocated to the acquisition of electronic information, as reference sources and scholarly journals become computer-based and the economic feasibility of the scholarly monograph is increasingly questioned.

The percentage of investment in digital information will grow from the current 5-10 percent of acquisitions budgets to 40-50 percent. There will be an ongoing need for investment in local collection building, however, because what has not been acquired and preserved cannot be made available to users and other libraries. Even as collections continue to expand, the gap between what is being published and what we can afford to acquire will continue to grow. As a result, there will be a dramatic decline in ownership: new information accessible through libraries will plunge dramatically.

Nevertheless, the role of the academic library as a depository and gateway for government information will expand, as traditional print-based distribution models are eliminated. The academic library will expand its role in scholarly publishing and communication. Project Muse at Johns Hopkins and High wire at Stanford, and the Journal Storage Project spawned by Mellon are examples of the library's central involvement in the management of current and retrospective electronic publications. More than 50 percent of reference transactions will take place over campus networks

Patron-initiated and Controlled Services will Expand Rapidly

Libraries are already beginning to employ self-circulation, computer renewals and recalls, direct interlibrary loan, and document delivery. Full-text databases are becoming commonplace. The role of library staff as interpreters and mediators of user information transactions outside of local collections and services will decrease. Inside the university, the librarians' role as instructor will be formalised in a separate college department focusing on information and network literacy. The technology of the World Wide Web that is evolving rapidly and unpredictable with the World Wide Web Consortium co-ordinates many activities in the areas of user interface, technology and society. The World Wide Web which was first announced by CERN in 1991, 2-3 years ago most people had not heard of it but by the end of 1996, there were 300,000 Web sites. Libraries are creating Web sites to help students to distinguish between relevant and irrelevant information. The Web is likely to have a profound impact on education, communication and research activities of the universities.

Examples:

- *The Web empowers individuals:* They can easily reach a worldwide audience. Anyone can publish material that would never have been published in the past, and it is instantly available to millions of people.
- *The Web offers us the best of both worlds. Anyone can publish:* Their views cannot easily be suppressed, for good or ill. And anyone can comment, validate and offer judgement or advice.

The E-mail for example is extremely valuable for communication between the library and its users. Users Borrowers are expected to return their books within about two weeks. Very many do without reminders, but for those who need reminding, for some reason e-mail is a more effective spur than other methods. Online catalogs will increasingly define accessibility and not just local ownership.

Thus the links between the local collection, the bibliography of a discipline, and the text of the publications/sources will become blurred. Remote use of online catalogs and databases is increasing rapidly at most colleges and universities.

An example, at Carnegie Mellon, already 75 per cent of catalog use is remote. Remote access to information necessitates new instructional efforts. Levels of all traditional collection circulation activity - general and reserve borrowing and interlibrary loan - will decline significantly. They will fall prey to the rapid growth in options for electronic document delivery and the implementation of electronic reserve systems. The new electronic journals already offer facilities unavailable to users of paper.

These include:

- The ability to search for particular content within a paper or a complete journal;
- The ability to move easily between the table of contents of a journal and the abstract.
- Facilities to annotate articles to create a personal virtual filing cabinet and
- The ability to move quickly from the article you are reading to one which it cites in its references, and that includes forward citing, example the ability to go to articles that cited the one you have just been reading but which were published later.

An example, the American Astronomical Society has digitised into electronic form all the articles in the last 20 years of its journal which can now be accessed. Academic libraries will house and manage campus usability laboratories focusing on the needs of the user and will involve users as part of the design team.

Reference assistance to users will be electronic-based, with more than 50 per cent of transactions taking place over campus networks in batched or real-time communication, up from the current neglible levels.

User profiles linked to SDI-type services will ensure delivery of relevant, cur-rent information to faculty and students on a scheduled basis. Academic librarians will increasingly pursue service goals as part of multiple consortia-based relationships. There will be joint investment in commercial services and acquisition of materials, in the purchase and use of technology, and in the hiring and development of staff.

Librarians will be Key Players in Developing Technological Innovations

Technology is currently poised to transform the fundamental nature of operations and services. From the early days of automation in the 1970s, academic libraries have moved to the cur-rent distribution and individualisation of technology and digital conversion and production. The challenge of the next decade will be the application of intelligence to the searching and retrieval capabilities of library systems.

The library will play a central role in the future development of the campus information environment. Rather than reacting to campus technology decisions, library staff will be integrally involved in determining what the next innovations will be. In the new world of the desktop workstation, academic libraries have a mandate to integrate high-speed access both to scholarly and institutional information. They need to provide tools for filtering, analysing, and manipulating information.

The predominant mainframe-based library management systems will be completely replaced by client-server technologies and applications that include robust full-text content and intelligent links to network-based sources. Automatic language translation software will be introduced, contributing to the development of a rcncwcd global acquisitions programmc for both based and digital sources. Campus network infrastructures will extend to all student, faculty, and staff work and living areas.

This will provide dependable connectivity for a growing array of applications, including distance learning. Wireless technology will be introduced and will receive its initial testing in library services. The retrospective digitising of library collections, particularly unique materials, will evolve as a central activity in academic libraries. Newly formed digital knowledge centers will manage the operations and partner with academic departments, publishers, and other libraries.

The Number of Librarians Working in Academic Libraries will Decrease

Libraries will increasingly view staff development as an integral and essential component of organisational success. With retooling of skills emerging as a three-to-five year cycle, participation in training courses will be mandated for all employee groups. As technology programmes advance and dominate library collection and service activities, technical staff as a percentage of total staff will increase significantly. This will produce a net reduction in the number of librarians employed in academic libraries.

It will also promote more effective working relationships between librarians and technologists, improving current conditions marred by distrust, inadequate communication, and lack of shared investment in planning. Academic libraries have not responded effectively to demographic cultural, racial, and ethnic shifts.

They will collectively enter the next century still recognising the important trends producing a more pluralistic society but without well-developed and well-coordinated strategic directions for the role and contributions of the library. Telecommuting, which is increasingly commonplace in commercial settings, will become a viable and acceptable option for *academic* library employees.

An expanding array of library operations and services will be performed from home, enabling improved competitiveness for the recruitment and retention of talented staff. Academic libraries and library education programmes will collaborate on the development of internship and certification programmes for new professionals. This will be necessitated by the anticipated rapid increase in retirements in the next 15 years, as well as by the need to develop new approaches to the preparation and orientation of the next generation of academic librarians. An example of a university library, De Montfort University in the UK that has been developing a digital library environment for some years past.

The lessons they claim to have learnt might be summarised under the following headings:

- The digital library will develop more quickly than people think;
- The digital library is still a complex, unstable entity for which little theoretical structure exists.
- Because of this inherent instability, investment and implementation are still high risk.
- Digital libraries operate in a global environment: new products and services can become *de facto* standards very quickly.
- Co-operation is therefore a key factor for maintaining competitiveness.
- The content of the digital library will become the dominant factor.
- Copyright issues will be resolved or side-stepped because the market will demand it.
- The economics of the digital library are not yet well understood.
- Library jobs and roles will change very rapidly.

THE IMPACT OF TECHNOLOGY ON EXISTING GENERATIONAL DIFFERENCES

This online collaborative environment has enabled people to access information, as well as interact with each other to share knowledge, like never before. It is no coincidence that in the face of this online landscape, the physical library is getting smaller. There is much debate in the library profession right now as to how the future will shape up, but there is little doubt that many libraries, public and special, are currently facing budgetary cuts and a reduction in the physical space available to them.

Teams of librarians are being replaced by the rise of solo operations, with little career development or ability to recruit more staff. In addition, services may be increasingly outsourced or long-established information centres closed. Quite simply, where people can go online to fulfil many of their information needs, there is little perceived need to visit a library or use the services of a librarian. There is also a generational shift, reinforced by technology advances, which may also be threatening the survival of the library. Quite simply, many still perceive the library to be a physical space, filled with books and policed by a bespectacled librarian, probably from an older generation, and trained in advanced forms of library cataloguing and indexing.

While they are valuable skills, the younger generation may little relish the thought of following in their footsteps – after all, they have grown up into a world that appears completely different, and that is dominated by instantly accessible online information. In the business world, for example, the proliferation of technology has had a completely transformative effect, enabling vast global expansion because the tools allow for different offices in all locations to streamline operations and communicate. Most people now use technology applications on a day-to-day basis, if only to function effectively in the workplace.

For younger generations, though, this technology drive has been even more revolutionary. From childhood, younger people have been using technology to help with everything, from doing their homework to socialising. And as those younger people have grown up and entered the workplace, so have the days of reading books or even just sitting in a classroom seemed increasingly numbered. E-learning, for instance, is becoming more popular, with many businesses employing sophisticated techniques for delivering employees with 'just-in-time' training at their desks.

Younger employees will also be far more adaptable to these technology tools, having most likely graduated from colleges that also employ tools, such as webinars, to deliver vital training. For this younger generation, the whole concept of the 'library', including the people who staff them, may appear somewhat old-fashioned and irrelevant. Meanwhile, the older generation may not be well-equipped to adapt to this new environment or to educate younger people on the continuing and, indeed, evolving value of library services. While certainly not ignorant of technology advances, the older generation is less likely to view technology as such an integral part of daily life.

Al Podboy has worked as director of library services at law firm Baker Hostetler for 30 years; he knows the firm's culture and its lawyers inside out, and he's also familiar with these changing times. "My generation and a lot of my peers have been working in their firms for a long time. I've seen a couple of generations come through the firm and I've seen the differences between them," he comments. He has also been a witness to intergenerational conflict – he refers to one example where a familiar criticism targeted at the younger generation is that they just don't read. "I get a bit annoyed by this to be honest. We live in a much faster environment than when I started. Younger people do read, just not necessarily books," he says. Such differences highlight a real problem: a potentially growing generation gap that could be particularly harmful for the survival of library services, where the older generation is less likely to keep up with new applications and younger people are less likely to be open to, or understand the worth of library services. And if that means fewer people even enter the library profession, the impending crisis could soon be worse than feared.

For Podboy, such generational differences need to be addressed proactively: "We have to introduce older people to technology and convince them that the younger people are not necessarily doing things wrong," he explains. "We need to ensure that people of my age understand what those technologies are and try to encourage them to adapt to them.

At the same time, though, we need to be able to teach younger people the older forms – the value of a book or of an older mentor, for example, where they can benefit from somebody's direct experience of a particular work or task." But bringing together different generations, so that they can appreciate the merits of different methods of working, may be particularly difficult in this modern landscape. Where Podboy, like many of his peers, stayed with the one firm for his whole career, the younger generations are far more likely to change jobs and even careers several times. According to a 2006 survey by *The American Lawyer*, for example, many associates in US law firms see jumping ship as a 'fundamental career milestone'.

Nearly two-thirds of third and fourth-year associates responding to the survey said they didn't expect to be, or didn't know if they'd be, at the same firm in five years as a partner or senior associate. Quite simply, attitudes to the workplace and lifestyle expectations between generations are often vastly different. Generations X and Y want flexibility, challenges, career-advancement opportunities, learning and development opportunities, and fast appreciation and recognition.

And much of their experience of this will be in a fast-paced, technologicallyenabled, online environment. In contrast, older generations are far more used to working in one company, and having one career for a lifetime, learning via traditional routes, and probably using, but not relying, on technology to function effectively. Not only do their attitudes differ widely, but it is less likely today that they'll even be in the same company for long enough to really benefit from the teachings of each other.

IMPACT OF INFORMATION TECHNOLOGY ON INFORMATION PROFESSIONALS

As quoted by Matson, new technology is, of course, very powerful and brings in 'an imperialistic thrust' not only into librarianship, but into everyday life. Not surprisingly, the new roles created by the changing technology have commanded attention and have made up a large part of recent literature about librarians. He added the resulting proliferation of online catalogs, librarian have been spurred by technological developments to become more efficient organisers and planners. They have, in short, brought their traditional skills to the service of the new technologies. As claimed by Hyams, the role of the New Information Professionals (NIP) in the learning environments is likely to be much more global. It is a call for librarians to rethink their job functions and the future of the academic library as center of technology. The change that's happening isn't at all like the automation change the librarian went through. It is a fundamental kind of change: 'To Who We Are and What We Do."

NEW ROLES, NEW SKILLS AND NEW PEOPLE

Researcher argue that library jobs and jobs for information professionals are changing at the same—or even greater as experienced in other parts of our economy and society. Are librarians, new and old, keeping pace with these changes? Are they stuck in a traditional mind-set about their jobs and the settings for those jobs? What are some of the new horizons available to librarians willing to 'think outside the box" as far as their careers are concerned? What prepares the librarian for these emerging jobs? The struggle of librarians in academic libraries to cope with the dynamic changes brought by technology is real. The new roles and skills include:

As Library Webmaster

The single most significant factor in the changing information jobs has been the Internet. It has changed everyone's job, some people's job descriptions', and the job market itself, example as Webmaster.

Definition of Webmaster

The essential assignment of the Webmaster as defined by Richmond is:

- "... a person who manages a Web; a mediator between Web authors and system administrator—ensures that applicable standards such as HTML validity and link liveliness are met; optimises the Web architecture for navigability; takes editorial responsibility for the content, quality and styles of the site; finds, creates and installs tools to create Web content and check consistency; develops and enforces the house style; liaises with graphic artist; provides first level user support..."

From this definition, it is clear that Webmasters must be responsible for several roles in their day to day activities.

Task Analysis of the Webmaster

Van der Walt strongly believe that Webmasters were originally depicted as members of an organisation who were early adopters of Internet and Web technologies and who saw the need to educate the rest of the library users in using those technologies.

His statement is strongly supported by the researchers who claimed that an area where early Web expertise could be found was the *academic,* and specifically *university,* environment.

Vander Walt listed several responsibilities of the Webmaster such as:

- Administration and daily management of a Web site such as home page design, Web-based online searching, searching Web sites, Intranets and Internal database publishing
- Understand the broad purpose and potential of a Web site—that is, what the site can accomplish and what it may be able to do in future
- Possess a thorough understanding of the organisation and have a background in marketing, familiarity with the Internet
- A solid understanding of programming languages and technology
- Keep up with and also recognise the significance of emerging technologies and business models, and be able to inform and educate the rest of the organisation
- Experiment with unproven technology to develop WWW sites and the Webmaster is a solo space explorer, often looking at way-out-in-front technology'
- A person with the necessary technical talent in user interfaces and a good knowledge of operating systems, as well as creative skills in graphic design, marketing, advertising, copy writing and event planning

The Growing Importance of the Webmaster

These basic responsibilities are slowly being enhanced. Today the Webmaster has become an integral part of an education venture vital to the entire strategic planning of the library. As a newcomer in the information retrieval field, the Webmaster forms an essential part of the online presence of any organisation, as it is he or she who leads the Web site development team in managing an effective and efficient Web site.

The value of librarians as webmasters in the university as claimed by Stover is for a number of reasons:

- First, to support the scholarly communication process because disseminating information is a function that traditionally been associated with librarians
- Second, librarians have a certain measure of expertise in the area of organising and providing access to information. What better way to share their skills with the academic community than by turning Web documents into one-stop-shopping malls that offer the end user subject access to a document along with the full-text of the document itself?

- Third, Web publishing gives us a higher profile on campus, which is an important asset these days because of the changing nature of higher education and changing role of librarians
- Fourth, the Web provides unique access to scholarly information because of its serendipitous nature, its immediacy, its hypertext structure, and its universal appeal. Why wouldn't librarians want to be involved with this exciting technology at the publishing level?
- Fifth, it provides our parent institutions a positive reputation in the national and international academic communities. This is more important ever given the current climate of declining enrollments that many colleges and universities face today.
- Sixth, Web publishing allows us to bypass the profit-based system of print publishing that has tormented librarians for years by gouging out huge chunks of money from their budget.

As claimed by Van der Walt, many Web sites are now becoming mission critical in the sense that they are seen as a marketing tool for the university and also as a support tool for the end-user or library customers. The Internet and World Wide Web are both essential elements in the IT infrastructure of any organisation. Thus the Webmaster can play an important role in managing the library assets according to the information center's strategic planning.

As Systems Librarian

Shearer describes the term Systems librarians as:

- "Individuals who are responsible of designing, supporting and developing systems to enhance access to and management of the library's collection. Ensuring that the computer-based systems are essential to the library's work at all times."

Responsibilities

- Evaluation, planning, implementation and maintenance of library automation and Internet access, network maintenance as well as web page design and maintenance.
- Evaluation and selection of databases and software and staff training.
- Maintains computer security and hardware.

Skills

- Knowledge of networking, Internet and software applications.
- Ability to master new computer hardware and software.
- Ability to diagnose and solve hardware, software and networking problems.
- Ability to communicate technology to the uninitiated.
- Ability to work in a dynamic and changing environment.

Electronic Access to What and by Whom

Selecting academic information resources requires a broader view. For any library, the determination of which databases to provide and who will access them has become an ever more complex due to the number of databases that are now available has grown by leaps and bounds over the past few years. Today's systems librarian is often involved in the decision of which database service to supply to end-user desktops. There are myriad choices of general topic and specialty products available online, on the Intranet, on CD-ROM, and via the Web, at all price points. In today's academic setting, the librarian not only has to take into account the resource for the library's own collection but has to weigh offering the database to a wider user base against what end users within the university are already accessing by way of their own desktops.

Thus the systems librarian must weigh the type of access to provide against questions of:

- Timeliness,
- System capabilities, and
- Client expectations of good service.

Access Policies

Schuhnan quote that once the library decides which databases to select, it must determine how to deploy them and who will have access to them. As electronic access to external databases becomes more prevalent throughout all academic areas, the systems librarian's budget and equipment come under greater pressure. Whenever contemplating the addition of a new database resource it's also a good opportunity to review internal corporate access policies. As quickly as events dictate change in resource selections, policy revisions will naturally be carefully thought about more frequently. Decisions such as supplying access to information for those with a 'need to know' are undergoing modification.

Increasingly, those with a 'need to know' occupy expanding outward circles within organisations. Schulman added, smart organisations are extending information resources access to more employees as competitors become more aggressive and move more quickly. They are finding that providing more employees with timely access to competitive information allows an organisation to respond to competitive threats more quickly.

As the system librarian continuously evaluate databases and the provision of access to them, here is a series of questions to ask each time considering a new source:

- Is this source unique or does it duplicate an existing resource.
- If it's a close duplicate, is it less expensive, easier to use, or unique in another beneficial way.
- How does this database fit in with the corporate mission.

- Who within the university will benefit from this database—all users, faculty members and university community.
- What is the cost-benefit ratio.
- What critical element does this database supply that overcomes a poor cost-benefit ratio.
- Does this resource fit within our existing budget.
- Does another resource have to be eliminated to bring on this resource, and, if so, what impact will that have to the budget and to those who depend on the resource under consideration for elimination.
- Will this resource improve service to our clients/customers? How?
- In what format will we purchase the database.
- How will this database be integrated into our other resources.
- What changes have to be made to the hardware/software configuration to accept this new database and how will this impact our budget? How will it impact access to other resources?
- How will we provide access to this resource?
- Who in which departments and at which levels within the university will have access to this resource? Directly? Indirectly.
- Will end-user training have to be provided?
- Will additional staff be required?
- What other departments should be involved in this decision?
- How much time and effort is involved in implementing access to this resource?
- When will the corporation see a return on investment?

Thus by using this list as a guideline and foundation for decision making should help the system librarian to revise the questions as the mission, budget, environmental influences changes and stay ahead of the game.

As In-House Content Providers

The meaning of In-house Content Provider refers to:

- "one who was interested in exploring the balance between making its content freely available on the Internet while protecting its print-based revenue stream."

Funke provide a comprehensive comment on the new role of the Information Professionals as an In-House Content Providers. He claimed that along with the new technologies comes interacting with different groups within an organisation such as the MIS people, an information professional must have the ability to effectively 'bring content to the table" and work effectively with MIS as a team to make this content readily available. In order for information professionals to effectively do this, they must keep up with the latest technologies related to text retrieval, content organisation, search technologies, and knowledge management.

Bringing Content to the Table

Making MIS people understand the importance and expertise of people who know content and how clients will use it can be a constant uphill battle. Many programmers in this situation view another 'player' either as a threat or someone who doesn't have their background. Unfortunately, the onus lies on the information professional to make programmers understand what we can contribute, the value we can provide.

For starters, before you can integrate content into a Web site, you must understand:

- The overall requirements of the current Web site, including servers,
- Their ability to handle various indexes; search engine capability; and
- How the parser is set up to integrate content.

The Information Professional can provide expertise on how to organise content on a site; how users might search for the content; and the search requirements needed to access the content.

Metadata

Many information professionals have taken courses such as cataloging and indexing. These courses can serve as a foundation for the resource-organising activities on the Internet involving metadata. Metadata provides document information on and from Web sites, producing an index or directory to the resource. With the tremendous growth of content on the Web, there is a need to standardise the organisation of the information.

As metadata standards are further defined and organisations embrace these new standards, many questions will need answering such as:

- What will be worth cataloging?
- How detailed should the descriptions of various resources be?

Information Professionals can play a major role in helping answer these questions.

Search Engines

Researcher added, the evaluation and use of search engines is a 'product' that Information Professionals should manage within their organisations because they:

- Understand and know how to use Boolean logic.
- Can evaluate search engines from the user perspective?
- Know how to implement effective user searching of content.

Some of the major Intranet search engines available these days include Fulcrum Surfboard, Verity, Microsoft Index Server, and Excalibur. Thus, when implementing the Boolean logic features of these search engines, most programmers, will say that users cannot grasp Boolean logic or that such control is unnecessary as long as the search engines do relevancy rankings of documents retrieved. Users can go beyond basic Boolean operators such as AND, OR, NOT, which programmers usually dictate for them, and take advantage of proximity operators such as NEAR and NEARIN.

From experience, when one explains the differences in search results to users, *e.g.*, the effect of using the Boolean operators and NEAR, end-user searchers understand and respond positively right away. Programmers may support their positions by doing a query to see how many searches were performed using each Boolean operator. Information Professionals should try search queries for this type of data, too. Request the tools to perform this kind of query. What some programmers find difficult to understand is that you just can't implement a feature without some user education. Information Professionals can play an important role by providing this guidance within their organisations.

Information Retrieval Agents

Making sense of the overwhelming amount of indexed information constitutes one of the biggest challenges of the Web. To help, we see a rising use of Web robots, called information retrieval agents. These agents know where to look for relevant information based on user direction, advanced search algorithms, and learned behaviour. Major players in this area include NewsBot, Agent ware, and Wise Wire. As organisations move towards managing knowledge, intelligent information retrieval agent software tools will playa major role and will require people with the ability to manage and evaluate these tools. Search agents work when a user sets up search queries to 'train the documents,' whereby the agents learn from human behaviour and use pattern recognition to find relevant information to automate the retrieval process.

Information Professionals with expertise in searching and content analysis can help manage and evaluate these tools. Note that several of the traditional electronic publishers have already begun exploring this technology, *e.g.*, LEXIS-NEXIS and UMI with WiseWire Professional, an agent technology that evaluates user's viewing habits. Like it or not, new technologies are changing the information professional's role and the opportunities to enhance one's role have become boundless. To take advantage of the opportunities, Information Professionals must keep up with the emerging technologies, recognise the opportunities to utilise our skill sets, and work with MIS to effectively implement change. At times it can be frustrating and overwhelming, but the opportunities to grow and learn outweigh any negatives.

AS KNOWLEDGE MANAGER

Peter Drucker has predicted that the most important profession in the next century will be knowledge worker, and knowledge workers are not the same as computer systems specialists. He claimed that the most competent ones are likely to be reference librarians using sophisticated hardware and software, tools which the end user does not know how to use. Certainly, those who have exploited the almost unlimited opportunity to provide more information have taken advantage of this development.

Still, Drucker assumed that this deluge of knowledge would drown us and force us to seek people to manage that knowledge. Knowledge workers would assess knowledge on behalf of those who had neither the time nor the inclination to do so. The concept of knowledge management embraces the need to organise large data files, and to link and integrate different but related files and databases to one another so that users can move between and among related resources efficiently. Thus, Church believe the transformation from librarian to knowledge manager is clearly underway; however, a deeper look at the direction that the Internet is taking business reveals the possibility of more far-reaching changes. As many library services processes move to the Internet, the use of information will become integrated with these processes. In this environment, information as a distinct function or resource may no longer exist.

Changing Roles and Responsibilities

The information transfer cycle is directly affected by Internet use. They should "embrace the entire new information transfer cycle, from the creation, restructuring and representation of information to its dissemination and use." They have an important and valuable role to tell users what users ought to see and read. It is to protect library clients from drowning in the information overflow and help them work smarter.

How their role as knowledge managers would evolve within the next few years, Church outline five key functions:

1. *Consultant:* Their role would involve less 'doing' and more consultation. This role would require remote support to endusers within the organisation. In effect, 'foot traffic' would be replaced by remote consultation for complex search strategies.
2. *Analyst:* Some information professional felt that their role would require increased value-added in the form of analysing and interpreting information that is presented to end-users.
3. *Intranet content manager:* With the integration of external data into corporate Intranets, a key function of the information services professional will be to source and manage the content which is accessible through the system.
4. *Product planner and marketer:* Data integration also forces information professionals to become product developers and planners, with responsibility for packaging information and marketing products, services and delivery strategies to internal audiences.

5. *Corporate knowledge manager:* Increased recognition of knowledge as a valuable strategic resource could heighten the importance of the information professional. It foresee a merger of all information functions into a single department or function. Being the Knowledge Manager just means that they create value to my organisation by facilitating access to high quality information and by networking people and their ideas together using the technological infrastructure.

These new responsibilities imply a totally different skill set. The emphasis will shift from:

- Technical skills in the library to communication,
- Facilitation, training and management skills.
- Interact with IT staff and managers beyond Knowledge Management (KM).

To adjust to these more far-reaching changes, information professionals must search beyond current bounds and think in terms of benefits to their organisations. Right now, information can be used to enhance competitiveness and productivity. These same benefits will remain in the future, no matter what the role involves.

If information is to be seamlessly integrated with transaction processes, then someone must scope out work-related behaviours to ensure that it is done in the most efficient and effective manner. And, if equal information and technology is available to everyone, then competition rests on the ability to interpret and apply these tools. Clearly the impending shift to knowledge management represents an exciting change for academic librarians. However, it's an opportunity that requires a great deal of preparation, and a new way of thinking.

AS COLLABORATORS/PARTNERSHIPS

All organisations are in the period of transformation including academic libraries and librarians should use this period of change to establish, refocus and strengthen partnerships with other professionals groups within their institutions.

There are two significant groups with which library professionals should establish strong collaborative relationships:

1. Faculty and
2. Technologists.

Creth suggest in order for a real partnership to succeed, librarians need to see themselves as part of the teaching and research endeavor, and participate as an active and integral member of the education team. He added, for some librarians this idea of a partnership with faculty may require incorporating a different concept of their importance in relation to the faculty and developing new expectations and different behaviour. In the most general sense, librarians need to be certain that their commitment to service does not display itself through behaviour that is like of a servant.

Library professionals also need to reshape and strengthen their relationships with the computer specialists in the university with reasons such as:

- To eliminate much of the waste that occurs in most organisations where computer and information technology remains untapped or barely utilised because the learning curve is too steep for so many people and because the design of the equipment and software is so often far from intuitive.
- The New Information Professionals can provide constant feedback to designers and programmers about what works, what does not work, what new functions are needed.
- They can become the voice of the inexpert user, the typical person who is not technically inclined but strongly needs the service that the technology promises to deliver.
- They are both dealing with changing and chaotic times, and their activities are centered around information technology, so they should naturally consider themselves partners in addressing the many challenges that exist.
- They need to be willing, to share the act of discovery, to be able to identify shared goals, and to work together as peers.

If, librarians are to be prepared to absorb and even help shape the magnitude of predicted change into this 21st century, then it will be important for librarians to realign their relationships within the university so that strong partnerships exist to provide us with necessary support as well as knowledge for meeting the challenges ahead.

AS EDUCATOR

Anderson emphasised that librarians have always played a key role in education. They have formed relationships with subject specialists to build library collections to support instruction in the classroom and provided instruction in the form of classes on library skills and have conducted library instructional orientations sessions to assist students doing research in their classes. Today, in the digital age, librarians can no longer be simply information providers or the 'keepers of knowledge'.

The changes in technology using electronically stored and retrieved information has changed the way patrons and students are able to access, retrieve and use information. The instantaneous access of information through the Internet has made vast amounts of information and data available to anyone with a computer, a modem and a provider. Digital information is changing the role of librarians from "a person who students ask for assistance in finding information to someone who needs to provide services and instruction regardless of place, time or format." But how do we make important and valid information available to our faculty and students that may appear on the Web tomorrow?

Big Six Information Skills

As educators, Eisenberg have suggested that librarians must acquire these skills; the ability to:

- Define the task,
- Information seeking strategies,
- Location and access,
- Use of information,
- Synthesis,
- Evaluation.

The librarian's role too has:

- Expanded with a much broader instructional and participatory role in the instructional process. This role can be one of actively participating in the building of on-line courses by providing assistance in finding current and valid information for instructors delivering instruction on the Internet.
- Extend into the area of providing instruction and librarians must be involved in creating independent thinkers.
- Enhanced their roles to knowledge navigators and instructors teaching the discipline called information literacy.
- Be one of teaching critical thinking and resource-based learning.

New vocabulary in education such as: living curriculum, critical literacy, information power, information literacy, and information problem solving mandate that we re-examine our roles as professional information providers and educators.

Students need to acquire the skills of evaluating information. This new vocabulary is bringing new challenges in library instruction. Changes in education such as the infusion of instructional technology and the use the Internet to deliver instruction has also changed how libraries and librarians can provide and assist instructors in teaching in the digital age.

New Trends in Instruction—Web Based Course Delivery

The trend in education towards distance learning and web-based courses is providing new challenges for information professionals as service providers as well as instructors. We are required to provide access to quality and valid information to support on-line instruction as well as provide on-line instruction both indirectly in the form of guides and on-line tutorials as well as directly in the form on courses to teach information literacy. Universities are recognising the necessity of requiring an information literacy course as part of the curriculum in the digital age.

As educators, the librarians are using a variety of tools and teaching techniques to assist students such as:

- *Provide instruction through learning guides and on-line tutorials:* Finding quality information is the biggest challenge our faculty and students are faced in the research and instructional process. With the advent of distance delivery of instruction and web-based pages for libraries using the vast amounts of information available on the Internet, it is essential that independent learners are skilled in locating information. Students can access these tutorials and guides from home or from the computers in the library and walk through self-paced instruction on any topic from "What is the Internet? To How do I do research?"
- *Provide access to guides to recommended search engines for the Internet:* Using search engines effectively and choosing the best search engines for your specific needs may be the most challenging skill that learners need to master. Guides to recommend search engines that introduce and compare search engines in a standard format are an invaluable tool for independent learners. Students can readily compare the different features of several search engines and access the search engines directly from your library's page.
- *Provide instruction in the area of Information Literacy:* Teaching Information Literacy in the electronic environment is a new and exciting role for librarians. Creating courses and formal instruction in the discipline of information literacy with the purpose of encouraging independent learners and critical thinkers to meet the challenges of the new information age is the role of the future for librarians. In today's workplace, employees are not only expected to work well with others, communicate well, find creative solutions to problems; they will also be expected to use the Internet and electronic information effectively to solve problems and conduct business. More and more businesses are moving towards conducting business on the Web for advertising, delivering services and products as well as using the Internet as a communication tool. Librarians must be involved in creating valuable employees with the current skills required to be successful on the job.

Librarians are the most appropriate professionals to lead the team of people in finding the answers to the challenges we are facing in the digital environments of electronic information and the Internet. They have always been the experts at teaching people how to use the tools to locate that information regardless of format. They are the most effective searchers and researchers and their basic role of teaching those skills has not changed. Thus, in this fast and ever-changing information environment, librarians need to make full use of information and multimedia technology to support a greatly expanded teaching venture. The technology and varied format of information is changing and making new demands on their profession. In this fast-paced world it is important that they change with the changing roles and challenges.

AS MANAGERS

Researcher address how change has affect everyone in the organisations from leaders to employees and clients—the needs to shift his or her mind-sets, seeing the organisation and their established and new roles sometimes highly threatening and unfamiliar activities.

Thus he added, employees need emotional support to adapt to change; support in learning new ways of working and relating. Linda claimed that information technology has changed a librarian's jobs; they have to readjust to new situation and develop new skills of managing the investments of an organisation—in people, technologies, and collections. As managers, they need to look for outcomes rather than just thinking about managing a resource at the resource level. The human resource in any organisation is the key to its success or failure.

Changes in Library Management

We have seen that the major external force that is technology had affected libraries; that means the library managers must use new structures in their management. *Strategic planning—strategic thinking*—should be a fundamental concept that librarians incorporate into their daily activities. Overall they need to give greater attention to strategic planning at the organisation and departmental level, and then integrating these strategic plans into the goals and activities of individual professionals. With a shifting organisational environment and culture, managers should shift their responsibilities and approach to one that is more consultative and supportive rather than one of authority and control.

The role of the manager should focus on:

- Coaching and mentoring staff.
- Development of staff.
- Developing shared values and vision among staff.
- Providing resources within framework of cost-benefit assessment.
- Taking pride in the accomplishments of others,
- Providing incentives to team work.

Library staff who are struggling to keep up with the demands in today's work environment require, indeed deserve, new ways for accomplishing their work. The redesign of the library organisation is imperative if we are to move rapidly and with an entrepreneurial spirit in the delivery of services in the current interactive high- speed communication environment.

Thus to be successful, libraries must reshape the prevailing corporate culture and build into their organisational structures and their approaches to work.

As managers, researcher stress that they must possess:

- The ability to identify, anticipate, and quickly respond to constantly changing customer needs.
- Capable of leaps forward and breakthrough performance.
- Must be ready to abandon formerly successful approaches to work, strategies, processing systems and services.
- Good communication at all levels, staff participation and training.

The librarians in transition that want to consciously manage their change efforts need to help their staff understand the change process and how they can positively participate. Creating an overall framework that shows the considered changes are a natural evolution from current practices, assessing that the organisation has the expertise and climate to implement the proposed changes. Instead of organising personnel around how librarians do their work, librarians must:

- Organise around customers and how they do their work.
- Reduce hierarchy, flatten the organisation, and eliminate redundancy in order to be more responsive to changing needs and new opportunities and developments.
- Give up their need for control and their desire to create stability.

We Live in a Time of Change

The information has change our profession and library managers today have to pick up new skills to adjust to changes and to be able to survive in the future.

AS INFORMATION RESOURCE MANAGER

The term Information Resource Manager refers to:

- "Individuals who are responsible for the provision of information resources—be they print or electronic or technical infrastructure—and the power of digital technology, which grows everyday. To provide the leadership to conceptualise and manage the broad array of information resources that are necessary to support its mission".

As an Information Resource Manager, the librarian would continually go through a ten-step process:

- *Step 1. Define the Customers:* Who are the library's primary customers?
- *Step 2. Understand the Customers Needs:* One of the best ways to help you analyse the needs of the workforce and effectiveness of your current information strategy, is to arrange an information audit examples:

- Implementation of custom survey designed to take an inventory of products, services and personnel related to information activities
- Interviews with key personnel
- Understand the users needs
- Analysis of surveys and interviews
- Creation of 'information strategy' designed to help maximize investment in users and services
- Recommendations

- *Step 3. Map Needs against Decisions and Sources:* This will list information originators and users; sources required and decision supported. It will also identify high pay-off opportunities, for example where certain information has multiple uses.
- *Step 4. Implement a Sourcing Strategy:* The source/needs map from step 3 will point to clusters of information needs that can give economies in purchasing. For example, purchasing a networked CD-ROM may be more cost-effective than doing multiple ad-hoc online searches.
- *Step 5. Define Information Policies and Standards:* Steps 1-4 will reveal, often to many people for the first time, the sheer wealth of information that is available. This step therefore involves:
  - Classification standards,
  - Ownership,
  - Life-cycle management standards
  - Agreed 'protocols and procedures' between owners and users.
- *Step 6. Select a Pilot Project:* Select a key decision process that involves people across several departments as a pilot.
- *Step 7. Select and Adapt Appropriate Technology:* With the selected pilot project acting as a focal point, now is the time to start detailed consideration example of the computer solution. The choices are bewildering, and are proliferating daily.
- Step 8. *Nurture the Intelligence Processes:* This requires encouraging interaction across departmental boundaries and subcultures. Therefore, the creation of events and forums to encourage this interchange is often a useful starting point.
- *Step 9. Focus Dissemination:* Issue weekly or monthly bulletins of key developments; it should be short and focused. They give organisation relevant and specific information that no external newsletter, with its generic coverage, can provide.
- *Step 10. Market the Capability:* Create two way interactions with library clients. Use all the techniques of marketing to reach the library's internal audience and consider carefully the incentives the library can offer to encourage the regular inflow of useful information.

AS TRAINER

Ben regard managing technological change is somewhat akin to the Queen's concept of progress in Through the Looking Glass. He claimed *"It takes all the running you can do, to keep in the same place. If you want to get somewhere else, you must run at least twice as that."* Thus to 'manage' this frenetic running pace, training is critically important. Trainers have to be very philosophical people, very adaptable, too. MacKellar claimed that two million anecdotes of unhappy and unavoidable crisis situations, however, do not replace the necessity of thorough preparation and competent training coverage, especially with basic tools such as Internet, CD-ROMs and other electronic sources. He added, in the documentation manual for Folio VIEWS, the following four statements are listed, emphasising the fact that trainers have to train users to do more than simply be able to push the right buttons:

- *Information* does not equal knowledge.
- Use of *information* can lead to knowledge.
- If you can't find the *information* you need, gaining knowledge can be difficult.
- If you can't use the *information* once you find it, gaining knowledge can be impossible.

So, what can trainers do to move users from button pushing to knowledge gathering? They can be patient, teach some underlying technology, and explain some basic search rules. Erlendsdottir consider training in libraries as in other organisations, is divided into two main categories:

1. *Maintenance training*—that enables the library to maintain its existing procedures and include induction training for new entrants to the library system or particular parts.
2. *Basic updating and improvement training in identified areas*—whereby training should be concerned with the whole person, concepts, skills and behaviour patterns.

As suggested, the technological training needs of the librarians in libraries depend on the IT level of the particular level.

Thus, the librarian must:

- Know the Art of the Search.
- Know what the systems contain example how the shopping streets of information are laid out.
- Know the back alleys as well as the main routes to the information example on the CD-ROMs.
- Bargain with the system to get the 'best answers' in the cheapest, quickest way.
- Consider using a greater range of visual and auditory challenges in the presentation.

- Keep abreast of the ongoing and latest technological advancements.
- Able to identify the body of core knowledge and skills required by them to run information and communication technology applications.
- Improve and promote the existing and new library services to reach their clients.

Training library users to use these technological resources, and to understand the cultural rules and the new environment such as functional setup, linking, split screens, exporting, cutting and pasting) are the challenges. Trainers are similar in a way to personal shoppers for Westerners who land in Hong Kong and don't know the environment or culture. Thus the trainer's end goal is to see these clients finally doing their own shopping in the information marketplace, hopefully with enough expertise to be able to pick up a few bargains.

Why the Need for Training

The three major benefits are:

1. Appreciate the gaps that may exist between what is currently being done and what needs to be done.
2. Opportunity to make corrections in their systems within a safe environment.
3. Develop 'ownership' and reduce or eliminate staff and users resistance to change, thereby adding longevity to the system.

Training for trainers is regard a necessity in academic libraries and it is the library's responsibility to structure training so as to help librarians clarify both their own expectations and the expectations of their clients and the organisation itself.

AS RESEARCHER

In a complex and rapidly changing environment, higher education must help students to become information literate. Information literacy enables students to recognise the value of information and use it to make informed choices in their personal, professional and academic lives. An information literate student effectively accesses, evaluates, organises, synthesises and applies information from a variety of sources and formats in a variety of contexts. Information literacy requires an ongoing involvement in learning and in evaluating information so that life long learning is possible."

As research and teaching increasingly rely on global networks for the creation, storage and dissemination of knowledge, the need to educate information-literate students has become more widely recognised. Students often lack the skills necessary to succeed in this rapidly changing environment, and faculty need training and support to make use of new technologies for effective teaching and learning. The current environment provides an opportunity for librarians to playa key role in the evolution of an integrated information literacy curriculum, in contrast to past efforts which were sporadic and rarely programmatically based. Librarians have always played a key role in research activities in the academic environment.

They have conducted library instructional orientations sessions to assist students doing research. Thus, to assist clients in their research activities, the librarian must acquire the information skills to manage the overload of information available in many formats propelled by technological advancements.

The Search Strategy

The best strategy involves identifying "what type of information need and which library resources will best provide that information." The time spent developing a well-organised search strategy will reduce the overall time and effort required to assist and conduct research. Following the steps in the *flowchart* below will lead to a well organised research report:

Follow chart

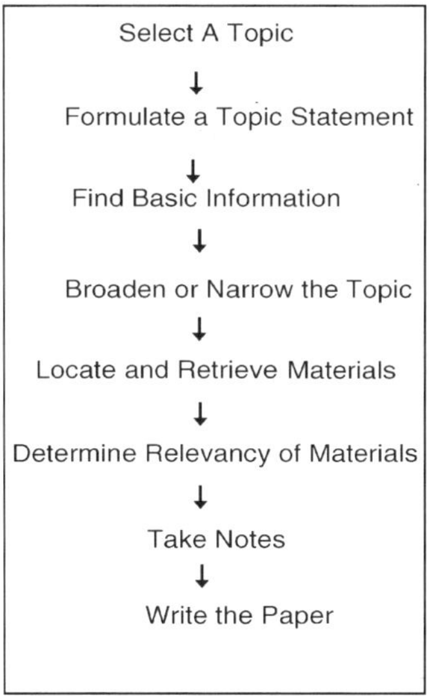

Select A Topic
↓
Formulate a Topic Statement
↓
Find Basic Information
↓
Broaden or Narrow the Topic
↓
Locate and Retrieve Materials
↓
Determine Relevancy of Materials
↓
Take Notes
↓
Write the Paper

Information Literacy Competencies

The impact on student who is information literate is able to:

- Identify and articulate needs which require information solutions:
  - Recognise a specific information need.
  - Focus and articulate the information need into a researchable question.
  - Understand that the type and amount of infor-mation selected is determined in part by the parameters of the need, as well as by the information available.

- Identify and select appropriate information sources:
  - Recognise the availability of a variety of sources and of assistance with using them.
  - Identify types of information resources in a variety of formats and understand their characteristics.
  - Select types of information resources appropriate to a specific information need.
- Formulate and efficiently execute search queries appropriate for the information resource:
  - Understand that different information sources and formats require different searching techniques, including browsing.
  - Select the search strategies appropriate to the topic and resource.
  - Understand that various resources may use different controlled vocabularies to refer to the same topic.
  - Use search language appropriate to the source, such as a controlled vocabulary, key words, natural language, author and title searches to locate relevant items in print and electronic resources.
  - Use online search techniques and tools to locate relevant citations and to further refine the search.
- Interpret and analyse search results and select relevant sources:
  - Understand that search results may be presented according to various ordering principles.
  - Assess the number and relevance of sources cited to determine whether the search strategy must be refined.
  - Recognise the components of a citation and differentiate between types of resources cited, such as a book, periodical, or government document, as well as the format.
  - Use the components of a citation to choose those most suitable for the information need.
  - Perceive gaps in information retrieved and determine whether the search should be refined.
- Locate and retrieve relevant sources in a variety of formats from the global information environment:
  - Understand the organisation of materials in libraries and use locally produced location guides.
  - Understand how to use classification systems and their rationale.
  - Use location information in the bibliographic record to retrieve locally owned resources.
  - Use local resources to locate information sources in the global information environment.
  - Understand that libraries have developed methods for locating and sharing resources not owned locally and use the appropriate

resource sharing system, such as interlibrary loan or document delivery, to retrieve information.
  - Understand that the Internet may be a useful resource for locating, retrieving and transferring information electronically.
- Critically evaluate the information retrieved:
  - Use a variety of criteria, such as author's credentials, peer review, and reputation of the publisher, to assess the authority of the source.
  - Assess the relevancy of a source to an information need by examining publication date, purpose, and intended audience.
  - Recognise omission in the coverage of a topic.
  - Recognise and evaluate documentation for the information source, such as research methodology, bibliography or footnotes.
  - Distinguish between primary and secondary sources in different disciplines and evaluate their appropriateness to the information need.
  - Apply evaluation criteria to all information formats.
- Organise, synthesise, integrate and apply the information:
  - Use appropriate documentation style to cite sources used.
  - Summarise the information retrieved.
  - Recognise and accept the ambiguity of multiple points of view.
  - Organise the information in a logical and useful manner.
  - Synthesise the ideas and concepts from the information sources collected.
  - Determine the extent to which the information can be applied to the information need.
  - Integrate the new information into existing body of knowledge.
  - Create a logical argument based on information retrieved.
- Self-assess the information-seeking processes used:
  - Understand that information-seeking consists of evolving, non-linear processes that include making multiple decisions and choices.
  - Describe the criteria used to make decisions and choices at each step of the particular process used.
  - Assess effectiveness of each step of the process and refine the search process in order to make it more effective.
  - Understand that many of the components of an information seeking process are transferable and, therefore, are applicable to a variety of information needs.
- Understand the structure of the information environment and the process by which both scholarly and popular information is produced, organised and disseminated:

  - Understand that information structure, *e.g.*, how information is produced, organised, and disseminated, can vary from discipline to discipline.
  - Understand that the value of a particular type of information resource may vary from discipline to discipline.
  - Understand that the information structure in a particular discipline can change and modify search strategies to accommodate these changes.
- Understand public policy and the ethical issues affecting the access and use of information:
  - Understand the ethics of information use, such as knowing how and when to give credit to information and ideas gleaned from others by appropriately citing sources in order to avoid plagiarism.
  - Respect intellectual property rights by respecting copyright.
  - Understand concepts and issues relating to censorship, intellectual freedom, and respect for differing points of view.
  - Understand the social/political issues affecting information, such as:
    - Privacy.
    - Privatisation and access to government information.
    - Electronic access to information.
    - The exponential growth of information.
    - Equal access to information.

CYBRARIANS

The word 'Cybrarian' was coined by Michel Bauwens, Information Officer at BP Nutrition in Antwerp, Belgium, to describe the staff in a virtual library. We may expand this definition to an Information Professional/Librarian who utilises digital and networked communications technologies to the fullest to retrieve, evaluate and disseminate information. While it is not currently possible to obtain a degree in 'cybrarianship', there are possibilities for advancing your knowledge of these technologies.

Characteristics of Cybrarians

So, what then are the characteristics of cybrarians. Keller commented:

- They remember the fundamental functions librarians perform: selection, description and intellectual access, interpretation, distribution, and preservation.
- They remember that they are present to serve the current, local population of readers first, but also perhaps remote readers as well, thanks to the networks.
- They remember also that they perform a vital role as custodians of

culture, assuring that the records of man's investigations and creative works survive for those not yet born.

- Many of them are subject specialists, expert and educated in a discipline as well as prepared to 'teach' in structured and unstructured settings.
- Many of them are technical specialists, catalogers, circulation librarians, conservationists.
- Some of them were either subject specialists or technical specialists or both and then became managers or leaders.
- All of them are comfortable with the constant on-rush of LT. and realise their fundamental functions must be performed regardless of the media or format of the information carrier.
- All of them are acutely aware of the need to be as responsive as possible to individuals even while translating a cacophony of individual needs and requests to systems and services intended to serve whole populations, whole communities.
- All of them will be ready to work with their colleagues in the next building, the next city or town, the next country or continent by using the communications potential of the networks.
- None of them will need a lot of sleep, for there will be more and more for them to do.
- Many of them will have strong entrepreneurial spirit.

8

Library Staff

LIBRARY STAFF DEVELOPMENT

Most university libraries throughout the world are engaged in some level of staff development. Benchmarking of staff development activities however is not widespread and little useful data exists to enable meaningful comparisons between university libraries within national borders, let alone provide meaningful international perspectives. Three studies in the first half of this decadc cxamined staff development policy and practice in the university library sector in Australia and the United Kingdom.

Significantly, the studies enabled limited international comparisons where none had been previously possible. In January 2008, two university library organisations – CAVAL in Australia and EMALINK in the United Kingdom - commenced a joint project to further develop this process of comparison by benchmarking staff development practices within their member libraries. Although located in different hemispheres and literally half a world away from each other, CAVAL and EMALINK were assessed as good candidates for a benchmarking study.

Both organisations are roughly similar in terms of their size, composition and orientation. Prior to 2008, they had also already shared expertise relating to staff development and key personnel had worked together as members of IFLA's Continuing Professional Development and Workplace Learning Section.

A collaborative project thus appeared to offer CAVAL and EMALINK a unique opportunity to provide value to their member libraries in two key ways:

- By identifying, comparing and generally sharing knowledge about current staff development practices and processes; and,
- By establishing common measurement points, indicators and best practice benchmarks to assist with planning improvements in future staff development practices and processes.

On the ground, the project aimed to obtain data and test various assumptions that would enable the development of a practical tool to facilitate ongoing benchmarking between CAVAL and EMALINK member libraries.

Longer term, the project hoped to inform the development of a marketable "dashboard" of indicators for benchmarking staff development activities in other libraries at national and international levels. CAVAL also planned to establish a database of indicators in order to build up a longitudinal data set to facilitate trend analysis.

In tandem with these aims, the project also sought to demonstrate how recent developments in information and communications technology (ICT), particularly social networking technology, have helped to facilitate international collaborative library research projects. Originally projected for completion in late 2008, the project encountered logistical challenges on the Australian side within several months of commencement. Rather than delay or compromise the entire project, CAVAL withdrew temporarily, thereby allowing EMALINK to push ahead with a pilot survey of its members in the United Kingdom. In this way, EMALINK was able to complete base level data collection already undertaken by CAVAL in 2006.

This chapter constitutes a progress report and case study of the CAVAL – EMALINK library staff development benchmarking project to July 2008. The chapter outlines the drivers for benchmarking in library staff development and discusses why applied research of this kind is of potentially such great value to university and other libraries in the context of current issues impacting staff development: for example, recruitment and retention of staff. Details are provided of the research methodology agreed by CAVAL and EMALINK, and the benchmarking dimensions investigated by the project. With preliminary data from EMALINK available in early July 2008, the paper reports on initial findings and considers important practical lessons in international collaboration learned to date.

STAFF DEVELOPMENT RESEARCH IN AUSTRALIA AND THE UNITED KINGDOM

Attempts to examine and benchmark staff development practice in Australian university libraries can be traced back more than twenty years; with more recent work in Australia and the United Kingdom attempting to update and expand that work. Both early Australian surveys by Trask and Gray revealed a paucity of human resource development in the university library sector, albeit balanced by an emerging recognition at that time of the importance of developing people.

In 2001 and then again in 2005, Smith explored the extent of commitment to staff development, linkages to strategic organisational priorities, and the focus of staff development activity. The overall picture presented by these 2001 and 2005 surveys was of a strong commitment to investment in human resource development – a picture very different to that found in the earlier 1983 and 1986 analyses.

Smith concluded that the major influences on the focus of staff development programmes in Australian university libraries included:

- Increasing scope and volume of electronic publishing, with consequent changes in required staff skills and knowledge;
- Increasing involvement of university library staff in teaching information literacy (with needs for skill development on the part of those staff doing such teaching);
- Changing organisational demographics (in particular ageing workforces), and actual or impending retirements of staff (particularly senior staff) – this resulting in the need for succession planning and development of new leadership and management capability; and,
- The imperative for regionally isolated libraries to grow and develop skills and capability within their existing workforce.

For the first time, the 2005 survey explored budget allocations for staff development. This was interesting as a measure in its own right of the level of commitment to staff development activity. It also enabled benchmarking against a comparable survey undertaken in the United Kingdom, and several other available benchmarks including those of the *American Society for Training and Development* and *UNESCO*. In 2004, motivated partly by the 2001 Australian study, Yeoh investigated staff development in a cross section of university libraries in England, Scotland and Ireland.

That survey found, inter alia:

- A strong commitment to staff development as part of institutional strategic organisational management;
- Formal written statements of commitment to staff development in just over half of the organisations surveyed;
- A planned and structured approach to staff development in most organisations; and,
- A structured appraisal and review of these activities in two thirds of organisations.

It was also keen to develop common staff development indicators and a database to enable longitudinal studies. In retrospect, the survey instrument developed by the project team was arguably too broad, encompassing 97 questions over 46 pages, and too complex; partly a outcome of trying to align the survey with international studies.

As a result of the CAVAL survey's complexity, details of staff development practice within member libraries were largely obscured by other issues relating to recruitment and retention and succession planning. Although providing a highly detailed and ultimately fascinating snapshot of human resources in CAVAL member libraries in late 2006, the project stalled after presentation of the preliminary findings in March 2007. "The research project generated an immense amount of data that is of varying degrees of completeness and indeed of value." The research instrument itself was complex, which potentially added further complications to the ability to undertake an effective comparative analysis and interpretation of the responses." Interestingly, researcher comments echo those of Ford, writing on benchmarking HRD: "choosing the wrong set of metrics is one of the surest ways to doom a benchmarking study." For CAVAL, the over-riding challenge of the 2006 *Benchmarking of Staff Development Practice in CAVAL Member Libraries* project was how to go about "extracting the desired key measurement points needed if benchmark levels of practice and processes are to be established within the membership of the consortium."

With resources allocated to the CAVAL project exhausted by early 2007 and other projects moving to the fore, further progress on benchmarking staff development seemed unlikely in the short term. As one door closes, however, sometimes another opens. Enter at this point EMALINK, the East Midlands Library Information Network, representing the 10 university and higher education libraries comprising the United Kingdom's East Midland University Association (EMUA).

WHY BENCHMARK BEST PRACTICE IN LIBRARY STAFF DEVELOPMENT?

Before reporting on the methodology and early findings of the 2008 CAVAL-EMALINK study, it is important to understand the significance of benchmarking best practice in staff development to libraries in general. Libraries, it was long argued, were simply the sum of their collections – print and later electronic.

A big library was ipso facto a good library. The majority of contemporary library measures still reflect this preoccupation with the physical item, even where electronic resources have taken precedence. The rise of the internet and increasing demands from customers have however progressively turned the focus of library managers to their people – arguably always their best information 'assets'. People and the environments in which they live and work are not static though, and the parallel processes of personal and professional development must be ongoing.

Thus libraries, particularly university libraries, have come to realise the significance of better understanding staff development through benchmarking. Many are returning to the origins of benchmarking as an organisational improvement tool, and Spendolini's simple elevator definition of benchmarking as "learning from others". Researcher that "changes in the academic library workplace mirror those of other workplaces in the new millennium."

Expanding on this theme, researcher observes:

- Following the nature of the work, the organisation of the institution is constantly shifting, requiring staff in all areas to perform a greater variety of tasks. The operations daily become more automated and more technical. The workforce becomes more diverse. The pace quickens. The budget tightens. And the tensions mount.

For libraries, particularly university libraries, there are also specific challenges to address. The last two decades have seen greatly increased emphases on access to information and knowledge management. Changes and developments in the ways and means of organising and accessing recorded knowledge have been both rapid and profound; with increasingly sophisticated information systems evolving as a result.

As IFLA acknowledges, libraries and those who work in them have an increasingly important role to play in such an environment:

- The quality of service provided to the public by library and information science institutions depends on the expertise of their staff. Constant flux in the needs of societies, changing technologies, and growth in professional knowledge demand that information workers must expand their understanding and update their skills on an ongoing basis.

As a consequence of this transformation, human resource professionals in libraries are observing a range of issues impacting on and influencing staff development.

Focusing on university libraries, the issues are as follows:

- The need for library staff to keep current with continuous changes in information technology and with information itself;
- A related need to coordinate technical training for library staff, and find the expertise and resources to provide it;
- A strengthening of libraries' traditional customer service orientation in order to compete with Internet search engines and online booksellers;
- Further development of libraries' orientation towards teamwork, made necessary by shrinking budgets, decreases in staff numbers, and the rise of multifunctional teams;
- Additional support required for both new and experienced managers;
- Growth of the teaching and training role of university library staff, particularly but not exclusively those in professional positions; and finally,
- The need to provide meaningful staff development as a means of recruiting and retaining staff.

The imperative to maintain and upgrade the skills, knowledge, and abilities of library and information staff has been recognised, and is reflected, in the significant priority allocated to human resource development (HRD) activity in many libraries. As a strategic organisational priority it is important that HRD is assessed and, where necessary, improved and that this be a continuing cyclical activity. Benchmarking has clear potential to achieve that end. Indeed, benchmarking has particular applicability for HRD because the activity naturally lends itself to cooperative and collaborative working between institutions. Ford proposes a series of metrics which may be usefully applied to benchmarking staff development. Some are relatively straightforward to measure and calculate, while others are more challenging.

In broadly escalating degrees of difficulty in measurement these metrics include:

- Expenditure on staff development activities expressed as a percentage of payroll;
- Average hours spent on staff development per employee per annum;
- Average staff development cost per participant per hour;
- Percentage of employees undertaking staff development activity per annum;
- Average percentage of positive ratings of staff development activities by participants;
- Average percentage of gains in learning reported by participants in staff development activities;
- Average percentage of improvement in on-the-job performance as a result of participation in staff development activities;
- Cost savings and efficiency gains as a result of participation in staff development activities.

The eventual goal is to take raw data and convert it to ratios or percentages that can be monitored easily over time – in effect, a staff development 'dashboard'. Although nowhere near this level of sophistication, IFLA's *Continuing Professional Development and Workplace Learning Quality Guidelines Project* has published useful best practice indicators for staff development.

IFLA requires that there be:

- Regular learning needs assessment.
- Broad range of learning opportunities, both formal and informal; formal offerings in a choice of formats, designed to meet identified needs, in modules structured to cover topics from introductory through advanced.
- Organizational commitment and leadership from staff development and continuing education administrators with expertise in adult continuing education.
- Widely disseminated information about continuing education and resources, accurately described.
- C[ontinuing] E[education] activities design that includes learning objectives aligned with identified needs; follows principles of instructional design and learning theory; selects course instructors on the basis of both subject knowledge and teaching ability; attends to transfer of training and feedback.
- Consistent documentation of individuals' participation in learning and recognition of continuing learning in hiring and promotion decisions.
- A minimum of 0.5 to 1.0 per cent of institutional budget earmarked for staff development, as stated in *The public library service: IFLA/*

UNESCO guidelines for developmen.

- About 10 per cent of work hours provided for attendance at workshops, conferences, in-service training, and other educational activities, and for informal learning projects.
- Evaluation of continuing education and staff development offerings and programmes.
- Research that assesses the state of CPD and examines the efficacy and outcomes of continuing education and staff development programmes.

CAVAL-EMALINK STUDY METHODOLOGY

In October 2007, Ian Smith and Graham Walton proposed that CAVAL in Australia and EMALINK in the United Kingdom undertake a joint study to identify best practice in staff development in member libraries.

They highlighted a number of benefits to individual member libraries, including:

- Acquisition of staff development data to inform and guide ongoing change processes;
- Opportunity to undertake national and international level comparisons; and,
- Opportunity for international partnering and skills exchange.

Within the context of developing and delivering the project, the proposal acknowledged that university libraries are busy organisations and that no funds had been budgeted for the project by CAVAL or EMALINK in 2008. It was considered crucial therefore that the work should not be time or resource intensive, particularly in relation to project management and data collection.

A relatively brief web based questionnaire was suggested to minimise the time and effort required for survey development, administration and analysis. Smith and Walton proposed that the project should be jointly overseen by a small team of nominated representatives from the CAVAL Human Resources Group and EMALINK. This working group would take responsibility for jointly developing and administering the survey questionnaire, analysing the data obtained, and producing a summary report for dissemination to individual member libraries. The proposed study methodology called for data collection to take place through a web based questionnaire, with questions taking no more than 20 minutes in total to complete.

In scoping the 2006 staff development benchmarking study involving CAVAL member libraries, Smith originally proposed eight benchmarking dimensions:

- Budget allocation for staff development expressed as a percentage of total payroll costs. Further, what elements are covered by that budget and what budget model is applied for staff development (*e.g.*, centralised or distributed)?

- Approval criteria and processes – how are staff development applications assessed and approved?
- Links between staff development priorities and strategic planning;
- Organisational approaches to the development, documentation and evaluation of staff development plans;
- Common themes and priorities in staff development plans;
- Application of *Rodski* results in setting staff development objectives - have staff development investments in turn improved *Rodski* ratings?
- Coordination of staff development in CAVAL member libraries – how and by whom?
- Evaluation of staff development programmes by the organisation and measurement of the return on investment (ROI).

By mid-July 2008, EMALINK had received an encouraging seven responses from a total membership of ten university libraries. In 2006, CAVAL received responses from all eleven members.

UNDERSTANDING THE VALUE OF BENCHMARKING

In the context of libraries, benchmarking may be defined as an ongoing structured process by which we evaluate the functions, work processes and services of other organisations (not always libraries) recognised for their leadership and innovation. This process of evaluation is undertaken for the purpose of organisational comparison and improvement. The concept of *competitive benchmarking*, later 'benchmarking', was first popularised by the Xerox Corporation in the late 1970s as an innovative response – at that time – to strong competition in a market segment that it had hitherto dominated.

Xerox refined the concept of benchmarking through the 1980s and eventually promulgated a ten-step benchmarking process. Despite there now being many competing process models for benchmarking, most can trace their origins back twenty years to the original Xerox process, and early variations. Other influences cited as significant in the development of the concept of benchmarking include the quality assurance movement and just-in-time manufacturing methods. Indeed, Deming's classic four step quality improvement process still forms the basis of many benchmarking exercises. Benchmarking is essentially concerned with understanding how processes work – through observing and studying work methods and practices – and then identifying good or best practice. Benchmarking seeks to learn from the observation of such good and best practice, and to make improvements necessary to reach identified standards of good and best practice. Assessment of improvement is based on review and comparison with other like organisations; hence the significance of a good match between CAVAL and EMALINK. Drawing on Deming's four step process, Ford and Longbottom each propose useful models for benchmarking; Ford specifically in the context of benchmarking human resource development (HRD).

It is Longbottom's 'PAIR' approach however that resonates through the methodology applied in the CAVAL-EMALINK project:

- Planning - investigation, measurement and examination of the strengths and weaknesses of current processes;
- Analysis – identifying potential benchmarking partners and then exchanging information, and observing and comparing processes;
- Implementation – adaptation and modification of processes based on learning from the analysis stage;
- Review – ongoing review and refinement with the intention of achieving continuous improvements.

Within the higher education sector, libraries have frequently been early and enthusiastic adopters of benchmarking techniques. University libraries in Australia, New Zealand and the United Kingdom, for example, have all been at the forefront in adopting and applying benchmarking processes to various aspects of their operations. In the case of Australia, the work of scholars has been important in outlining suitable frameworks and encouraging the adoption of benchmarking methods in university libraries. Noting the need to identify benchmarks which would assess efficient use of resources and the quality of the contributions which university libraries make to the realisation of university objectives, McKinnon *et al* proposed a range of criterion reference benchmarks with the intention firstly of identifying attributes of good practice and then using those attributes as benchmarks for further evaluation.

The *Council of Australian University Librarians* has encouraged benchmarking between its members and has facilitated a range of studies in various operational areas including client satisfaction with library services, performance and effectiveness of document delivery services, availability of sought materials, cataloguing, and the re-shelving of library materials. Several trans-national benchmarking projects have also been undertaken with Australian libraries as a key partner, for example between libraries in Australia and New Zealand and Australia and the United Kingdom.

MANAGING STAFF DEVELOPMENT

There can be no doubt that the need for professional development, continuing education, or workplace learning in regard to technology is vital for today's libraries. Never before have the profession's tools undergone such extreme and rapid transformations, and these transformations are not about to cease, as illustrated in the various thesis compiled in Core *Technology Competencies for Librarians and Library Staff*. It is, therefore, incumbent upon library administration to develop, implement, encourage, and support policies on staff competency and development. It is, also, necessary for both professional librarians and paraprofessionals to—at the very least— be proficient in the current trends of technology, if not embracing the changes by keeping pace with them. In short, with a little innovative leadership, learning options are endless, as well as accessible, user-friendly, and exciting.

BARRIERS TO LEARNING

The "graying" of today's library is perhaps the most cited obstacle for staff development in technology. Long and Applegate, for instance, provide statistical data that reveals the willingness to learn of library staff according to their generation. Many professional librarians who received their degrees prior to 1995, or before the study of computers in Library Science programmes in the United States, understand the importance of keeping up with technology, yet a surprisingly large percentage of support staff is unwilling to adapt to the technical changes or to explore the possibilities that new technology brings.

Time constraints are another barrier to staff development. Workers who are given the time to develop skills are more apt to do so. However, many employees say there is little time to complete their usual tasks, much less learn new skills, regardless of whether employers allow the time for it. One thing is clear and that is that management needs to understand their employee's learning needs, as a number of investigations note the lack of managerial support in staff development. In fact, even professionals must often be self-motivated and seek out learning opportunities on their own.

E-LEARNING, WEBINARS, AND LEARNING 2.0

E-Learning, or learning delivered through electronic tools, is clearly the most popular form of staff development today. Both professionals and paraprofessionals may choose from a myriad of sources for such learning. Among the many options are webinars from WebJunction, OCLC, EbscoHost, and Gale Cengage Learning, to name a few. However, Learning 2.0 has not only gained considerable attention, but it has also been implemented, studied, and documented, thereby, raising its stature and effectiveness.

Developed by Helen Blowers and based on Web 2.0 technology, Learning 2.0 is an incentive-based model programme for training library staff in new technologies. Students, who are self-directed, are asked to complete "23 Things," or online interactive projects on, for example, RSS feeds, flickr, wikis, podcasts, and LibraryThing. Kingsley and Jensen's paper on Learning 2.0's implementation at the University of Alaska Fairbanks Rasmuson Library stands as the most comprehensive study to date of the freely shared model, illustrating the programmes success rate and offering some concluding recommendations, such as making staff development mandatory.

ADMINISTRATION AND STAFF DEVELOPMENT

Not only are the tools with which library staff work changing, but so, too, are the philosophies and practices of management, especially in regard to staff competency and development. Mosley and Kaspar describe the challenges of hiring and retaining competent employees that can meet the ever-changing demands of library service. They suggest that management needs to look to the future by reconsidering job descriptions and job postings by avoiding the use of traditional library wording.

Management also must consider incentives when encouraging staff development. Incentives, such as the MP3s, PDAs, and laptops offered by Blower's pilot Learning 2.0 programme at the Public Library of Charlotte and Mecklenburg County, are not always possible, especially in the current economy. However, there are other methods of motivation. For instance, the University of Arizona Library restructured their monetary compensation, or wage, plans, which were based upon a traditional hierarchical scale. Their innovative and team-based "pay-for-skill" programme rewards employees for developing advanced capabilities, along with the willingness to learn and take on more responsibility.

METHODS OF TRAINING

There are various methods of training, which can be divided in to cognitive and Behavioural methods. Trainers need to understand the pros and cons of each method, also its impact on trainees keeping their background and skills in mind before giving training. Cognitive methods are more of giving theoretical training to the trainees. The various methods under Cognitive approach provide the rules for how to do something, written or verbal information, demonstrate relationships among concepts, etc., These methods are associated with changes in knowledge and attitude by stimulating learning.

The various methods that come under Cognitive approach are:

- Lectures.
- Demonstrations.
- Discussions.
- Computer based training (cbt).
  - Intellegent tutorial system(its).
  - Programmed instruction (pi).
  - Virtual reality.

Behavioural methods are more of giving practical training to the trainees. The various methods under Behavioural approach allow the trainee to Behaviour in a real fashion. These methods are best used for skill development.

The various methods that come under Behavioural approach are:

- Games and simulations.
  - Behaviour-modeling.
  - Business games.
  - Case studies.
  - Equipment stimulators.

- In-basket technique.
- Role plays.

Both the methods can be used effectively to change attitudes, but through different means.

INSTRUCTIONAL SYSTEM DEVELOPMENT MODEL (ISD) MODEL

Instructional System Development model or ISD training model was made to answer the training problems. This model is widely used now-a-days in the organisation because it is concerned with the training need on the job performance. Training objectives are defined on the basis of job responsibilities and job description and on the basis of the defined objectives individual progress is measured. This model also helps in determining and developing the favourable strategies, sequencing the content, and delivering media for the types of training objectives to be achieved.

The Instructional System Development model comprises of five stages:

- This phase consist of training need assessment, job analysis, and target audience analysis.
- This phase consist of setting goal of the learning outcome, instructional objectives that measures Behaviour of a participant after the training, types of training material, media selection, methods of evaluating the trainee, trainer and the training Programme, strategies to impart knowledge, *i.e.*, selection of content, sequencing of content, etc.
- This phase translates design decisions into training material. It consists of developing course material for the trainer including handouts, workbooks, visual aids, demonstration props, etc, course material for the trainee including handouts of summary.
- This phase focuses on logistical arrangements, such as arranging speakers, equipments, benches, podium, food facilities, cooling, lighting, parking, and other training accessories.
- The purpose of this phase is to make sure that the training Programme has achieved its aim in terms of subsequent work performance. This phase consists of identifying strengths and weaknesses and making necessary amendments to any of the previous stage in order to remedy or improve failure practices.

The ISD model is a continuous process that lasts throughout the training Programme. It also highlights that feedback is an important phase throughout the entire training Programme. In this model, the output of one phase is an input to the next phase.

Another Method is Management Development Method

- The more future oriented method and more concerned with education of the employees. To become a better performer by education implies that management development activities attempt to instill sound reasoning processes. Management development method is further divided into two parts:

- The development of a manager's abilities can take place on the job.

The four techniques for on the job development are:

1. Coaching.
2. Mentoring.
3. Job rotation.
4. Job instruction technique (jit).

OFF THE JOB TRAINING

There are many management development techniques that an employee can take in off the job.

The few popular methods are:

- Sensitivity training.
- Transactional analysis.
- Straight lectures/ lectures.
- Simulation exercises.

TRAINING AND SUPPORT TO USERS

The importance of the library as a resource centre and the endeavor of the management to exploit the resources gathered over the years with a lot of investment, need not be over emphasized. However, it has been the experience of many a library, especially those attached to organisations, the use of their resources appear to be little compared to the efforts put in building up the resources. As such there appears to be a constant need to initiate outreach programmes in order to enhance the usage of the library to the maximum extent. Library is looked upon as a centre for learning.

The Library has to strive to repackage the material that is received in the library in the form of Alerts, reviews, digests, abstracts and databases to enhance library utilization and improve readership. Also, in view of the rapid developments in Information and Communication Technologies, the role of a librarian is not like what it used to be a few decades ago. Added to IT, satellite communication systems, networking, Internet and intellectual property rights, have all made the library environment more complex. Further, the budgetary constraints, inadequate infrastructure, falling standards in human resources are all compelling the librarian to change his attitude from a mere custodian of information to that of a facilitator. As the library is a service institution there should be close interaction between the information providers, processors and users to enhance the effectivity of any resource centre Keeping in view the above factors, National Institute of Rural Development (NIRD) conducted a learning programme on. This programme provided a forum for the users of information and the library personnel to come together, to understand each others way of dealing with information and how the information barriers can be overcome and what best practices are to be adopted to increase the utilization of the resources of the Library through various training programmes.

LIBRARY UTILIZATION AND READERSHIP ENHANCEMENT (LURE)

When CORD conducted the one-day programme LURE I in 1991, had a modest goal to find out the ways and means to increase the library utilization by adopting innovative methods tolure the readers. This was based on a feeling that we have been investing in the library huge amounts of money year after year, trying to equip the library with more relevant reading material and also recruit trained personnel to make the resources more useful. While we are trying to build up a tempo, we had a feeling somewhere along the line that the readers or users are still not coming along with us. This feeling lead us to an introspection which gave rise to the impetus for conducting a programme for the first time on LURE in 1991. As stated earlier, the learning programme provided an opportunity for interaction between the library professionals and our own users in understanding the lacunae in promoting exploitation of library resources. In the first workshop on LURE in 1991 several issues were thrown up such as the following:

ISSUES FOR CONSIDERATION

As the reader is reluctant to come to library, it may be necessary that the library has to go to the reader. Naturally, that situation will determine the kind of services that are planned or envisaged to enhance the usage of the library. The issues that influence the usage hinge upon how the information needs are gauged and the methods that are adopted to identify those needs. Some of the other major issues identified are:

- Focus of the parent organisation
- Information collection
- Information processing
- Information search in the Internet era
- Information dissemination
- Information barriers

The workshop offered a set of simple but effective steps to increase the library use with suggestions like involvement of users in procurement of literature, client based services etc., The other major recommendations include:

- The book selection and acquisition are both important and modalities like participatory practices have to be followed;
- User education and user services have to be frequently conducted by the library to improve the interaction between users and the library personnel;

- A brochure on the library highlighting the library collection, cataloging and classification system followed and the services offered would be more useful;
- immediate computerization of all activities of library;
- creation of new services like abstracting, alerting service, reference and making digests on specific topics etc.,
- augmentation of facilities for document supply and other physical facilities like proper sign boards, stools to reach higher shelves, etc., and
- strengthening of the resource sharing at the local level.

These recommendations were taken seriously as they were particularly important in the over all development of the library utilization. Fortunately, most of the suggestions would be implemented with a telling effect on the positive response of the readers.

LURE – II

After a gap of nearly two years, CORD thought of again reviewing the library utilization with the completion of library automation. Accordingly, in 1993 a second programme on LURE was conducted. This time with a difference. The impetus came from the management of parent organization. There was a constant refrain from the management that with automation is there any improvement in the utilization of library resources? How many faculty are visiting the library? What is the ratio between faculty and participants of various training programmes that visit the library? What special arrangements were made to familiarize the participants with the new automation etc.,

These were a few of the questions that were bothering the management. Also, with computerization of library procedures, a new barrier is likely to be perceived by the users. Such 'Automation anxiety' may have to be taken into consideration in designing training programmes on library initiation.

Accordingly, the participants were chosen from not only the users of the library but also the participants of the then running courses, besides other librarians of neighbouring institutions. The programme was conducted in 3 sessions. In these sessions several papers based on cases illustrating the circulation facility, visitors register, pattern of usage of library on different dates and use of various information products of CORD were presented. These studies provided a picture of the pattern of library usage after the automation which appeared to be promising and provided the guidance as to how to increase awareness and access to information. Several suggestions emerged based on the discussions and some of which are as follows:—

- **Information Products:**
  - The coverage of indexing and abstracting services done through CORD Index and CORD Abstracts is found to be satisfactory.

However, emphasis may have to be given to the immediate interest of the faculty members depending on their research and training programmes.

  - The journals that are covered in CORD Alerts may have to be displayed at a designed place for their immediate location and identification of articles given in the service.

- **Maintenance:**
  - Upkeep and maintenance of various sections will provide the necessary incentive for the users to browse.
  - Library staff should be trained and motivated to assist the readers.
- **User Studies:**
  - Though the faculty members are patronising the library, there is a scope for improvement.
  - Visitors to the Library are not always recording their visits in the prescribed register and so it did not reflect the total visits made by the academic staff in comparison with non-academic staff. A strict vigil on the visitors register may have to be maintained to satisfy the management.

The other major recommendations include:

- Promotion of library with a professional image is essential;
- Library staff should be trained in inter-personnel communication skills;
- There is a need to display current journals in more attractive and useful manner like displaying latest issues at a prominent place, rearranging of primary journals in alphabetical sequence, etc.,
- NIRD publications should be displayed prominently for outside visitors.
- A marketing approach to its library and information products is essential. For this purpose Library counters and surrounding areas should be used for display of not only for acquired publications but also NIRD publications.
- There are about 3000 participants in a year coming to NIRD to participate in the training programmes, who should be given orientation tour to the library for better appreciation of the resources. Also, a session on information resources, and information management relevant to the theme of any course wherever possible should be arranged apart from display of the publications pertaining to the training programme.
- A faculty directory, user manual, training of staff on information technology etc., are other suggestions that emerged from the programme.

After LURE-II in 1993 there was marked improvement in the appreciation of library services, the physical facilities and the environment in the library. Non-book material like CD-ROMS, videos, electronic journal have slowly started to show their presence. In the mid 90s internet opened gates to the Information sources world wide, and made possible access to information from a remote location. As a result it has become more important to look into the problems of transforming a traditional library into an information clearing house.

LURE – III

Against this backdrop a 3rd LURE programme was conducted in the year 1998 after a gap of 5 years. This learning programme was made into a National Workshop inviting papers from all over India on various themes such as library utilisation; techniques of readership enhancement; evaluation of library services; internet and changing role of the librarian etc. Participants from several parts of the country made their presentations based on their own back-home experience in user education and identification of user needs. This workshop revealed various kinds of experiments that are on-going in several parts of the country by innovative librarians and demystifying the Internet for the librarian and the user. Information search in the Internet era has totally changed the way the readers look for information. Searching Internet should become a matter of routine in any special library, to make the expression "Internet is Librarianship" truly applicable. Some of the other major recommendations of the workshop were:

- Continuous study of user needs.
- Development of communication skills of the library personnel.
- Role of parent organization in recognising the contribution of their libraries and supporting their activity.
- Design and update of user manual in the fast changing information technology environment.
- Change of attitude of librarians to the market driven economy and interact with the users more closely and make users appreciate the library services.
- A thematic approach to all the library services have to be *i.e.*, the information products of the library like CORD INDEX, CORD ABSTRACTS should follow the themes identified for the research and training of the institute.
- The Selective Dissemination of Information (SDI) service can perhaps be concentrated on a faculty or a discipline at a time. Once a faculty is studied for a period of 6 months or so as a focussed group the impact on the group and its activities perhaps be quantitatively measured.

CORD is giving continuous training to the Library staff in the above areas in order to serve the clientele for effective use of Library Resources. They are also deputing the staff to other training programmes to get trained in these as well as new emerging areas. Simultaneously providing training and support to the users for better utiliztion of the resources without any barriers.

Thus a new era emergd where information driven activities gained importance which will hopefully energize the users as well as information specialists to come together and work for the better uilization of information following the best practices in information dissemination through regular training programmes.

One common characteristic of the statewide networks is the active involvement of the State Library:

- The State Library of Ohio has strong influence over OPLIN operations and development as a result of its authority to appoint all of the network's board members.
- The State Library in West Virginia operates SLN.
- In Wisconsin, the State Library influences BadgerNet planning and operations through its seat on the BadgerNet Council.

Although MSLN's governing board is the Maine Public Utilities Commission (MPUC), the state librarian is responsible for suggesting policy and for representing the interests of libraries before the MPUC. Furthermore, the Maine State Library has staff members responsible for assessing the needs of MSLN members and for preparing an annual report that outlines the network's needs and presents an annual budget request.

INTERNET TRAINING FOR ACADEMIC LIBRARY STAFF

Educational institutions are being encouraged by the Government and other organizations to upgrade their resources for research and education. Consequently the academic libraries of the higher education institutions are also being upgraded. Internet has proved to be boon in this endeavor. Internet has helped these libraries to be interconnected and share their resources and also to access resources in remote locations. Internet connections have been growing in the recent years with good connectivity and access.

But are these libraries fully geared up especially in terms of their employees' skills to be able to fully utilize the Internet for the benefit of the academic community? It has already been widely discussed that training is essential for the staffs to work in a network and automated environment. The Library Association Working Party on Training cites in its Policy Statement that training "is of fundamental importance to all levels of staffs working in all types of library", contributing to "greater efficiency and continuity, with real cost benefits". Since technology keeps on changing it becomes even more necessary for the staff to be trained in Internet.

OBJECTIVES

The present study aims to understand the status of Internet training for the academic library staff within greater Guwahati. Since the importance of Internet is growing in today's academic environment therefore the issue of training the academic library staff in handling Internet is becoming important. So this study will investigate the various training methods used in the academic libraries, the content of such training, problems encountered and whether any evaluation is undertaken for such training. The investigation will also try to reveal the attitudes of the library managers with regard to training their staff on Internet. In order to understand the status of Internet training for the staffs of the academic libraries a sample of six academic libraries was taken. A questionnaire-based survey of the sample was conducted. The questionnaire contained both close-ended questions and open-ended questions.

The questionnaire was prepared based on some existing studies already done on understanding the Internet training of academic library staff. Comprehending the importance of the study the author personally went to the respective libraries to collect the data.

INTERNET AND ITS USE IN ACADEMIC LIBRARIES

Many of us by now are familiar with Internet especially those working in the academic libraries. This is because the academic libraries have been the pioneer in the field of automation and Internet. Internet has become essential for today's education and research in the academic institutions. Library being a hub of research and academic activities are therefore being provided with Internet connections. The Internet is a unique information resource, bringing a wide range of material from around the world to a local machine. One of the earliest usages of the Internet was to access the OPAC *i.e.* the Online Public Access Catalogues of different libraries or within a campus. The union catalogues which lists the holdings of several libraries was another important tool accessible through net.

Another area of growing importance for academic libraries is that of electronic journals. Big publishing houses like Elsevier, Springer, ACM etc. are providing packages of their journals to libraries in electronic form via Internet. So at nominal subscription the libraries can access to these costly journals, which are becoming increasingly popular with the users.

Thus grew consortia based subscription in India. INDEST, INFONET and CSIR Consortium are the examples of library consortia for sharing journals and bibliographic information. These consortia based journal subscription are available through the Internet. The Indian National Digital Library in Engineering Science and Technology *i.e.* INDEST was set up by the Ministry of Human resource Development (MHRD) for subscription to electronic resources for 38 institutions including IISc, IITs, NITs, IIMs, etc. Over 6000 e-journals are accessible through this consortium, which has its headquarters in IIT Delhi. Infonet Contortia is set up by UGC and operated through its INFLIBNET Centre, Ahmedabad. Over 100 Universities are its members. It covers disciplines like Arts, Sciences, Mathematics and statistics etc. About

4000 full text electronic journals from 25 publishers are currently accessible. CSIR e-journal Consortia provides access to 3300+ e-journals from 11 publishers to all CSIR S and T staff of different CSIR institutions located around India.

These consortia not only provide full text access but they also give access to bibliographic databases like COMPENDEX, INSPEC SciFinder Scholar, and Web of Science etc. Many open access materials important for education and research are available on the Internet. They are very useful in the context that they are not fee based and also don't have restricted access and are thus becoming very popular with students and researchers. Communicating with users is very important in academic libraries.

Widespread access to the Internet has also created new means of communicating with users. In some cases, Internet technologies (*e.g.* e-mail and publishing on Web pages) are used to reproduce an existing service in another medium, such as online "suggestion boxes". However, there is "added value" to such a service as users can mail in their suggestions from terminals on or off campus at a time convenient to them. E-mail enquiry or reference services also represent an extension of mainstream library activity - although some academic librarians initially had concerns about being able to meet the demand of such a service. Reference and enquiry services in academic libraries in the main seek to teach their users how to search for information themselves, rather than answering the enquiries themselves, as is more likely to be the case in a special library.

A significant number of British academic libraries have adopted electronic mail enquiry or information services - at the University of Hull the "e-mail help line" is treated as an extension of the Enquiry Desk service. Anecdotal evidence suggests that electronic enquiry services are not overwhelmed, and most users do stay within the parameters of the service. The most successful e-mail enquiry services have developed their procedures and boundaries prior to the service going live.

As many enquiries fall into the category of Frequently Asked Questions, these can thus be answered by existing position statements. Electronic mail also has great potential to cut down on the mountain of paperwork involved in sending out recall notices, notifying readers that items can be collected etc. Some library systems allow students to renew loans (provided no other reader is waiting for the book) directly via the OPAC or to request a renewal via e-mail. Similarly, weblogs or simply blogs are now becoming very popular on the Internet as a communication medium. A library weblog can be used to:

- Providing news information for users
- Providing links to recommend internet sources
- Book reviews, information about new books
- Providing entertainment or amusement for users

- Providing news or information for librarians
- Book discussions
- Provide news or information for the trustees
- Provide research tips
- Communication among the librarians (in a library system).

The library can make good use of the electronic mail system of Internet *i.e.* E-mail to communicate reservation alert, current awareness services like SDI, new arrivals of books and journals, receiving interlibrary loan request and sending overdue notices to the users. In addition to these specialist services academic librarians also make use of the Internet information that is available to all users. Much bibliographical and price information can be found from online bookstores and Web sites for professional organizations and publishers. A wide range of factual information from government and NGO sources is available too.

Although librarians have more skepticism about the well-publicized Web search tools than most users, such services can be valuable, particularly for easily defined topics (such as names or abbreviations) and the sheer range of material indexed, subjects covered and the speed with which they search can make them useful when a clear starting point is not obvious. They may not always retrieve a full answer, but may give helpful clues.

Internet resources are just another information medium academic librarians are extending their skills to encompass it. So they may offer a current awareness service to teaching and research staff to inform them of new Web sites and discussion lists; they will apply established criteria to assessing the content of information sources or the effectiveness of secondary services like search tools.

The hypertext nature of the Web makes it easy to make additional explanation or instruction for a resource as an optional choice. This concept of instruction at the point and time of use is harder to achieve in the physical library.

WHY INTERNET TRAINING IS NECESSARY

In the Internet age there is acute need of Internet specialists. These specialists will be armed with the necessary skills and training to help the users to locate their information pin pointedly and efficiently on the net. Libraries specially the academic libraries would have a great demand for these specialists.

Internet connectivity in the academic libraries is growing day by day. So, the present administration of the academic institutions should take necessary steps to equip the library staff with the required skills and training on Internet. Training can help to understand many essential aspects of the Internet such as follows:

- Are we using the right type of Internet connection for our needs? Are we getting a good deal?

- How quickly can we find what we looking for on the Internet? We should be able to find useful information about virtually any topic in less than a minute. If you're taking longer, you're doing something wrong.
- How do we know if we are safe? Most people who contract viruses or other nastiest thought they were protected.
- Are we using e-mail correctly? Or are we really annoying we our colleagues and they are too polite to tell us? We might be unpleasantly surprised to learn the truth.
- How do we avoid those terrible pop-up windows?
- How do we know if information is real or a hoax?
- How can we make surfing faster?
- How can we get the maximum satisfaction without spending more time on net?

As noted by Paula L. Matthews while employing Internet in academic libraries one of the important issues for the administrator is the implementation library staff training. "A lack of training can result in:

- Poor staff performance;
- Lack of motivation;
- High staff turnover;
- Resistance to change;
- Costly errors or accidents;
- Unfulfilled objectives;
- Undesirable low standards of service.

Academic librarians may well draw on training materials available on the Internet for the higher education community. Recently the issue of whether librarians should learn HTML (Hyper-Text Markup Language) was debated on a North American discussion list.

The conclusion was that knowledge of basic HTML was necessary in order to prepare presentations and information guides, which are an integral part of the librarian's professional role. As an increasing number of academic libraries experience some measure of "convergence" with other academic support services, library staff has many opportunities to augment their IT skills and collaborate with colleagues in other services. The combination of technical knowledge and the ability to evaluate information sources is a powerful argument for the continued need for LIS professionals in higher education. The users of the Academic libraries including some faculty member do not have net skills.

In such cases the academic library staff has to come forward to help them. For readiness the staff should have some kind of net skills. The transition of traditional library resources to technology based library resources has put a lot of pressure on the academic library staff. Unless the staff is kept up to date on Internet skills he will face more pressure to work in such conditions. So training of staff has become a necessity in today's context.

TRAINING AND DEVELOPMENT: CONCEPT, IMPORTANCE AND METHODS OF TRAINING

Changes in technology, especially information technology, generate knowledge spreading up at tremendous speed, as well as its quick obsolence. In the period between 1900 and 1950, the amount of human knowledge doubled, and Since, then it has doubled every 5 to 8 years. Knowledge is becoming obsolete so quickly that all of us need do double our knowledge every 2 to 3 years in order to keep up with the changes. On the other hand, the increasing complexity, turbulency and uncertainty of the environment requires different and greater knowledge. Modern business requires more and more knowledge and skills that are still inadequatly present in the formal school education, *i.e.*, the gap between business reqiurements and the knowledge acquired at school is growing.

The period of mass producing is over and the customers are very selective. Increased consumer demands require new solutions and knowledge. Due to increasing competition, the organisation is required to constantly revise its product and service mix, managerial methods, and to increase productivity. Modern conditions of dynamic competition, sophisticated information technology, knowledge economy, market globalisation, has changed the relation to importance of human resources in organisation. These conditions actualise the human capital as the strategic resource of every organisation. Differences between the organisations exist exactly due to the differences between human capital, *i.e.*, the organisations human resources, ways of their management and development.

In a more and more global, complex and turbulent environment, knowledge is the only reliable source of competitive advantage. Traditional factors of manufacturing as the soil, Labour and capital did not disappear, but their significance is not primary anymore. Knowledge is viewed as the key of realisation of a competitive advantage. And therefore the question of where the corporative knowledge is located, how to release it and develop to achieve organisational goals has become very important.

Since, the organisational knowledge is largely located inside the human mind, *i.e.*, the head of employees, as carriers of knowledge and activities, human resources are becoming the key factor of business success. Organisational development is always conditioned by human knowledge and skills. That is why, contemporary organisations pay more and more attention to the development of their emplozees. Thus, employee education and training are becoming an optimal answer to complex business challenges, and the management of human resources is taking central role in modern management.

Through the process of employee training and development, the management of human resources provides constant knowledge innovation, creates conditions for mutual knowledge and experience exchange and proactive behaviour, in this way contributing to competitive advantage and satisfaction of all participants in business procedures. As a consequence of these procedures a learning organisation has formed. The aim of this chapter is to point to the fact that education and development of human potential are the basic factor for creation of basis for transformation from traditional to a learning company. Learning organisation is organisation that promotes learning of all of its members and it transforms permanently. Individuals and societies that do not have enough knowledge are in inferior position, compared to societies and organisations that have it and even permanently acquire new knowledge. That is the reason why we say that success is not among the educated but among those that are learning permanently, and everything changes except knowledge acquirement, which is constant.

EMPLOYEE TRAINING AND DEVELOPMENT

Understanding the phenomenon of employee training and development requires understanding of all the changes that take place as a result of learning. As the generator of new knowledge, employee training and development is placed within a broader strategic context of human resources management, *i.e.*, global organisational management, as a planned staff education and development, both individual and group, with the goal to benefit both the organisation and employees. To preserve its obtained positions and increase competitive advantage, the organisation needs to be able to create new knowledge, and not only to rely solely on utilisation of the existing. Thus, the continous employee training and delopment has a singnificant role in the development of individual and organisational performance.

The strategic procedure of employee training and development needs to encourage creativity, ensure inventiveness and shape the entire organisational knowledge that provides the organisation with uniqueness and differentiates it from the others. Education is no longer the duty and privilege of those in higher positions and skilled labour, but it is becoming the duty and need of everyone. The larger the organisations, the more funds they spend on education and provide their employees with greater and diverse possibilities of education and development.

Understanding the tremendous significance of education for the modern organisation and confident that it represents a good and remunirative investment, present day organisations set aside more and more resources for this activity. Most of the organisations invest 3 to 5 per cent of their revenue into adult education. It is estimated that the organisations that desire to keep the pace with changes need to provide their employees with 2 per cent of total annual fund of working hours for training and education. Thus, it is necessary to accept the model of permanent, continuous learning.

That truth has been known for more than two centuries. Denis Diderot, a French philosopher and literate of the Age of Enlightment, wrote the following: "Education shouldn't be finished when an individual leaves school, it should encompass all the ages of life . . . to provide people in every moment of their life with a possibility to maintain their knowledge or to obtain new knowledge". The only way for present day organisations to survive is the imperative to innovate or perish. Since, this depends on the knowledge the organisation possesses, this imperative could be read as: learn faster than competition. The logical sequence is: knowledge creation – innovation – competitive advantage. If knowledge is good, is it not true that the more knowlegde we have, the better we are? Many organisations which consider knowledge as a good thing are trapped into the pitfall of gathering as much knowledge as possible. Knowledge that is not necessary is exatly what it is: unnecessary. And the efforts to obtain it are wasted efforts.

The only important knowldege is the knowledge with strategic importance to the company, knowledge that helps to increase the value of the company, knowledge with significance to the strategy of the company. It is not about knowledge for the sake of knowledge, but rather knowledge according to the needs, applicable knowledge, knowledge to create innovation and competitive advantage. Obtaining knowledge, learning, education, all could have a real effect on the quality of labour only if they are harmonised with the needs of a particular organisation, its goals and the goals of its employees. The further choice of educational contents and educational methods, and the efficiency of educational effectiveness control depend on clearly defined educational goals and needs, answers to the questions of which knowldege is necessary to realise the strategy and the survival of the organisation in general, which employees need to possess this knowledge and will this knowledge solve certain problems. Employee training and development does not imply only obtaining new knowledge, abilities and skills, but also the possibility to promote entrepreneurship, introduce employees to changes, encourage the changes of their attitude, introduce the employees to important business decisions and involve them actively in the process of decision making.

To precisely define expectations and attract skilled workforce, more and more employment advertisings offer a certain number of annual hours or days for education. The most wanted resources are the people with particular knowledge, skills and abilities. Managers must learn to manage them, and the organisations to employ and retain them. Knowledge based organisations must preserve their competitive advantage by retaining skilled workforce, workers of knowledge, strengthening their motivation and improving the reward and compensation systems according to the workers' performances.

Within the context of learning organisation, it is not sufficient for the worker only to add value to the organisation based on his knowledge, but he also has to receive knowledge. He gives as much knowledge as he receives. For the present day employees the wage by itself.is not a sufficient incentive, but they also need investment into themselves in a sense of investing in their knowledge. Empolyees no longer work for money alone, nor can they be influenced by traditional attractive financial packages.

CONCEPT OF A LEARNING ORGANISATION

Every individual should appreciate lifelong learning, and every successful organisation has to become a permanently learning organisation. Many successful organisations describe themselves as learning organisation or one of their strategic goals is to become such an organisation. Companies such as Coca-Cola, Motorola, General Electrics and Cisco have assigned vice presidents for knowledge, learning or intellectual capital whose task is to create knowledge management systems that enable them to quickly adopt development tendencies, influencing in that way the customers, competitors, distributors and suppliers.

The organisation is not only the user of knowledge, but also its creator. Peter Senge described in the book named "The Fifth Discipline", the learning organisation implies free flow of knowledge, *i.e.*, lifting of all barriers on developing knowledge and new ideas at the very beginning. In the future it will not be possible to "unthread things from above" and for all the others to follow the "big brother's" instructions anymore. The top organisations of the future will be distinguished by their knowledge about how to encourage engagement and develop the learning potential on each organisational level. Peter Senge's model of a learning organisation is very interesting Since, it recognises the organisation as a whole, *i.e.*, in his organisation, through their functions and sectors within the organisation, all the employees influence the course of business procedures, and the knowledge creation, consequently the creation of new values both for the organisation and its customers. With this definition, Senge has made significant qualitative progress compared to the classical organisation, Since, he emphasised the necessity of ability development through the process of learning.

Besides Senge, Chris Argyris was a great populariser of a learning organisation as well. In his book "Teaching smart people how to learn", he says: "Any company that aspires to succeed in the tougher business environment must first resolve a basic dilemma: success in the marketplace increasingly depends on learning, yet most people don't know how to learn.

What's more, those members of the organisation that many assume to be the best at learning are, in fact, not very good at it. I am talking about the well-educated, highpowered, highly committed professionals who take up key leadership positions in the modern corporation." Organisations learn only through the learning individuals. Individual learning does not guarantee organisational learning. But without it there is no organisational learning as well. The ablity to learn faster than the competitors may be the only sustainable competitive advantage.

Thus, the learning organisation is the organisation that learns and encourages people to learn in the organisation. It motivates information exchange between employees and creates staff with different knowledge. Chris Argiris explains this: "On the other hand, there is a problem of existence of individuals within the organisation who know how to learn, but that doesn't create automatically conditions for the organisation to learn as well. This is due to the indisputable view that knowledge is still the only private property the man owns. This means that individual learning, and even learning of all the employees, doesn't imply the existence of a learning organisation. To have a learning organisation, it is necessary to know how to transfer individual into organisational knowledge, *i.e.*, into organisational learning." The starting point of knowledge management concept is in the fact that power does not come from knowledge, but from the exchange of knowledge.

It starts from the synergic effect. By exchanging knowledge, combining individual knowledge, we get much more qualitative knowledge than the individual knowledge. Obtaining and sharing knowledge is the core of the learning organisation. The reasons to become a learning organisation are the following: people are developing (greater motivation, flexibility of employees, people are more creative, improved social interaction), better working teams and groups (knowledge sharing, mutual dependence), benefiting organisations (greater work productivity, more qualitative products/services/ procedures, competitive advantage, profit).

9

Public Library

INTRODUCTION

A public library is a library that is accessible by the public and is generally funded from public sources and operated by civil servants. There are five fundamental characteristics shared by public libraries. The first is that they are supported by taxes; they are governed by a board to serve the public interest; they are open to all and every community member can access the collection; they are entirely voluntary in that no one is ever forced to use the services provided; and public libraries provide basic services without charge.

Public libraries exist in many countries across the world and are often considered an essential part of having an educated and literate population. Public libraries are distinct from research libraries, school libraries, and other special libraries in that their mandate is to serve the general public's information needs.

Public libraries also provide free services such as preschool story times to encourage early literacy, quiet study and work areas for students and professionals, or book clubs to encourage appreciation of literature in adults. Public libraries typically allow users to take books and other materials off the premises temporarily; they also have non-circulating reference collections and provide computer and Internet access to patrons.

SERVICES OFFERED

In addition to print books and periodicals, most public libraries today have a wide array of other media including audiobooks, e-books, CDs, cassettes, videotapes, DVDs, and video games, as well as facilities to access the Internet and inter-library loans. Readers' advisory is a fundamental public library service that involves suggesting fiction and nonfiction titles.

Public libraries may also provide other services, such as community meeting rooms, storytelling sessions for infants, toddlers, preschool children, or after-school programmes, all with an intention of developing early literacy skills and a love of books. In person and on-line programmes for reader development, language learning, homework help, free lectures and cultural performances, and other community service programmes are common offerings. One of the most popular programmes offered in public libraries are summer reading programmes for children, families, and adults. In rural areas, the local public library may have, in addition to its main branch, a mobile library service, consisting of one or more buses furnished as a small public library, serving the countryside according to a regular schedule.

Public libraries also provide materials for children, often housed in a special section. Child–oriented web sites with on-line educational games and programmes specifically designed for younger library users are becoming increasingly popular. Services may be provided for other groups, such as large print or Braille materials, Books on tape, young adult literature and other materials for teenagers, or materials in other than the national language.

California and Nevada now offer a new service called Link+. This new programme links county libraries across the two states, allowing patrons access to books their library may not have in their collection.

Librarians at most public libraries provide reference and research help to the general public, usually at a reference desk but can often be done by telephone interview. As online discussion and social networking allow for remote access, reference is becoming available virtually through the use of the Internet and e-mail.

Depending on the size of the library, there may be more than one desk; at some smaller libraries all transactions may occur at one desk, while large urban public libraries may employ subject-specialist librarians with the ability to staff multiple reference or information desks to answer queries about particular topics at any time during regular operating hours. Often the children's section in a public library has its own reference desk.

Public libraries are also increasingly making use of web 2.0 services, including the use of online social networks by libraries. Public libraries in some countries pay authors when their books are borrowed from libraries. These are known as Public Lending Right programme.

DIGITAL DIVIDE

As more commercial and governmental services are being provided online, public libraries increasingly provide Internet access for users who otherwise would not be able to connect to these services. Part of the public library mission has become attempting to help bridge the digital divide. A study conducted in 2006 found that "72.5 per cent of library branches report that they are the only provider of free public computer and Internet access in their communities". A 2008 study found that "100 per cent of rural, high poverty outlets provide public Internet access, a significant increase from 85.7 per cent last year".

The *American Library Association* (ALA), addresses this role of libraries as part of "access to information" and "equity of access"; part of the profession's ethical commitment that "no one should be denied information because he or she cannot afford the cost of a book or periodical, have access to the internet or information in any of its various formats."

In addition to access, many public libraries offer training and support to computer users. Once access has been achieved, there still remains a large gap in people's online abilities and skills. For many communities, the public library is the only agency offering free computer classes and information technology learning.

As of 2008, 73.4 per cent of public libraries offered information technology training of some form, including information literacy skills and homework assignment help. A significant service provided by public libraries is assisting people with e-government access and use of federal, state and local government information, forms and services.

Internationally, public libraries offer *information and communication technology* (ICT) services, giving "access to information and knowledge" the "highest priority." While different countries and areas of the world have their own requirements, general services offered include free connection to the Internet, training in using the Internet, and relevant content in appropriate languages. In addition to typical public library financing, *non-governmental organizations* (NGOs) and business fund services that assist public libraries in combating the digital divide.

ORIGINS AS A SOCIAL INSTITUTION

The culmination of centuries of advances in the printing press, moveable type, paper, ink, publishing, and distribution, combined with an ever growing middle class, increased commercial activity and consumption, new radical ideas, massive population growth and higher literacy rates forged the public library into the form that it is today. Public libraries are not a new idea; Romans made scrolls in dry rooms available to patrons of the baths, and tried with some success to establish libraries within the empire.

Naturally, only those few that could afford an education would be able to use the library, where those less than rich or without control of money; women, children and slaves could not. In the middle of the 19th century, the push for truly public libraries, paid for by taxes and run by the state gained force after numerous depressions, droughts, wars and revolutions in Europe, felt mostly by the working class.

Matthew Battles states that:

> "It was in these years of class conflict and economic terror that the public library movement swept through Britain, as the nation's progressive elite recognized that the light of cultural and intellectual energy was lacking in the lives of commoners."

Libraries had often been started with a donation, an endowment or were bequeathed to various, parishes, churches, schools or towns, and these social and institutional libraries formed the base of many academic and public library collections of today.

Andrew Carnegie had the biggest influence in financing libraries in the United States of America, from the east to west coast. From just 1900 to 1917, almost 1,700 libraries were constructed by Carnegie's foundation, insisting that local communities first guarantee tax support of each library built.

The establishment of circulating libraries by booksellers and publishers provided a means of gaining profit and creating social centers within the community. The circulating libraries not only provided a place to sell books, but also a place to lend books for a price. These circulating libraries provided a variety of materials including the increasingly popular novels.

Although the circulating libraries filled an important role in society, members of the middle and upper classes often looked down upon these libraries that regularly sold material from their collections and provided materials that were less sophisticated. Circulating libraries also charged a subscription fee, however the fees were set to entice their patrons, providing subscriptions on a yearly, quarterly or monthly basis, without expecting the subscribers to purchase a share in the circulating library.

Circulating libraries were not exclusively lending institutions and often provided a place for other forms of commercial activity, which may or may not be related to print. This was necessary because the circulating libraries did not generate enough funds through subscription fees collected from its borrowers. As a commerce venture, it was important to consider the contributing factors such as other goods or services available to the subscribers.

Many claims have been made for the title of "first public library" for various libraries in various countries, with at least some of the confusion arising from differing interpretations of what should be considered a true "public library". Diffi-culties in establishing what policies were in effect at different times in the history of particular libraries also add to the confusion.

The first libraries open to the public were the collections of Greek and Latin scrolls which were available in the dry sections of the many buildings that made up the huge Roman baths of the Roman empire. However, they were not lending libraries.

The "halls of science" run by different Islamic sects in many cities of North Africa and the Middle East in the 9th century were open to the public. Some of them had written lending policies, but they were very restrictive. Most patrons were expected to consult the books on site. The later European university libraries were not open to the general public, but accessible by scholars.

PUBLIC LIBRARIES IN INDIA

Public library is largely regarded as the People's University. It has tremendous developments in India from the early period to till date at various stages. Most of the Indian states now have free public library services to develop the people of India at different levels.

ANCIENT PERIOD

- "The history of the development of the public library may be said to be as old as that of education in India". During Vedic times, the pupils stayed in the *guru-gruha* for several years for education. Since ancient times, India is being very much pertinent in search of knowledge and wisdom. Oral communication was the best means amongst the people of India and writing was not available. "The earliest written and recorded materials found in India are the inscriptions on stone pillars of King Asoka; these inscriptions could be called the first outside open libraries".
- Later, *Ashrams* came into existence in India and students study under the supervision of well-known teachers. They kept many manuscripts for use of the teachers and students as well as for the visitors. Many students joined ashrams and such big ashrams were known as *vidyapeeth*, where numbers of teachers are engaged to teach the students. These educational institutions collected many different manuscripts and other materials which can help in their teaching and daily routine.
- They kept and preserved carefully. "The reading materials, of course, related to many subjects formed the source material for transmitting knowledge in different streams of education and culture. The collections might be likened to modern libraries since they were carefully maintained and extensively used by students and teachers alike". Such *ashrams* or *vidyapeeths,* where manuscripts and other reading materials were reserved, may be regarded as a kind of library as they serve information and knowledge to the students and community in different ways.
- Pandey S K Sharma stated that; "In India, since the ancient times libraries have been functioning as light houses for those who wanted to read and to extend the boundaries of various disciplines. References are available to prove that Nalanda University had its own multistoried library in AD 600 with massive collection of manuscripts. The collection of the library was housed in three buildings, each having nine floors and three hundred rooms. This library was opened by the then Emperor of India, King Davapal. The library was open for any body that was known scholar and took interest in reading, interpreting and even copying the documents kept in the library. Chinese traveller Whuen Sang is known to have consulted this library in the seventh century and to have taken from here hundreds of treatises to China

and Japan. This library was completely destroyed by Bakhtiar Khilaji, who invaded India in AD 1205. And burnt the library. The library kept on burning for about six months".

Libraries in ancient India also developed at other famous centers of learning, such as *Vikramshila* and *Odantapuri.* Universities of ancient India, like Taxila and Vikramshala also have valuable collection on *tantras* and manuscripts in their libraries.

MEDIEVAL PERIOD

Muslims mostly rule the Medieval Period of India. Historically, it is also known as Mughal Period. There were great changes not only in social and political, but also on education and library system during this period. The Muslim rulers made great contributions to Indian culture and libraries played a significant role in the sociocultural development of the nation. "The period of Mughal is considered as the golden period of Indian history for its educational, literary, and library activities". Babur, king of Kabul invaded India and annexed Delhi to his kingdom. "He established the first Mughal Imperial Library in 1526".

Babur inherited manuscripts from his father and kept in his library and also collected books from different sources of his kingdom. Babur died in 1530 and was succeeded by his son Humayun. Humayun much lived in Agra and established library in his palace. He set up a library at Agra Fort, which was managed by Lal Beg.

In his library, he kept books, gilded pen cases, portfolios, picture books and beautiful works of calligraphy. After the death of Humayun, his son, Akbar, succeeded him in 1356. Akbar is regarded as one of the greatest Mughal king. Akbar improved the management of library with some technical works. He appointed Sheik Faizi to manage and control library services.

Akbar was very interest in manuscripts and appointed calligraphers to copy good manuscripts. He established a separate library for women at Fatehpur Sikri and made great improvement to the library. At the time of his death in 1605, the Imperial Library has twenty-four thousand books.

Jahangir, another rule of Mughal period, made a law that when a wealthy man died heirless, the property should be used for building and repairing schools, monasteries, libraries, and other institutions. Some wealthy and scholars, like Abdul Rahim Khan-i-Khanan, Shaik Faizi, Gulbadan Begum and ruler of Mysore and Jaipur also have their private libraries.

Some Hindu learning centers also have libraries. "The libraries of these centers contain huge collections of manuscripts on religion and philosophy as well as other subjects like medicine, science and history". Christian missionaries have also contributed for the libraries since the coming of Vasco da Gama in India. During the Mughal period, library technical works, *viz.* Accessioning, Classification and Cataloguing were also carried out in some ways. The head librarian was known as *"Nizam"* and the assistant librarian *as "Muhatin"* or *"Darogha"*. Other staff of libraries during Mughal period is Scribes, Book Illustrators, Calligraphers, Copyists, Translators, Bookbinders and Gilders.

THE BRITISH PERIOD

The Britishers came to India primarily to establish trade and commerce. Some of them were very interested for the upliftment of rich cultural heritage of India. "A number of Academic institutions were established during the British period by the East India Company and by the Christian missionaries".

The University of Calcutta was established in 1857 and its library was opened in 1873. Other Universities, University of Bombay and University of Madras were established in 1879 and 1907 respectively. There were only nineteen Universities in India before 1947. Universities were equipped with libraries in accordance with the Indian University Act of 1904.

The Bengal Royal Asiatic Society set up library in 1784, Bombay Royal Asiatic Society in 1804 and Calcutta Public Library in 1835. Establishment of these libraries enlightened the community and may be regarded as the foundation of the concept of public libraries to the Indian people.

Some of the important libraries set up in 19th. Century in India are Andrews Library, Surat in 1850, Gaya Public Library, Gaya in 1855, Long Library, Rajkot in 1856, Connemara Public Library, Madras in 1860, Government Library, Janagarh in 1867, Adyar Library, Adyar in 1886 and Dahi Laxmi Library, Nadiad in 1892.

Apart from these, other libraries, like Gujarat Vernacular Society along with a library, in Ahmedabad 1848 and Barton Library, Bhavnagar in 1882 were also established. Some of the Indian states also established public libraries.

Such as Baroda established Baroda State Library in Baroda in 1877, Cochin established Public Library and Reading Room in Trichur in 1873, Dhar established Victoria General Library in Dhar in 1856, Indore established General Library in Indore in 1852, Jaipur established Maharajah's Public Library in Jaipur in 1899. Others states also established such kind of libraries, *viz.* Jammu and Kashmir in 1879, Kahtiawar, in 1886, Kolhapur in 1850, Nizam's Dominion in 1891 and Travancore in 1829.

The first significant date in the development of public libraries in India is 1808 when the Bombay Government initiated a proposal to register libraries, which were to be given copies of books published from the 'Funds for the Encouragement of Literature'.

The contributions of His Highness the Maharaja Sayajirao III, Gaekwar of Baroda towards library movement in India cannot be overlooked. He is remembered today as the Father of Library Movement in India. At the age of 18, in 1881, he was entrusted with full power of the government of Baroda in the Gujarat speaking region of the Bombay Presidency and the Peninsula of

Kathiawar. Baroda's population was predominantly rural, the main occupation was agriculture. The people in general were economically poor and socially backward. Education was the foundation to reconstruct a new social and economic life and education should be the right of the humblest villager.

He introduced free and compulsory education in his princely states. Baroda became the first territory not only among the native states but also in British India to have compulsory free primary education. He opined that primary education was to be the very base and decided to preserve it by means of libraries, which were the only agencies for perpetual universal self-education.

He decided to establish library as an experiment in one of the towns of a *taluka* and in order to implement his idea immediately; he issued orders to his ministers. "In conformity to his ruler's instructions, the Minister of Education prepared a detailed plan to open Circulating Libraries in the State, which was approved in March, 1907. Every public library instituted through the State's financial assistance was to be named as Circulating Library".

In 1906, he went to America as "an observer, a student desirous of acquiring all the knowledge and experience that could enable him to make his own State a model one in India". He was very much impressed by the library services of America for the development of the people in their social, economic and educational life. He then invited an American, William Alanson Borden, a pupil-assistant of Charles A Cutter, who is working as Librarian of the Young Men's Institute, New Haven, Connecticut to come and established library services in India.

In response to his invitation, Borden reached Baroda on November 6, 1910, and became the Director of State Libraries. It can be traced back that public library movement started since 1910 in India. Borden makes a survey of libraries in Baroda and concludes that there were over 241 libraries, holding a little over 100000 volumes. But he did not find any of those libraries adequately housed, nor did he find them shelved in such a manner as to make them most attractive to readers or convenient to those in charge.

He then make proposal for the best services of libraries in the State as:

- Should Your Highness feel disposed to grant me the necessary authority, I propose to organize a Department of Public Libraries, to rank with the other Departments of Your State, with the necessary equipments of officers and clerks, etc. and to bring all the libraries under its control and management;
- To unify all the collections of books in Baroda City into one Central library;
- To add to this Central library, general and technical books;
- To erect a suitable library building of fireproof construction, with reading grooms, study rooms, Women's Library, Children's library, Lecture hall, Library school, and executive offices;

- To make that library to be Free Public Library of Baroda City, and also the main storehouse for all the valuable historical documents and papers now in private hands in the State, but which the owners would probably be glad to have stored in a safe place;
- To make it also the center from which traveling libraries should start and from which the books, new and old, could be distributed to the various branch libraries in the different towns, cities, and villages of the State.

The Maharaja apparently accepted Borden's proposals, and ordered that the whole scheme might be implemented in parts. The Library Department was created under Order No.9/19, January 30, 1911, for organizing libraries in Baroda. As the Director of state libraries, he planned a network of free public libraries consisting a state central library, four district or divisional libraries, forty-five town libraries, and more than a thousand village libraries-all integrated into one chain system.

Borden played a leading role for the establishment, management and organization of public libraries in India. As a result of system, within two decades 85 per cent of the Baroda urban and rural population had access to libraries.. Borden developed library classification scheme to suit Indian libraries.

Another great contribution of Borden was the establishment of the first library school in India, in which he trained his own assistants and successors. Borden conducted the first formal library-training programme in India at Baroda in 1911. He was instrumental in the foundation of the Baroda Library Club and its journal, "Library Miscellany", published quarterly in three languages between 1912 and 1919.

University of Madras created the post of University Librarian in 1923 and Dr. S R Ranganathan joined the post on 4 January 1924. Ranganathan published his Five Laws of Library Science in 1931, Colon Classification in 1933 and Classified Catalog Code in 1934.

He also prepared Model Public Library Bill and drives to legislate library bill in Indian states. He made a tremendous contribution for the development of libraries in India. Scholars, educationists and people of library bent of mind founded Calcutta Public Library in 1835 and the same was opened on 21 March 1836 for the public.

In 1944, Calcutta Public Library was shifted to a new and spacious building, constructed in honour of the Governor-General of India, Lord Metcalf. Indian War of Independence broke out in 1857 resulted in to Europeans of Calcutta withdrew their support for the library management in 1899. Consequently, the management and establishment of the library were gradually waning and by the end of the century, the activities of the library came into standstill.

Lord Curzon, the then Viceroy and Governor-General of India visited Calcutta in 1899 and found a miserable condition of Calcutta Public Library. He bought the rights of the Library from the proprietors and later merged it with the Official imperial Library consisting of government departmental libraries of the East India Company. He then declared open of a new Imperial Library of India on 30 January 1903 in the Metcalf Hall. In 1948, one year after the independence of India, Imperial Library was transformed into National library of India and was housed to the Viceroy's Palace in Calcutta, namely, the Belvedere Palace.

POST-INDEPENDENCE PERIOD

Public libraries in India made a tremendous growth after the independence of India in 1947. The central and the state governments took a number of steps forward for the development of the nation from the point of education and considered library as essential part of it.

The programmes executed by provincial and central governments since 1910 for the social and adult education of the populace paved the way for the enactment of library laws and rules for grants-in-aid in the country. Hence public library became part of the education budget.

To enhance the level of literacy of 16 per cent in 1941, the government undertook some programmes such as extension services, continuing education, social education, non-formal education and adult education. The government further initiated steps for the development of community and organized some projects in this regard. Libraries were considered to be an essential part of the Community Development Project that was launched during the first plan period.

In order to accelerate the pace of socioeconomic development, the government considered public libraries to be an integral part of development projects.. The Connemara Public Library in Madras became the State Central Library in 1950 under the provision of Madras Public Libraries Act 1948, and became one of the three depository libraries in 1955.

Delhi Public Library was established in 1951 as the first UNESCO Public Library Pilot Project under the joint auspices of UNESCO and Government of India to adopt "Modern Techniques to Indian Conditions" and to serve as a model public library for Asia.. In 1954, the Delivery of Book Act was passed to include newspaper.

The act obligated every publisher in India to deposit one copy each of its publications to the National Library in Calcutta, the Asiatic Society Library in Bombay, Connemara Public Library in Madras, and Delhi Public Library in New Delhi The Advisory Committee for Libraries as constituted in 1957 by the Government of India, with K P Sinha as the Chairman.

The Committee submitted its report in 1959 with a drafted Model Library Bill. The Planning Commission constituted a Working Group on Public Libraries in 1964 and the Commission submitted its report in 1965 with a Model Public Libraries Act. The model bill was sent to all the states/UTs, which do not have Public Libraries Act.In 1972, the Government of India, Planning Commission constituted Working Group on Development of Public Libraries to make recommendations for library development. Raja Rammohun Roy Library Foundation, an autonomous body under the Department of Culture, Ministry of Education, was established in 1972.

The main objective of the Foundation was to assist state library services in developmental works. In 1979, a library section was established in the Department of Culture under the Ministry of Education, which section was under the charge of an Under Secretary. The objective was to promote the development of public libraries in India.A Working Group on Modernization of Library Services and Informatics was appointed by the Planning Commission in 1983 and submitted its report in 1984 with the formulation of National Policy on Library Services and Informatics. Delhi Public Library became a copyright library in 1982.

National Literacy Mission was adopted in 1986, which emphasized education for women and also establishment of rural libraries. Library networks and systems were strengthened at the national level institutions in the development of literature in neo-literates. Fourteen states namely, Tamil Nadu, Andhra Pradesh, Karnataka, Maharashtra, West Bengal, Manipur, Kerala, Haryana, Mizoram, Goa, Orissa, Gujarat, Uttaranchal and Rajasthan have enacted Public Libraries Bills during 1948 to 2006.

The Government of India, Department of Culture, appointed a Committee on National Policy on Library and Information System in 1985. The National Policy on Education, 1986 states that a nationwide movement for improvement of existing libraries and the establishment of new ones will be taken up, provision will be made in all educational institutions for library facilities, and the status of librarianship improved.

The National Book Policy, 1986 also had an impact on libraries, as:

- Provision of reading material for children by all the agencies involved;
- That 10 per cent of the annual education budget of the governments be used to purchase books for libraries.

These goals are to be achieved by using formal, non-formal, and open channels of learning.. Rural libraries should become the focal point for postliteracy and continuing educational programmes. Publishers, voluntary organizations, and school library programmes undertaken as part of the "Operation Blackboard Scheme" of the National Education Policy on Education, 1986 were given assistance. The following five libraries were regarded as national importance and may be stated in a very brief manner.

National Library, Kolkata

National Library, Kolkata was established in 1836 in the name of Calcutta Public Library. It was not a Government institution running on a proprietary basis. The then Governor General, Lord Metcalf transferred 4,675 volumes from the library of the College of Fort William to the Calcutta Public Library. This and donations of books from individuals formed the nucleus of the library. Prince Dwarkanath Tagore was the first proprietor of the Calcutta Public Library. Both the Indian and foreign books, especially from Britain, were purchased for the library. In the report of 1850 we find that the library started collecting books in Gujarati, Marathi, Pali, Ceylonese and Punjabi.

The Government of Bengal and North Western Provinces regularly made by individuals as well as donations. The Calcutta Public Library had a unique position as the first public library in this part of the country. Such a well-organized and efficiently run library was rare even in Europe during the first half of the 19th century. Because of the efforts of the Calcutta Public Library, the National Library has developed rare books and journals in its collection.

The Imperial Library was formed in 1891 by combining a number of Secretariat libraries. Of these, the most important and interesting was the library of the Home Department, which contained many books formerly belonging to the library of East India College, Fort William and the library of the East India Board in London.

But the use of the library was restricted to the superior officers of the Government. Lord Curzon, the then Governor General of India, was the person who conceived the idea of opening a library for the use of the public. He noticed both the libraries, Imperial Library and Calcutta Public Library, were under-utilized for the want of facilities or restrictions. So, he decided to amalgamate the rich collection of both of these libraries.

He was successful in effecting the amalgamation of Calcutta Public Library with the then Imperial Library under certain terms. The library, called Imperial Library, was formally opened to the public on 30th January 1903 at Metcalf Hall, Kolkata.

The aims and objectives of the Imperial Library, well defined in a Notification in the 'Gazette of India' *as 'It is intended* that it should be a library of reference, a working place for students and a repository of material for the future historians of India, in which, so far as possible, every work written about India, at any time, can be seen and read.

Librarian of the British Museum, London, was appointed as the first Librarian of the Imperial Library. After his death, the famous scholar and linguist Harinath De took over the charge of the library. After his death J. A. Chapman became the librarian. Mr. Chapman showed keen interest in the affairs of the library and worked hard to improve its status. After his retirement, Khan Bahadur M.A. Asadulla was appointed as the librarian and he continued as the librarian till July 1947.

The policy of acquisition broadly adhered to by the Imperial Library was enunciated by Lord Curzon in his speech at the opening ceremony of the library, "The general idea of the whole Library is that it should contain all the books that have been written about India in popular tongues, with such additions as are required to make it a good all-round library of standard works of reference."

After the independence the Government of India changed the name of the Imperial Library as the National Library, with an enactment of the Imperial Library Act 1948 and the collection was shifted from the Esplanade to the present Belvedere Estate. On 1st February 1953 the National Library was opened to the public, inaugurated by Maulana Abul Kalam Azad. Sri B.S. Kesavan was appointed as the first librarian of the National Library.

The reviewing Committee in its report of 1969 suggested that the following should be the basic features of the National Library; Acquisition and conservation of all significant printed materials produced in the country to the exclusion of ephemera:

- Collection of printed materials concerning the country wherever published and also acquisition of photographic record of such materials that are not available within the country;
- Acquisition and conservation of manuscripts having national importance;
- Planned acquisition of foreign materials required by the country;
- Rendering of bibliographical and documentation service of retrospective materials, both general and specialized;
- Acting as a referral centre purveying full and accurate knowledge of all sources of bibliographical activities;
- Provision of photocopying and reprographic services; and
- Acting as the centre for international book exchange and international loan..

Khuda Bakhsh Oriental Public Library, Patna

Khuda Bakhsh Oriental Public Library, Patna was open for the public in October 1891 with 4000 Oriental manuscripts. Maulvi Khuda Bakhsh donated his entire collection to the nation by a deed of trust.Acknowledging the immense historical and intellectual value of its rich and valued collection, the Government of India declared the Library as Institution of National Importance by an act of Parliament in 1969. The Library is now fully funded by the Ministry of Culture. This autonomous institution is being governed by a Board with the Governor of Bihar as its ex-officio Chairman and Director is carrying the responsibility of dayto-day management of Library affairs.

Rampur Raza Library, Rampur

Rampur Raza Library, Rampur was founded by Nawab Faizullah Khan in AD 1774. It was brought under the management of a Trust till the Government of India took over the library on 1 July 1975 under the Act of Parliament, which declared it as an institution of National importance. It contains very rare and valuable collection of manuscripts, historical documents, specimens of Islamic calligraphy, miniature paintings, astronomical instruments and rare illustrated works in Arabic and Persian languages besides 80,000 printed books. Nawab Faizullah Khan who ruled the state of Rampur, from 1774 to 1794, established the library with his personal modest collection kept in the Tosha Khana of his Palace.

Now the Library occupies the position of an autonomous institution of national importance under Department of Culture, Government of India and is fully funded by Central Government. The Library has now attained an International status of higher studies.

Thanjavur Maharaja Serfoji's Sarasvati Mahal Library, Thanjavur

Thanjavur Maharaja Serfoji's Sarasvati Mahal Library, Thanjavur is one among a few medieval libraries existing in the world. It contains very rare and valuable collections of manuscripts, books, maps and paintings on all aspects of Art, Culture and Literature.

The *Encyclopaedia Britannica* in its survey of the Libraries of the world mentions this as "the most remarkable Library in India". The Library houses a rich and rare collection of manuscripts on art, culture and literature. Conceived and christened as the Royal Palace Library by the Nayak Kings of Thanjavur. And the Maratha rulers nourished it for intellectual enrichment.

In 1918 this library was made as a public library. A body constituted by the Government and financed by the Central and State Governments now administers the library. During the reign of Nayaks of Thanjavur, "Sarasvati Bhandar" was formed and developed. The Maratha rulers who captured Thanjavur in 1675 A.D. patronized the culture of Thanjavur and developed the Royal Palace Library till A.D. 1855.

The Sarasvati Bhandar was situated within the Palace campus and the Manuscripts used for the purpose of reading by the Royal personages. Among the Maratha Kings, King Serfoji II, was an eminent scholar in many branches of learning and with great enthusiasm he took special steps for the enrichment of the Library.

It is a fitting tribute to the great collector Serfoji that the Library is named after him. Till the survival of the last Maratha Queen, the Library was the Palace property. After that, the Library together with the Palace properties formed the subject of litigation in Civil Courts.

The Royal Family members voluntarily came forward to delete this Library from the suit properties formed an Endowment and dedicated this Library to the public with one lakh rupees for its maintenance and upkeep. The Government of Madras in their G.O. Ms. No.1306 Home dated 5th October 1918, took possession of the Library under the Charitable Endowment Act and framed scheme for the Library management. In 1983, the Library was declared as an Institution of National Importance. The

Government of Tamil Nadu abolished the Five Member Committee of administration and made it as a Registered Society as per G.O. 209 (EST) dated 1-2-83. The Society was constituted and got registration on 9-7-1986 under the Tamil Nadu Registered Societies Act of 1975.

The Society consists of ex-officio members of Central and State Governments, nominated Scholars, Member from the Royal family and the Director of the Library. The Hon'ble Education Minister of the Government of Tamil Nadu is the ex-officio Chairman of this society.

Harekrushna Mahtab State Library, Bhubaneswar

Harekrushna Mahtab State Library, Bhubaneswar was conceived during 1st Five-year Plan under the advice of Government of India and was completed in 1959, enshrined within a beautiful land of 3 acres in a prime location of Capital City of Bhubaneswar. In 1967, it was named as Gandhi Bhawan commemorating birth centenary of Mahatma Gandhi, the father of the nation. In 1987 it was renovated and entire space of the four storied building was utilized for the functioning of two Libraries *i.e.* State Library for the entire State of Orissa and another Public Library for Bhubaneswar City.

In 1987, Government decided to rename the State Library and the Public Library as Harekrushna Mahtab State Library and the Bhubaneswar Public Library respectively. The former is a Reference Library and lending of books is not permitted whereas the latter is a Lending Library for the public of Bhubaneswar City. These two Libraries have managed to function over the limited space. Total readers seats available are about 350 against the present demands of 600-700 readers per day.

LIBRARY LEGISLATION IN INDIA

Since the beginning, the public libraries served as the local information centers making the source of knowledge readily available to the public. The local community from the local fund or individual munificence could not achieve the services of a public library. Public leaders, scholars and learned societies have realised that the only way to establish and develop a public library system is through legislation. The UNESCO Public Library Manifesto, 1972 stated that, "The public library should be established under the clear mandate of law", which is substantiated by the IFLA/UNESCO Public Library Manifesto 1994 as;

> "The public library shall in principle be free of charge. The public library is the responsibility of local and national authorities. It must be supported by specific legislation and financed by national and local government. It has to be an essential component of any long-term strategy for culture, information provision, literacy and education".

Libraries are recorded under the Article 246 of Indian Constitution, Seventh Schedule List II of State List No.12 and the Indian Constitution Act, 1956,

"Libraries, museums and other similar institutions controlled or financed by the State; ancient and historical monuments and records other than those to be of national importance." Provision of public library service is the responsibility of the State Government as the subject matter of libraries is relatable to entry 12 of the State List in the Seventh Schedule to the Constitution of India. Dr. S R Ranganathan regarded as the pioneer of library legislation in India. "The concept of legislation for libraries is a contribution of S R Ranganathan to Indian public libraries". He made library legislation obligatory for the implementation of the second law of library science, "Every reader his/ her book". Ranganathan the second law can be properly carried out only by legislation. Dr. S R Ranganathan strived a lot for library legislation and prepared different library bills for the Indian Union and constituent states; such as;

- Model Library Act for constituent states of India;
- Bengal;
- Bombay;
- Central Province and Berar;
- Old Madras state which later became Act in 1948;
- United Province;
- Cochin;
- Travancore;
- Union Government;
- Madhya Pradesh;
- Union and Constituent States;
- Constituent States;
- Union;
- West Bengal;
- Kerala;
- Uttar Pradesh;
- Mysore which became Act in 1965;
- Assam;
- Gujarat and Model Library Bill.

Public libraries also considered as community information centers providing access at local level to a wide range of knowledge and information for the benefit of the individual and society as a whole. To ensure sustained development and information network services public libraries should be based on legislation.Public library legislation may be in various forms depending upon the government structure. It can be simple, allowing the establishment of public libraries but leaving standards of service to the level of government directly responsible for the library, or more complex, with specific detail on what services should be provided and to what standard.

But no British Government passed library Act for creation of public library system in Indian states.. There have been different efforts to work out library legislation models in India. In the pre-independent and post-independent of India, there have been five models of public library bills suggested by experts and national level professional associations and organizations.

MODEL PUBLIC LIBRARIES ACT OF DR. S R RANGANATHAN

The first Model Public Libraries Acts was prepared by Dr. S R Ranganathan in 1930 and revised in 1957 and 1972. It was discussed at the First All Asia Educational Conference held at Banaras during 26-30 December 1930. It was introduced in West Bengal Legislature in 1931 and in Madras Legislature in 1933. The Bill could not be passed due to financial clauses on library grant, library cess etc. Salient features of final version are:

- Establishment of public libraries in city, rural and other areas;
- Constitution of State Library Authority *i.e.* Minister of Education;
- Constitution of State Library Committee as an advisory body of the State Library Authority;
- Constitution of Local Library Authority for each city and one for each district;
- State Library Authority, Government and Local Library Authority may determine library rate in such a manner and may determine collection of library cess from time to time.

MODEL PUBLIC LIBRARIES BILL OF MINISTRY OF EDUCATION

The Government of India, Ministry of Education appointed an Advisory Committee for Libraries in 1957, under the Chairmanship of Shri K P Sinha, former Director of Public Instruction, Bihar. This committee recommended the need for library legislation for each state. As a follow-up action of the Advisory Committee, the Ministry of Education, Government of India appointed a committee under the Chairmanship of Dr. M D Sen. The Committee drafted Model Public Libraries Bill in the year 1963.

The salient components of this Bill are:

- Constitution of State Library Authority as an apex body to advise the Government in the matter of library developments;
- Constitution of State Library Directorate for direction and controlling of library services;
- Constitution of District Library Committee in each district;
- Treatment of employees as government servant;
- Collection of library cess at the rate of 6 paise per rupee on house tax and property tax.

MODEL PUBLIC LIBRARIES BILL OF THE PLANNING COMMISSION

The Planning Commission, Government of India, constituted a 'Working Group on Libraries' in 1964 to plan and advice on the development of Libraries during the Fourth Five Year Plan. The Working Group recommended a Library Development Scheme to be implemented during the Fourth Plan period with a financial commitment of ₹.309 million, which was appended by Model Public Libraries Bill and submitted its report in 1965. Bill was not considered even by a single state.

The Bill included the following features:

- Establish, maintain, develop and integrated adequate public library service in the state;
- Constitution of Committee of Experts to prescribe the standards of service;
- Constitution of State Library Council to advise the government for the promotion and development of library service;
- Establishment of State Library Directorate to control, direct and supervise library system in the state;
- Establishment of State Central Library, State Regional Libraries and District Libraries;
- Treatment of employees in the system of State Government Servants
- Government shall be the financial source and shall maintain the public library system in the state.

MODEL PUBLIC LIBRARIES BILL OF INDIAN LIBRARY ASSOCIATION

The Indian Library Association (ILA) formed in 1933, has keen interest in library legislation. The ILA discussed library legislation at its various seminars organized in 1964, 1978 and 1981. Consequently, ILA Council at its meeting held on 23 June 1989, keeping in view of the developments and experiences gain from the existing Acts, resolved to prepare a Model Library Bill.

Accordingly, as asked by ILA, Dr. Velaga Venkatappaiah, Chairman, Central Sectional Committee on Public Libraries of the ILA prepared a Model Public Library Bill. ILA accepted the draft Bill with minor changes at its National Seminar on Public Library Legislation in 1990 at the final product of the Model Public Libraries Bill was published in 1991.

The Bill was circulated to all the states and union territories but few states reacted favourably to the Bill. This Model Bill was again discussed in a National Seminar on Library Legislation and revised as the Model State Public Library and Information Service Act in 1995. In view of emergence of Information Technology at all levels, the model act was again revised in 2000.

The important components of this Bill are:

- State Library and Information Service, based on a State Policy;
- Constitution of State Library Authority at the apex level with Minister of Libraries as Chairman as policy making and executive body;

- Establishment of Directorate of Public Libraries for directing, controlling and supervising;
- Constitution of City, District Library Authority for rendering service from district to village level;
- Provision for network of Public Library and Information Services from state to village level;
- Constitution of State Library and Information Service;
- Collection of Library cess on house tax and property tax, entertainment tax, professional tax, vehicle tax, etc.;
- Constitution of State Boards for education, book production, co-ordination, etc.;
- Accountability of public expenditure and services.

MODEL UNION LIBRARY ACT

The Government of India appointed a committee to explore the possibilities to establish a National Central Library at New Delhi in 1948. Dr. S R Ranganathan, a member of the committee drafted a Library Development plan in 1950 with a 30-year programme and a draft Library Bill for the states and Union Public Library Act.

This was revised in 1959 and again in 1972. However, libraries falls under the state list of the constitution and it may not be possible to pass Bill as a Union Act, unless and until the constitution is suitably amended for this purpose.

The main features of this model Act are:

- Constitution of a National Library Authority;
- Establishment of national central libraries;
- Constitution of National Library Committee as an advisory body to the National library Authority;
- Constitution of National library fund;
- Amendment to the delivery of Books and Newspaper Act, 1954.

The IFLA/UNESCO Public Library Manifesto 1994 reads that, "The public library is the local center of information, making all kinds of knowledge and information readily available to its users". Public libraries, to become an enthusiastic source of information and knowledge for the local community, needs certain forms of developments in terms of infrastructure, collection and the trinity of library as well. It cannot survive by the local contributions and dedication alone, but through the support of government.

"The pubic library, as a democratic institution operated by the people for the people, should be established and maintained under the clear authority of law; supported wholly or mainly from public funds; open for free use on equal terms to all members of the community regardless of occupation, creed, class or race". Efforts have been going on well under the initiatives of professional associations and learned societies in this context. "In India, the post independence era was favourable to the establishment of public libraries based on legal basis"..

STATES WITH LIBRARY LEGISLATION

During the last six decades, 14 Public Library Bills were enacted in different states of India, such as:

- Tamil Nadu: The Tamil Nadu Public Libraries Act 1948;
- *Andhra Pradesh*: The Andhra Pradesh Public Libraries Act 1960;
- *Karnataka:* The Karnataka Public Libraries Act 1965;
- *Maharashtra*: The Maharastra Public Libraries Act 1967;
- *West Bengal:* The West Bengal Public Libraries Act 1979;
- *Manipur:* The Manipur Public Libraries Act 1988;
- *Kerala*: The Kerala Public Libraries Act 1989;
- *Haryana:* The Haryana Public Libraries Act 1989;
- *Mizoram:* The Mizoram Public Libraries Act 1993;
- *Goa:* The Goa Public Libraries Act 1993;
- *Orissa*: Orissa Public Libraries Act, 2001;
- *Gujarat:* Gujarat Public Libraries Act, 2001;
- *Uttaranchal:* Uttaranchal Public Libraries Act, 2005,
- *Rajasthan:* Rajasthan Public Libraries Act, 2006

Tamil Nadu

Tamil Nadu is the first state that enacted Public Libraries Act in independent India. It came into force with effect from 1 April 1950. The objectives of the Act are contained in its Preamble as, 'An act to provide for the establishment of public libraries in the province of Tamil Nadu and the organization of comprehensive rural and urban Library Service therein". It has 19 sections.

The salient features of this Act are given below:

- This Act facilitates establishment of Public Libraries in the State.
- Constitution of State Library Committee for the purpose of advising the government on such matters relating to libraries.
- Provision for appointment of Director of Public Libraries to control, direct and supervise public libraries.
- Constitution of Local Library Authorities, one for the City of Madras and one for each district.
- Every Local Library Authority shall levy in the area a library cess in the form of a surcharge on property tax or house tax at the rate of six paise per rupee.
- The Government shall contribute Library Fund to each of the Local Library Authority, except the City of Madras, to the amount of library cess collected.

- The Act amended Sec.9 of the Press and Registration of Books Act, 1867, Central Act XXV of 1867 to the effect that every printer shall deliver five copies of each book to the State Government out of which four will be deposited in the State Central Library, Madras.

Tamil Nadu was very rich in public libraries. The Connemara Public Library was opened for the public in 1896 and became the State Central Library from 1 April 1950. There is a tremendous growth and development of public libraries since an enactment of Tamil Nadu Public Libraries Act 1948 being the first state in India with Library Legislation.

As on March 1998, the state has public library service units, as–1 State Central Library, 29 District Central Libraries, 1548 Branch Libraries, 506 Village Libraries, 649 Part-time Libraries, and 8 Mobile Libraries. The Department of Public Libraries has been offering extension services, like–Mobile Library Service, Home Delivery Service, Library Service for Children, Library Service for Police Personnel, Library Service for state workers and remote settlers in the hills, Hospital Library Service, Rural Library Service, Part-time Library Service, Library Service for Students, Library Service for research scholars and Library Service for competitions for various civil services.

Andhra Pradesh

The state of Andhra Pradesh was formed in 1956, comprising Andhra areas of composite Madras state and Telengana area of Hyderabad area, whereas Madras Public Libraries Act in force in Andhra area. To solve administrative problems on two acts in operational in one state; both the acts were amalgamated, modified and up-to-date as Andhra Pradesh Public Libraries Act 1960.

It received the Governor assent on 18th. February 1960. Andhra Pradesh is the second state that has enacted Public Libraries Act in independent India. Its Preamble reads that, *"An Act to* consolidate and amend the laws relating to the establishment and maintenance of Public Libraries in the State of Andhra Pradesh and matters connected therewith".

It has seven chapters. Important features of this Act are as below:

- Constitution of 'The Andhra Pradesh Granthalaya Parishad', as a corporate body, having perpetual succession and power to the provisions of this Act.
- Constitution of Directorate of Public Libraries to direct, supervise and control Public Library System.
- Constitution of Zilla Granthalaya Samastha, one for the City of Hyderabad, one for the district of Hyderabad and one for each districts.
- Provision to collect library cess by every Zilla Granthalaya Samstha in its area as surcharge on property tax or house tax up to eight paise per rupee.

- The accounts of Zilla Granthalaya Samstha shall be open to inspection.
- Provision of Government Grant-in-aid to private libraries.
- Provision for constitution of a Library Service for the Zilla Granthalaya Samstha for the appointment of Librarians.

Andhra Pradesh is one of the leading states in India for the promotion of library services in India. It is the second in India with Public Libraries Act in 1960.

The structure of public library services can be classified into three categories consisting of:

- *Government Libraries:* 1 State Central Library, 6 Regional Libraries, and 1 Mobile Library,
- *Zila Grandhalaya Samstha Libraries:* 23 District/City Central Libraries, 1448 Branch Libraries, 355 Village Libraries, 3 Mobile Libraries, and 576 Book Deposit Centers,
- *Aided Libraries:* 1238 Gram Panchayat Libraries, 37 Cooperative Society Libraries, and 680 Private Libraries.

Karnataka

Karnataka is the third state in an independent India that have enacted Public Libraries Act. The objective of this Act can be seen in its Preamble that reads, '*An* Act to provide for the establishment and maintenance of Public Libraries and the organization of a comprehensive rural and urban library service in the State of Karnataka '. Important features of this Act are given below:

- Constitution of State Library Authority to meet twice in a year, Minister of Public Libraries as its Chairman and State Librarian as *ex-officio* Secretary.
- Provision for creation of an independent Department of Public Libraries with a profession as its head, to supervise, direct and control library services.
- Provision for the establishment of State Library as apex of public library system in the state.
- Constitution of Local Library Authority, City Library Authority and District Library Authority.
- Provision for setting up of Advisory Library Committee for Branch and Village Library Services.
- Collection of library cess on tax on lands and buildings.
- Additional sections in State Central Library
- State Bureau of Copyright Collection
- State Library for the Blind
- State Bureau of Inter Library Loan
- State Bibliographical Bureau
- State Bureau of Technical Service.

Karnataka is the third state in India that enacted Public Library Bill in 1965. The Belgaum Native General Library, established in 1848 by M.J.D. Invararity, was regarded as the first library started in Karnataka state. There were other seven libraries or reading rooms in Belgaum, namely, Library at Chikkodi established in 1886, Nippani Library in 1875, Gokak Library in 1865, Athani Library in 1865, Sampagaon Library in 1866, Khanapur Library in 1868, and Saundatti Library in 1870.

The existing public libraries in Karnataka are-1 State Central Library, 1 Indira Priyadarshini Chidren's Library, 1 Public Technical Library, 27 District Central Library, 19 City Central Library, 14 Mobile Libraries, 490 Branch Libraries, 107 Service Stations, 31 Reading Rooms, 5766 Gram Panchayat Libraries, 21 Aided Libraries, 200 Slum Libraries and 600 Reading Rooms in Slum Areas.

Maharashtra

Consequent upon the constitution of Maharashtra state, The Maharashtra Public Libraries Act, 1967 succeed Kolhapur Public Libraries Act 1945. The fourth state in an independent India that has enacted Public Libraries Act is Maharashtra state. Preamble of the Act read that, "To provide for the establishment, maintenance, organization and development of public libraries in the state of Maharashtra".

Important features of this Act are:

- Constitution of State Library Council. Minister for Education shall be the ex-officio President of the Council. The Council will advise the State Government on all matters connected with the administration of this Act.
- Constitution of a separate department of Libraries and the appointment of a professional Director;
- Establishment of Maharashtra State Library Service;
- Establishment of State Central library and a Divisional Library for each Division;
- Constitution of District Library Committee in each of the district. Chairman of the Education Committee of a Zilla Parishad in the district shall be ex-officio President of the Committee.
- Constitution of Library Fund by the State Government for carrying out the purpose of this Act. The State Government will contribute not less than a sum of twenty-five lakhs to the Library Fund every year.

The Birtishers started public libraries in Maharashtra after defeating Marathạs in 1818 but no Indians were allowed membership of these libraries till 1830. Pioneer libraries estab-lished by Indian in Maharashtra were at Ahmednagar in 1838, Bombay in 1845, and Poona in 1848. In 1939, the government constituted a Library Development Committee to prepare a plan for public library development in the state of Bombay. The report was implemented from 1955 to 1967. After an enactment of Maharashtra Public Libraries Act 1967, public library system was developed through voluntary organizations with grants from the government. As on 1998, Maharashtra has different categories of public libraries as–1 State Central Library, 6 Divisional Libraries, 31 District Libraries, 63 Taluka Grade A Libraries, 144 Taluka Grade B Libraries, 58 Taluka Grade C Libraries, and 3842 Recognized Libraries.

West Bengal

The West Bengal Legislature passed this Act and assent of the President was first published in the Calcutta Gazette, Extraordinary on the 7th January 1980. West Bengal enacted the Public Libraries Act in 1979 to become the fifth state of India with library legislation. Its preamble stated that, *"An Act to provide for the* establishment of Public libraries in the State of West Bengal and to regulate, guide, central, supervise and to grant recognition to the existing libraries in the State as also to provide for a comprehensive rural and urban library service in the State of *west Bengal".*

Some of the important salient features of this Act are:

- Constitution of State Library Council for the purpose of advising the Government on the matters of public library services. Minister-in-Charge of Library Services shall be the Chairman of the Council;
- Constitution of the Department of Libraries to supervise and direct the maintenance of Public Libraries;
- Constitution of Local Library Authority for each district. The District Magistrate shall be the Chairman of the Local Library Authority. Provision for constitution of Executive Committee for Local Library Authority;
- The Government is empowered to appoint District Library Officers and District Librarians in districts. The Government, in consultation with the Local Library Authority may place a person in charge of a District Library to be called as District Librarian;
- Financial management of local libraries rests upon the Local Library Authority. Means of augmenting funds are:
- Contributions, gifts and income form endowments;
- Grants from the government
- Collection of Local Library Authority under the Act.

In 1780, Mr. John Andrews run a commercial library in Fort William and the first public library; Calcutta Public Library was established during the British period in 1836, which is now known as National Library. By 1900, there were 50 public libraries in Bengal. The state government took up a seven tier library development scheme, which envisaged setting up of public libraries at different levels-State Central Library; District Library; Sub-Division/Area Library; Rural Library; Village Library; and Delivery Stations/Book Deposit Centers. By 1996, West Bengal has one State Central Library, 22 District Libraries, 120 Sub-Divisional/Town Libraries, and 2276 Rural/Area/Primary Unit Libraries. There are also around 3000 non-governmental/non-sponsored public libraries. West Bengal is the fifth state in India with Library Legislation in 1979.

Manipur

Manipur is the sixth state in an independent India that has enacted Public Libraries Act in 1988. The preamble stated the objectives of this Acts as, "An Act to provide the establishment and maintenance of Public Libraries in the State of Manipur and matters connected therewith".

Salient features of this Act are given hereunder:

- Constitution of a State Library Committee, to advise the State Government on all matters arising under this Act and to exercise and perform such other powers and duties as may be prescribed.
- Constitution of a separate Department of Public Libraries under the Director, as its head.
- Constitution of District Library Authority for each district to supervise library services in the area of its jurisdiction.
- Provision to constitute Executive Committee and Sub-Committees of District Library Authority to enquire into and report or advice on any matters, which it may refer to them.
- Constitution of Library fund formed mainly with the contribution of the State Government.

Manipur is the sixth state in India with Public Library Acts in 1988. Manipur Club established in 1927 was changed over into Manipur Book Club/Manipur Club Library and again changed into Jubabati Memorial Library in 1933. But the library had a setback during the Second World War.

Imphal Public Library, also known as Khwai Public Library was established in 1938 but was functioning till 1960 and later it was demolished in 1994. District Library and Children's Library-cum-Museun were merged on 26 August 1970 and came to be known as State Central library.. There are 9 District Libraries, 1 State Central Library, and 215 Libraries organized by Voluntary Organizations..

Kerala

Kerala Public Libraries Act, 1989 is also known as Kerala Granthasala Sanghom, 1989. Kerala enacted its pubic Libraries Act in 1989 to become the seventh state in India with library legislation. Preamble of this Act stated its objectives as, *"An Act* to consolidate and unify the library laws in the State and to provide for the recognition in the entire library system in the State of

Kerala with a view to the development and maintenance of comprehensive rural and urban library service and for matters connected therewith or incidental hereto".

Important features of the Act are:

- Constitution of Kerala State Library Council with Executive Committee to advise the government on all matters connected with this Act and to supervise and direct all maters relating to library service in the state;
- Secretary of the State Library Council shall be the Chief Executive Authority of the State Library Council;
- Constitution of District Library Council to supervise, co-ordinate and control the Library service under its jurisdiction and to promote co-operation between libraries and cultural and educational institutions in the country;
- Constitution of Taluk Library Union, with the power to supervise, coordinate and control the library services in the Taluk and to give directions and advise to affiliated libraries in regard to their day to day function and management;
- The Government may make every year a grant to the State library council with a maximum of one per cent of the education budget of the State.
- The State Library Council shall maintain a fund called State Library fund. Library cess collected and grants of State and Central Government will be credited to the State Library fund.
- Transfer of Kerala Granthaala Sangham with its staff, assets, and liabilities to the State Library Council.
- Collection of Library Cess in the form of a surcharge on the building tax or the property tax at the rate of 5 paise for the whole rupee.

Christian missionaries started libraries in Kerala during the 19th century. The history of public library movement in Kerala started in 1829 with the establishment of Trivandrum Public Library. There are more than 5000 public libraries in Kerala now, one in every 8 square kilometers.

Public libraries can be grouped into four categories, as–Libraries directly run by the Government, Libraries run by the local bodies, Grant-in-Aid libraries affiliated to the Kerala Grandhasala Sangham, and Libraries run by the Local Library Authorities.

The Kerala Grandhasala Sangham was established in 1947 and was registered under Section 9 of the Travancore Company Act, 1939 and in 1948 the Government approved it as the Central Agency of the Libraries. It plays an incredible role for the promotion, development and encouraging the people of the state through library services. Kerala enacted Public Library Bill in 1989 to become the seventh state in India with Library Legislation.

Haryana

Haryana is the eighth state in India with library legislation. The preamble stated its objectives as, "An Act to provide for the establishment, maintenance and development of Public Libraries in the State of Haryana and for matters ancillary *thereto.*"

Some of the important features of this Act are:

- Constitution of State Library Authority to advise the Government on all matters for the promotion of library services in the State. Minister-in-charge of libraries will be the Chairman;
- Establishment of State Library Directorate to execute the programmes approved by the State Library Authority;
- Establishment of State Central library;
- Constitution of District Library in each district and Municipal/City/ Town library; Block library; Village library; and Smaller book deposit centers;
- Provision for three types of library funds, such as State Library Fund, District Library Fund, and City/Town/Block/Village Library Fund;
- Levy of Library cess in the form of surcharge on property tax and house tax as decided by the government from time to time;
- Provision to recognize state library associations, and co-operative institutions by the State Library Authority.

Before the creation of this separate state, some public libraries were already established, Guru Gobind Singh Municipal Library in 1926, Shri Parmeshwari Yuvak Librray in 1927, and Sri Bal Amar Samiti Library in 1932. A State Central Library was started in 1967 by th4 Government of Haryana.

Besides it has started 12 District Libraries, 11 Sub-Divisional Libraries and 11 Municipal Libraries. Many philanthropic trusts and local bodies/ organizations had also established public libraries, which took active role in the promotion of reading habits and library services in the state. The Haryana Library Association was founded in 1967. The Haryana Public Libraries Bill was passed in 1989 and independent Directorate of Libraries was established in January 1993.

Mobile library services to reach the interior of the remote villages with reading facilities were started and the people are very much encouraged for the development of libraries at villages and panchayat levels as a social education center and community information center as well.

Mizoram

Mizoram is the ninth state of India to have library legislation. Preamble of this Act stated its objective as, "An Act to provide for the establishment, maintenance and development of comprehensive public libraries system in the State of Mizoram".

Important features of this Act are:

- Constitution of State Library Council to advise the Government on all matters relating to libraries and also in regard to promotion and development of libraries in the State;
- Constitution of the Department of Public Libraries to control and supervise the public library system in the State;
- Constitution of State Library, District Library, Sub-Divisional Library and Village Libraries;
- Provision of grant-in-aid to recognized libraries;
- No library cess. All expenses shall be made from the Government funds.

Goa

Goa is the tenth state to have library legislation in India. Preamble of this Act stated that, "An Act to provide for the establishment, maintenance and development of Public Libraries in the State of Goa and for the matters ancillary hereto".

Important salient features of this Act are:

- Constitution of State Library Council with the Minister-in-charge a the Chairman to advise the Government on all matters arising under the Act;
- Constitution of State Library Directorate for controlling and directing the public library system in the State;
- Organization of State Library, District Library, Taluk Library, and Village library;
- Creation of Public Library employees similar to the employees of State Government;
- Recognition of one State Library Association as co-operating institution;
- State library fund from different sources, *viz.* Government contribution, Government Grants, and any other contribution from the public;
- Levy of Library Cess in the form of a surcharge on Indian Made Foreign Liquor at the rate of 50 paise per bulk litre of beer.

Under the order of the Viceroy, *Dom Manuel de Portugal e Castro*, a public library, Publica Livraria was opened and attached to Academia Militar in 1832 and it was named as Bibliotheca Nacional de Goa in 1959 and came under the administration of Education and Health Services department.

The Government of Goa constituted a State Level Expert Committee in 1978 and State Library Advisory Board in 1983 for the development of library services in the state. The public libraries of Goa can be categorized into five levels, as State Library, Taluka Libraries, Village Libraries, Government Aided

Libraries, and Municipal Libraries. Goa is the tenth state in India with Public Library Act in 1993.

Orissa

The establishment of Diamond Jubilee Library at Kendrapara in 1897 and at Baripada in 1898 started the development of public library and followed by establishment of other libraries in the state. Three Government functionaries, Department of Information and Public Relations, Department of Sports and Culture, and Department of Housing and Urban Development operated public libraries in the state for some times.

In 1975, the Department of Cultural Affairs, Government of Orissa took complete charge of Public Libraries from the Department of Education. There is one State Library, 13 District Libraries, four Sub-Divisional libraries, six Ex. District Board Libraries, and four Memorial Hall Libraries.

Gujarat

Objective of Gujarat Public Libraries Act provided in its preamble is to provide for the promotion and development of public libraries in the State of Gujarat and for that purpose to constitute State Library development Council and for the matters connected therewith or incidental thereto.

Important features of this act are:

- Constitution of State Library Council with Minister—in-charge of Libraries as its Chairman;
- Establishment of Public Library Department with Director as its head of office;
- Establishment of District and Taluka Libraries at the headquarters of taluka;
- Constitution of District and Taluka Library Advisory Committee;
- Formation of State Library Development Fund;
- Recognition of libraries run by voluntary organizations.

The first considered public library in Gujarat was called, "Himabhai Institute of Library" established in 1849 in Ahmedabad. Other pioneer public libraries are Andrews Library established in 1850, Lang Library in 1857, Lakhajirao Pusthakalaya in 1868, Bhagavatsihji Library in 1884, State Library in 1865, Barton Library in 1882, Takhsinhi Library in 1877, and Victoria Jubilee Library in 1891.

There are two State Central libraries, 18 District Libraries in all the districts, 45 Taluka Libraries, 129 Mahila Libraries run by voluntary organizations, more than 300 Book Service Centers and Mobile Library service.

Uttarakhand

Uttarakhand is the 27th State of Indian Union, separated from Uttar Pradesh and coming into existence on 9.11.2000. The State comprises ten districts, namely Uttarkashi, Dehradun, Tehri Garhwal, Chamoli, Pithoragarh, Nainital, Uddam Singh Nagar, Pauri Garhwal and Hardwar. Public Libraries within these districts were automatically came under the Uttarakhand administration.

The State literacy rate is 72.28 per cent. The state government is very interested to serve the people through public libraries and the Uttaranchal Public Libraries Bill was enacted in 2005 to become the thirteenth state in India with Library legislation. Some of the well established libraries by the state government of Uttar Pradesh were taken over while coming up into existence.

Rajasthan

Libraries were established in Rajasthan as early as 14th. Century and maintained in the form of *Pothi-Khanas* consisting rich collections of manuscripts on different disciplines. Rana Kumbha's Saraswati Bhandar Library was established in 1448. Raja Man Singh established library, *Pothi-Khana* in 1592 by keeping rare and important manuscripts.

Pioneer Public Libraries were established in Bharatpur in 1907, Sikar in 1908, Kota in 1910, Fatehpur in 1910, and Jodhpur in 1915. There are 5 Divisional libraries, 24 District Libraries, and 8 Tehsil Libraries with 600 Book Deposit Centers on 15 August 1956. Mobile van was also provided to Division Libraries to supervise library services in the state.

STATES/UTs WITHOUT LIBRARY LEGISLATION

Public library systems and services of Indian states and Union Territories are highlighted hereunder.

Arunachal Pradesh

Arunachal Pradesh, formerly known as North East Frontier Agency, introduced library service since 1950s. During the Seventh Five Year Plan period, the state government took up the scheme of developing libraries in the state and set up a number of libraries at block and circle levels. Mobile library system was introduced in the state capital. The state has six categories of library, such as – one State Library, two Branch Libraries, 13 District Libraries, 2 Sub-Divisional Libraries, 20 Block Libraries, and 45 Circle Libraries.

Assam

In 1865, George Williamson, a tea-planter of Golaghat bequeathed 10,000 pounds for the purpose of educational and set up of libraries in Assam and the government taken up as an experiment measure to established public libraries at the initiatives of British government in 1902-1903 at Dhubri, Guwahati, Nagaon, Jorhat, Tezpur, Shillong, Sibsagar, Goalpara, Dibrugarh, Hailakandi, etc. and then handed over to the Local Boards. The people were awakened and established rural libraries in some areas. The Assam Library Association came into existence in 1938 and extended all possible help to established public libraries in different areas. The Central Library, established in 1954 at Shillong and the Assam Government Public Library established in 1903 was amalgamated in 1956 and renamed as the State Central Library.

In 1955, seven District Libraries were set up at Guwahati, Nagaon, Jorhat, Dibrugarh, Tezpur, Dhubri and Silchar. Book Mobile Service along with 70 Deposit Centers for Circulation of Books was organized to villages in 1959. Assam is running one State Library, one Branch Library, 22 District Libraries, 14 Sub-Divisional Libraries, and one Children Library.

Bihar

The ancient Educational and Cultural Centers like Nalanda, Vikramshala, Patiliputra and Taxila had magnificent libraries and Bihar Library Association was founded on 15 October 1936. The Association popularized importance of libraries and in 1937 prepared a Draft Scheme for the development of libraries in Bihar.

There is one State Central Library at Patna, having seven wings, *viz.*, State Reference Library, State Lending Library, State Library for Blind, State Bureau of Inter-Library Loan, State Bibliographical Bureau, State Bureau of Technical Service, and State Institute of Library Training and Research.

At present, there is one State Central Library, six Divisional Libraries, seven Special Libraries, 17 District Central Libraries, two State Libraries, 11 Sub-Divisional Libraries, 328 Block Libraries, and 4422 Village Libraries in Bihar. The library service is at the government level is under the control and supervision of the Commissioner of Education. In the state of Jharkhand area, there are five District Libraries, four Sub-Divisional Libraries and other Village Libraries are under the public library sector. The state of Jharkhand came into existence on 15 November 2000 by separating some areas of Bihar state.

Himachal Pradesh

Under the scheme of Integrated Library Service formulated by the Union Ministry of Education, a small library system was introduced in 1952. A State Central Library was established in Solan in 1959, and within two years sic District Libraries were opened. The State Central Library created four departments, namely, reference, Lending, Periodicals, and Children Section for the benefit of the readers.

Membership registration is free of charge to all the residents of Himachal Pradesh. It has one State Central Library, 11 District Libraries, 15 Community Central Public Libraries, and 101 Senior Secondary School Libraries in the state.

The School Libraries are also used as public libraries after the school hours. Two Mobile units are set up in 1961 to cater the needs of the community particularly in the rural areas of the state.

Jharkhand

The state of Jharkhand, separated from Bihar, is having 18 public libraries established by the state government.

These public libraries may be classified into four groups as below:

- Three State Public Libraries, one each at Ranchi, Chaibasa, Dhanbad and Dumka.
- One Divisional Library at Hazaribagh;
- Five District Libraries, one each at Gumla, Lohardaga, Daltonganj and Godda; and
- Eight Sub-Divisional Libraries, one each at Garhwa, Lahetar, Pakur, Simdega, Chatra, Sahebganj, Saraikela, and Khunti..

The library building are, generally, not functional to cater more readers at a time. Furniture is inadequate and water supply system is poor. No electricity connection was available to some of them due to non-payment of bills. Collection and subscription of periodicals/newspapers are not adequate to serve the library users as well.

Jammu and Kashmir

The state is divided into 14 districts. The Christian missinaries started education. Until 1947, the state has only two public libraries, namely, Sri Pratap Singh Library in 1893 in the city of Srinagar and Sri Ranbir Singh Library in Jammu.

The State government establishes the department of public Libraries in 1961 for the establishment and promotion of public library services in the state. The state has 2 Central Libraries, one each in the province of Jammu and Kashmir, 14 District Libraries, 51 Tehsil Libraries, and 18 Block Libraries.

Madhya Pradesh and Chhattisgarh

The state of Madhya Pradesh including Chhattisgarh lies in the heart of the country came into existence on 1 November 1956. Madhya Pradesh was divided into two states, *viz.*, Madhya Pradesh and Chhatisgarh on 1 November 2000; hence the state of Chhattisgarh came into existence.

It has 5 Regional Libraries in Bhopal, Gwalior, Jabalpur, Rewa, and Indore, 42 District Libraries, 6 Information Centers, 80 Private Public Libraries, and 15800 Gram Panchayat Libraries. The Madhya Pradesh Library Association was formed in 1957.

Meghalaya

Meghalaya has taken up the State Library of Assam established in Shillong in 1903 as its State Central Library. It has one State Central Library, four District Libraries, and Libraries run by voluntary organizations in different localities. The Meghalaya Library Association was established in 1994.

Nagaland

Nagaland has established a State Central Library at Kohima in 1981 functioning under the Directorate of Art and Culture. It offers computer facilities and reprographic services to its readers. There are eight district libraries and four of them have completed computerization. 330 Rural libraries are registered under the department of Art and Culture.

Punjab

The first public library in Punjab, known as Punjab Public Library was established at Lahore in 1884. Other pioneer libraries are Dyal Singh Public Library was established at Lahore in 1896 through a trust created in the name of Dyal Singh, Sir Ganga Commercial Public Library established in 1923, and Dwarka Das Public Library at Lahore in 1921. Pioneer Municipality Libraries in the state were established in Ludhiana in 1878, Lahore in 1884, Patiala in 1897, Amritsar in 1900, Kapurthala in 1904, and Sangrur in 1912. There are 2 State Central Libraries at Chandigarh and Patiala, 14 District Libraries, and 97 Municipal Libraries. Dr. A.C.Wooner founded the Punjab Library Association in 1915 at Lahore.

The Association organize training, seminar, conferences and also publish some library literatures.

Sikkim

Sikkim public libraries came into existence under the influence of academic libraries in the state. After 1975 the Government of Sikkim realised the importance of public libraries and has started a few libraries but public libraries have not made much progress in a systematic way. All the four districts have a separate District Library at the district headquarters. These libraries were controlled, supervise and administered by the Cultural Department of the Government of Sikkim.

Tripura

From the nucleus of "Ujjayanta Palace Library", the then Maharaja Birchandra Manikya established a library in the Royal Palace in the year 1896 in Agartala was called as "Birchandra Library" and declared open to the public. This library was taken over by the government in 1953 and named as Birchandra Public Library and from 1977; it was designated as a State Central Library and renamed as Birchandra State Central Library.

Libraries are look after by the Government of Higher and Technical Education and at present the position of public library in Tripura is – one State Central Library, 3 District Libraries, seven Sub-Divisional Libraries, 10 Block Level Public Libraries, two Rural Libraries, and 1 Children Library. The departments of Social Education and Panchayat Raj also run some public libraries in the state.

Uttar Pradesh

Uttaranchal state came into existence on 9 November 2000 separating some areas from the state of Uttar Pradesh. Some libraries were established in the early days, such as, Raza Library, Rampur in 1750, Allahabad Public Library, Allahabad in 1763, Maulana Azad Library, Aligarh in 1877, Bharati Bhawan Library, Allahabad in 1889 and Lyall Library, Aligarh in 1899. The state has a State Central Library at Allhabad, 69 District level libraries, 62 other prominent public libraries run by voluntary organizations..

Andaman and Nicobar Island

Andaman and Nicobar Island, one of the Union Territories of India, have never experienced the services of libraries until a small library was set up in the cellular jail in the early 1930s. The prisoners were allowed to read books, newspapers and magazines in this library. The Government took initiatives in establishing school libraries. In 1957 an Information Centre was set up at Port Blair.

In 1964, this Information Centre was converted into District Library and later on considering the public interest the District Library was enlarged and reorganized into the State Library in 1977. Library service is under the Department of Education and financed by the Andaman and Nicobar Administration and the department came forward with an idea of spreading education through the libraries. At present, there is one State Central library, one State Library, two District Libraries, 12 Zonal Libraries, and three Public Libraries..

Dadra and Nagar Haveli

In the Union Territory of Dadra and Nagar Haveli, there is a State Central Library at the capital city Silvasa and Public Library, known as Central Libariy at Naroli, Kanvel, Randha, Kilvani, Dapido, Amoli, Dushni and Mandoni. The Central Library at Silvasa and Naroli were established in 1954 and 1965 respectively.Central Libraries at Silvasa, Dadra and Kanvel are functio-ning in their own buildings whereas the remaining libraries were in a rented building and primary schools. There are no public libraries run by voluntary organizations in this Union Territory. The library services were under the control and supervision of the Director of Education..

Daman and Diu

The Assistant Director of Education under the control of the Department of Education supervises library services in the Union Territory of Daman and Diu. There are 3 Municipal Libraries at Moti Daman, Nani Daman, and Diu. Establishment of a Central library, 2 District libraries, and 1 Mobile Library is under consideration..

Lakshadweep

There was no library service in this Union Territory before independence. The first public library was established at Karavati in 1951. However, the island has the apex library of this Union Territory established in 1958 as Freedom Fighters Central Library, which was subsequently named as Lakshadweep Central Library.

It has well organized public library system in which Lakshadweep Central Library serves as the State Central Library and each of the ten constituent inhabited islands Androtti, Amini, Agatti, Bitta, Chetlat, Kadmat, Kalpeni, Karavatti, Kilton, and Minicoy is provided with a public library by the Administration of Lakshadweep. These libraries were earlier known as Reading Room-cum-Library.

Library services are looked after by a Library Development Officer who performs the supervision function under the overall control of the Director of Social Welfare and Culture. To develop and sustain library movement, the administration has constituted a state level committee known as 'Lakshadweep State Library Committee' in 1994 comprising 10 members including Library Development..

Pondicherry

The history of Library in Pondicherry began with the establishment of a '*Bibliotheque Publique*' in 1827 with a modest stock of books collected from several Government establishments functioning in this region. The British Indian Government also donated some books to this library from time to time.

It was renamed as '*Romain Rolland Library*' in 1967 after the French scholar Romain Rolland. The General Assembly, in 1892, authorized the opening of the library at Karaikal and constituted a Commission to advise the administration on measures to be taken for the development of the Library. The Library was originally named as '*Bibliotheque Coloniale*'.

This library was renamed as '*Bibliotheque Publique*' in 1952 and subsequently categorized as Regional Library and called as Government Public Library. The first library was actually started by the 'Association of Old Students' in 1918 at Mahe.

The Old Boys Association donated all the books and furniture of Mahe Public Library. In 1964, the Union Territory Administration has evolved a policy of opening Branch Libraries at rural areas of the territory and the number of Branch Libraries opened in four regions are, 46 in Pondicherry region, 14 in Karaikal region, 3 in Mahe region, and 2 in Yanam region.

The Director of Education from 1954 to 1991 controlled the library services. Since 1991, Director of Art and Culture is the head of the Library services. There are three Assistant Library and Information Officers to look after the library services under the Director of Art and Culture..

National Capital Territory of New Delhi

Before the independence, Delhi was very poor in library services, particularly in public libraries, due to political structures, lack of educational facilities, and attitude of the authorities. Harding Library was established in 1862 and housed in a portion of the Town Hall.

In 1942, Delhi Municipal Committee changed the name of the library to the Harding Municipal Public Library, which was further rechristened in 1970 as the Hardayal Municipal Public Library after the famous freedom fighter and intellectual Lala Hardayal. The British Council Library and American Information resource Centre are also being developed for the public and function with the latest technology which enrich public library services in Delhi. Marwari Seth Kedar Nath Goenka in the Chandi Chawk area of Delhi set up the Marwari Library, the first of any type founded through community awareness in Modern India, in 1915. Under the UNESCO's Pilot Project, the Ministry of Education, Government of India, founded Delhi Public Library in 1951. It was very much developed and became one of the depository libraries in India. The Delhi Public Library consists of the Central Library, Zonal Libraries, Branch Libraries, and Sub-Branch Libraries in addition to the Community libraries, Resettlement Colonies libraries, Sports libraries, and an adequately good network of Mobile Library Services to link up the remote urban and rural areas spread over the Union Territory of Delhi.

CONTRIBUTION OF RAJA RAMMOHUN ROY LIBRARY FOUNDATION

1972 was a significant year in the history of library movement in India. The country was celebrating the silver jubilee of its independence from the British Administration in 1972. Coincidentally it was an International Book Year with the slogan of 'Books For All' emphasizing promotion of reading habits among the masses. Not only that, it was the auspicious occasion of the bicentennial birth anniversary of an Indian social reformer, who stressed the need of modern education for the development of the nation.

In this august year, Raja Rammohun Roy Library came into being in May 1972. It is the nodal agency of Government of India to support public library services and systems and promote public library movement in the country. Raja Rammohun Roy Library Foundation is an autonomous organization, established and sponsored by the Department of Culture, Government of India. It is registered under the West Bengal Societies Registration Act, 1961. Its headquarters is located at Kolkata. In view of the expanding activities, the Foundation has opened zonal offices under the Assistant Field Officers for monitoring the impact and implementation of the assistance rendered by the Foundation such as-Eastern Zonal Office at Calcutta; Northern Zonal Office at New Delhi; Southern Zonal Office at Chennai and Western Zonal Office at Mumbai.

Objectives

Raja Rammohun Roy Library Foundation is a national agency for the promotion of library services in general and public library services in particular. The main objective of the Foundation is to promote and support public library movement in the country by providing adequate library services and by developing reading habits all over the country with the active cooperation of State Government and Union Territories and of Voluntary Organizations operating in the filed of library services, cultural activities, adult education and the like.

Objectives of the Foundation may be listed as below:

- To promote library movement in the country;
- To enunciate a national library policy and to help build up a national library system;
- To provide financial and technical assistance to libraries;
- To provide financial assistance to organizations, regional or national engaged in the promotion of library development;
- To publish appropriate literature and to act as a clearing house of ideas and information on library development in India and abroad;
- To promote research in problems of library development;
- To advise the government on all matters pertaining to the library development in the country; and
- To propagate the adoption of library legislation in the country.

Assistance Programme

The Foundation promotes public library services rendering book and financial assistance to the public libraries under different schemes of assistance. The scheme of assistance is of two types, *viz.*, Matching and Non-Matching schemes.

Matching Schemes

Assistance under Matching Scheme is given from the resources shared on matching basis with the States/Union Territory Administrations on the basis of developed states 50;50; developing and lagging states 60;40 and North-Eastern States 90;10. This revised matching scheme is effective from 2005.

The Matching assistance can be given to achieve its main objectives for:

- Assistance towards building up of adequate stock of books and reading materials.
- Assistance towards development of rural book deposit centers and mobile library services.
- Assistance towards organization of seminars, workshops, training courses and book exhibition.
- Assistance towards storage and display of books including reading room furniture.

- Assistance to public libraries below district level for increasing accommodation.
- Assistance to public libraries below State Central Libraries to acquire TVcum-VCP sets for educational purposes/Computer for library application.
- Assistance towards Networking of Public Libraries.

Non-Matching Schemes

The Foundation fully gives assistance under this scheme from his own resources to implement its objectives for:

- Assistance towards building up of adequate stock of books through central selection.
- Assistance to voluntary organizations providing public library Services
- Assistance to children libraries or children's section of general public libraries including women section and senior citizen section.
- Assistance to public libraries towards celebration of 50 years, 100 years and 125 years.
- Assistance towards collection and compilation of library statistics through official and non-official agencies.
- Assistance to centrally sponsored libraries.
- Assistance towards organization of seminars/conferences by national level library organizations.
- Assistance towards establishment of children's corner.

Promotion of* District Youth Resource Centres *(DYRCs)

The development of DYRCs is being made commensurate with the decision of the inter Ministerial Steering Committee constitutes for the purpose with the representative from Ministry of Sports and Youth Affairs, Ministry of Culture, Raja Rammohun Roy Library foundation and Nehru Yuvak Kendra Sanghatana.

The DYRCs are assisted for the following purpose:

- Towards building up adequate stock of books.
- Towards acquiring storage materials and library furniture.
- Towards construction of library building.
- Towards acquisition of computers with accessories.

Promotional Activities

RRRLF has undertaken a number of promotional activities for qualitative improvement of library services. It is associated and interacts with different national and international library professional associations like IFLA, ILA, IASLIC and different state level library associations.

Some of the promotional activities taken up by the Foundation for the qualitative improvement of library services may be given as below:

- It organizes seminars and conferences on the topics related to the development of public libraries in India.
- It plays a major role in the preparation of National Policy on Library and Information Systems and also issued guidelines on public library systems and services.
- It instituted 'RRRLF Fellowship' to eminent men and women in the field of library services who have contributed significantly to the library movement particularly, public library movement in the country through active involvement in the movement, organizational initiative, intellectual leadership or are dedicated to the propagation of the reading habit among the mass. Fellowship carries a cash award of ₹. 25,000 besides a plaque and a citation detailing the services rendered by the Fellow in the country.
- 'RRRLF Best Library Award' for the Best State Central Library in India. The Award carries a Citation and a cash incentive of ₹. 1 lakh.
- 'RRRLF Best District Library Award' in each of the six regions. The Award carries a Citation and cash incentive of ₹. 50,000.
- The Foundation instituted 'RRRLF Best Rural Library Awards' one for each state since 2005.
- 'Raja Rammohun Roy Award' was introduced annually to the best contributor of an article covering the area of development of Public Library Systems and Services or suggesting measures for the promotion of reading habits.

Research Cell and Special Library

A research cell along with a special library on Library and Information Science and statistics unit supported by a computer unit are providing necessary input to its various activities. About 5000 important books and journals on Library and Information Science and allied fields have been acquired in the library. Besides carrying on Research Projects on public library or allied subject, the Research Cell renders advisory and consultancy services whenever required. It has prepared and published a report on loss of books in libraries for the Government of India.

Publications

The Foundation has brought out many useful publications for the promotion and development of public library services in the country.

Some of its significant publications are:

- Indian Libraries; Trends and Perspectives
- Raja Rammohun Roy and the New Learning
- Directory of Indian Public Libraries
- RRRLF Newsletter

- Granthana-Indian Journal of Library Studies
- Annual Report
- Books for the Millions at their Doorsteps..

Modernization Programme

The Foundation is taking steps to meet the new technologies of information for the promotion of library services. It has a Computer Section for building-up data bank of Public Libraries for the country.

This section is planned to give information storage, retrieval and data processing support for all the application areas. It has keen interest with enthusiasm to computerized state libraries in India. It gave computers to the state and district libraries to carry out Foundations' zeal to computerize such libraries. The work is going on to computerized shortly.

Achievement

The Foundation has taken pains in promoting and developing library services in the country since its inception. Central Government's grant allotment is increasing over the last years and state contributions for matching scheme is also increasing as well.

This increased shows that the works carried out by the Foundation is growing and the State Government gives emphasis for the promotion of public libraries through the Foundation.

During the VIII Five Year Plan period the total plan grant from the Government of India was ₹.1175.50 lakhs with an average annual plan grant of ₹. 235.10 lakhs and contribution of States under matching scheme reaches ₹. 645.97 lakhs. The Government of India allotted an amount of ₹. 3233 lakhs as plan grant during IX Five Year Plan period. The annual average plan grant was ₹. 646.60 lakhs and the state contribution reaches ₹. 1977 lakhs.

During the last three years of the X Five Year Plan period, the plan grant stepped up to ₹. 1150.21 lakhs including a special grant of ₹. 150.21 lakhs for North-Eastern States and contributions received from various state governments also reaches ₹. 769.59 lakhs.

Plan grants and State contribution of matching scheme may be given in Table 5.1 and Graph as below:

Table. Plan Grant and State Contributions.

Rupees in lakhs

Five Year Plan	Plan Grant	Average Annual Plan Grant	State Contribution
VIII	1175.70	235.10	645.97
IX	3233.00	646.60	1977.00
X	1150.21	383.40	769.59

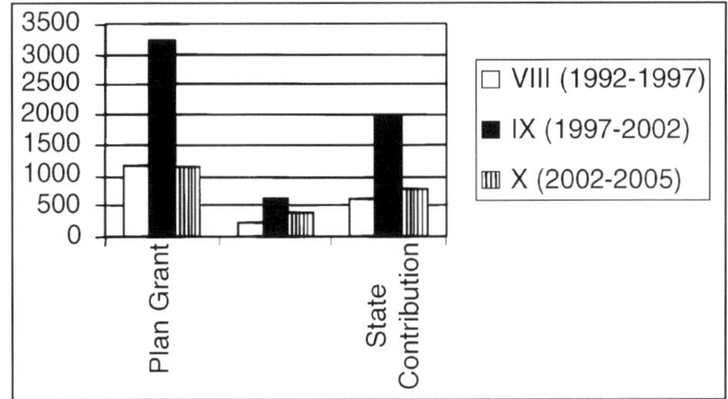

Fig. Plan Grant and State Contributions.

Over the last thirty-two years, the Foundation has covered about a little thirty-one thousand libraries at different levels for assistance. The RRRLF assistance to libraries/kendras is illustrated in Table and Graph as below:

Table . Assistance to Libraries Cover by RRRLF.

Category of Libraries/Kendras, etc.	No of Libraries Covered
State Central Libraries	28
Divisional and District Libraries	451
Sub-divisional/Taluka/Tehsil Libraries	501
Towns and Rural Libraries	30134
Nehru Yuvak Kendras	272
Jawahar Bal Bhavans	49
Others	128
Total	31563

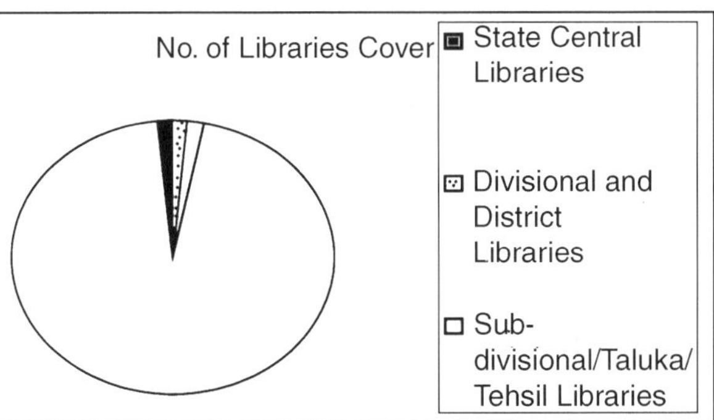

Fig . Assistance to Libraries Cover by RRRLF.

State Library Committee

The Foundation renders matching as well as non-matching assistance to support and promote public library services in the States and Union Territories in accordance with rules and procedures. Every State/Union Territory Administration are advised to set up State Library Committee (SLC) consisting of the following members and will meet at least twice a year:

- Secretary/Director or person nominated by the Department controlling library services-Chairman
- Director or Officer-in-Charge of the Department, if he is not the Chairman
- Director of the Foundation or his representative
- Nominee of the Chairman of the Foundation;
- President or Secretary of the State Library Association;
- A representative of the Education Department, if library service is controlled by a separate department;
- An educationist or an author or a person representing the state level organization connected with book production to be nominated by the State Government; and
- Librarian of the State Central Library or any other public library nominated by the State Government shall be the Convener of the State Library Committee. Where this is not feasible, the State Government will nominate a suitable official looking after library service as the Convener.

The functions of the State Library Committee shall be:

- To prepare perspective and annual plan of library services in the State with particular reference to the assistance programmes of the Foundation;
- To ensure payment of State Government/UT Adminis-tration contribution and availing of the matching grant from the Foundation;
- To select books according to the felt need of the community and in conformity with the guidelines prescribed by the Foundation;
- To scrutinize and recommend proposals for other schemes of assistance to the Foundation;
- To ensure proper utilization of assistance by the Foundation; and
- To perform any other activity conducive to the development of library in the State or Union Territory.

Foundation's assistance is available for all categories of public libraries, *viz.*, State Central Library, Regional/Divisional Libraries, District Central Libraries, Subdivisional Libraries, Tehsil Libraries, Taluka Libraries, Block Libraries, Branch Libraries, Municipal Libraries, Town Libraries, Rural Libraries, Panchayat Libraries, Village Libraries, etc. directly maintained or aided or recognized by the State Government.

State Library Committee will decide number and categories of libraries for assistance under different schemes and consolidated list of books for different categories of libraries. However, Textbooks, costly books and foreign publications should not ordinarily be selected. The maxim "the best reading for the largest number at the least cost' should be the guiding principle for selection of books.

The Foundation buys books at a graded rate of discount as mentioned below:

1	to	10 copies	-	10% discount
11	to	25 copies	-	15% discount
26	to	100 copies	-	20% discount
101	to	200 copies	-	25% discount
201	to	500 copies	-	30% discount
501	and	above	-	35% discount

The Foundation also gives assistance to Public Libraries to acquire new computer or upgrade as the case may be for either of the following items, with accessories for educational purposes once in 10 years:

- One TV-cum-VCP sets with accessories together with five educational videocassettes
- Computer System
  - One Server
  - Three clients for State Central Library
  - UPS in capacity rage of 0.5 kva to 3 kva
  - One Laser Printer and one Dot Matrix Printer; one Laser Printer, one Inkjet Printer and two Dot Matrix Printer for State Central Library.
  - Library Software
  - Network Equipments
  - Others;
    a. One Web Camera
    b. Two Barcode Reader
    c. Two Speaker
    d. One CD-Writer
    e. One Scanner
  - Cost of power cabling and installation of LAN
  - Cost of Retro Conversion of total holdings.

Assistance is also given to both Government and Non-government libraries for construction of a new building or extension of the existing building. Maximum amount given to District Level Library is ₹10 lakh and ₹8 lakh for Sub. Division/Town Level Library once in ten years. For other libraries ₹ 4 lakh can be given for construction of library building.

NATIONAL POLICY ON LIBRARY AND INFORMATION SYSTEM

John Martin said, "Policy is a statement of a specific goal or goals which are to be achieved, or to be pursued; a statement of the means by which realization of the goals will be brought about; an assignment of the responsibilities for implementation of the means, and a set of rules or guidelines regulating the activity". National Policy on Library and Information Science is to "provide a framework for properly planned and co-coordinated development of library and information structure in a country, resulting thereby in an enhanced and user-oriented information services to its user population".

The need for the formulation of National Policy on Library and Information Systems was brought to the notice of the Government of India by Indian library profession since 1950s by Dr. S.R.Ranganathan and in the recommendations of the Library Advisory Committee Report, 1958. Afterwards, professional organizations, like RRRLF, NISSAT and National Library urged upon the Government the necessity of enunciating such policy. The matter was discussed in the annual conference of IASLIC in 1979 at Roorkee and ILA in 1984 at Jaipur. Consequently, Indian Library Association submitted a draft policy statement to the Government in 1985. The Planning Commission Working Group in its report Modernization of Library Services and Informatics for the 7th Five-Year Plan emphasized the need of such policy. The Raja Rammohun Roy Foundation, after nine years of its inception, took up the task in 1981 and after careful deliberations submitted a Draft National policy on Library and Information Systems to the government in July 1984.

On the basis of the draft policy submitted by the Raja Rammohun Roy Library Foundation and Indian Library Association, the Government of India, Ministry of Human resources Development, Department of Culture, set up a Committee in October 1985 under the Chairmanship of Professor D.P.Chattopadhyaya for the formulation of a National Policy on Library and Information Systems and the final report was submitted in May 1986 which includes:

- The Public Library system;
- The Academic Library System;
- Special Libraries and Information Systems;
- The National Library System and the Bibliographical Services;
- Manpower Development and Professional Status; and
- Modernization of Library and Information Systems.

Though the government has not adopted the recommen-dations as the official policy, but it serves as suggestive model for the development of libraries as a whole.

The recommendations under the Public Library System are as follows:

- The most important task before the government is to establish, maintain and strengthen the free public libraries in the country and enable them to work as a system.
- The main thrust in this area should go to the rural public library. A village or a village cluster with an adequate population should have a community library, which will also serve as an information center. Resources of different agencies engaged in the work of public health, adult education, local selfgovernment and such others may be pooled to build up this composite center.

- An important link should be established between the community library of the village and the village primary school. If the school does not have a library of its own, the community library should provide the children with an adequate book-corner.
- The community library should also importantly cater for adult education and make adequate audio-visual aids available to attract the illiterate villagers.
- The district library should serve as an apex library for each district with public libraries at city, town and village levels constituting important components in the district library system. In addition to the usual services to be rendered by it, it should also provide for learning facilities and recreation for the handicapped. Wherever possible, district libraries and comparable city public libraries should provide literature in Braille. The district library and branch libraries should also arrange mobile and circulating library services within its area wherever it is necessary and feasible. Special services should be rendered to hospitals, prisons, and the infirm in their homes.
- Libraries for special groups should be built in areas of tribal concentration or minority communities to develop their distinctive cultures. The government will provide all encouragement for such communities to develop their own libraries through voluntary effort.
- Each public library should have a section for children and, in addition, separate libraries for children with attractive books and audio-visual supporting materials should be established wherever possible.
- The district library will take the leadership in establishing linkages between all other public libraries of the district and work towards resource sharing within the area.
- The key role of public libraries as chief sustaining agencies of distance education should be recognized and they should be adequately equipped with the relevant resources for this purpose.
- All the libraries within a state should form part of a network extending from the community library of the village through intermediary levels to the district and to the State Central Library. This State network should eventually connect with the national level.
- The role of the State Central Library is crucial in networking and the establishment of uniform library procedures within the States. The State Central Library/Directorate of Public Libraries has to perform as the coordinating agency for public libraries in the State.
- To bring about the development of the public libraries in a State it is vital that each State enact its own library legislation. The Central Government should revise the Model Public Library Bill, which it has already prepared, in the light of experience gained in recent years

and urge upon the States the importance of enacting such legislation. Finances for library development should be found by each State either from its general revenues or from local taxation.
- The Central Government should assist the State in the development of public libraries in a larger way than it has done so far. The Raja Rammohun Roy Library Foundation as the national agency for co-coordinating and assisting the development of public libraries be suitably strengthened enabling it to discharge its responsibilities effectively.

NATIONAL KNOWLEDGE COMMISSION

National Knowledge Commission was set up by the Prime Minister of India, Manmohan Singh to prepare a blueprint to tap into the enormous reservoir of our knowledge base so that our people can confidently face challenges of the 21st. Century. The Commission has a designated time frame of three years from 2nd. October 2005 to 2nd. October 2008.

The Commissions' Terms of References are:
- Build excellence in the educational system to meet the knowledge challenges of the 21st. century and increase India's competitive advantage in fields of knowledge.
- Promote creation of knowledge in Science and Technology laboratories.
- Improve the management of institutions engaged in Intellectual Property Rights.
- Promote knowledge applications in Agriculture and Industry.
- Promote the use of knowledge capabilities in making government an effective, transparent and accountable service provider to the citizen and promote widespread sharing of knowledge to maximize public benefit.

The Commission headed by Mr. Sam Pitroda as its Chairman and there are other 5 members, who are renowned persons in different fields of knowledge. It is a high-level advisory body to the Prime Minister of India, with a mandate to guide policy and generate reforms. The Commission is the world's first body of its kind.

The prime focus of the Commission is on five key areas of the knowledge paradigm, such as:
- Access
  - Literacy
  - Language
  - Translation
  - Libraries
  - Networks
  - Portals

- Concepts
  - School Education
  - Vocational Education
  - Higher Education
  - Medical Education
  - Legal Education
  - Management Education
  - Engineering Education
  - Open and Distance Education
- Creation
  - Science and Technology
  - Intellectual Property Rights
  - Innovation
  - Entrepreneurship
- Application
  - Traditional knowledge
  - Agriculture

Besides the Working Group on Libraries, other four Committees were set up with specialists and professionals in different areas of Libraries under the Chairmanship of Mrs. Kalpana Dasgupta.

Such Committees are:

- Committee on database creation and networking;
- Committee on private collections;
- Committee to set standards and modalities for collection development, systems and services;
- Committee on staffing pattern and staff requirement of libraries.

Terms of References of the Working Group on Libraries are given below:

- To redefine the objectives of the country's Library and Information Service sector;
- To identify constraints, problems and challenges relating to the sector;
- To recommend changes and reforms to address the problems and challenges to ensure a holistic development of information services in all areas of national activity;
- To take necessary steps to mobilize and upgrade the existing library and information systems and services, taking advantage of the latest advances in Information Community Technology;
- To explore possibilities for innovation and initiate new programmes relevant to our national needs, especially to bridge the gap between the information rich and the information poor within society;
- To suggest means of raising standards and promoting excellence in Library and Information Science education including re-orientation and training of working professionals;

- To assist in setting up facilities to preserve and access to indigenous knowledge and the nation's cultural heritage;
- To set up adequate mechanisms to monitor activities for securing the benefits of acquisition and application of knowledge for the people of India;
- To examine any other issues that may be relevant in this context..

The Notional Knowledge Commission's Working Group on Libraries, after consultations of more than 20 state representatives and NGOs and many more interest groups and professionals in the field, ready its first recommendations for submission to the nation. Moreover, the Commission submitted its first recommen-dations to the Prime Minister in December 2006 on the following areas:

- Libraries
- Translation
- Language
- Knowledge Networks
- Right to Education
- Vocational education
- Higher Education
- National Science and Social science Foundation

The Commission argued Libraries as Gateways to knowledge and continued that a "Library is not a building stacked with books-it is a repository and source of information and ideas, a place for learning and enquiry, and for the generation of thought and the creation of new knowledge. Public libraries in particular have the potential to bridge the gap between the 'information poor' and the 'information rich' by ensuing that people from all sectors and settings of society and the community across India have easy access to knowledge seek".. The Commission clearly incorporated roadmap for the execution of its recommendations on libraries under different points of consideration. It gave a Library Charter that is incorporated below.

Recognising that the library's objectives are to:

- Disseminate knowledge as widely as possible;
- Serve as a major vehicle to facilitate creation of new knowledge;
- Facilitate optimal use of knowledge by all sectors, such a government, industry, rural sector and civil society;
- Ensure that people from all sectors and all parts of the country have easy access to knowledge relevant to their needs, in their own language.

The library undertakes to:

- Serve as local center of information and a gateway to national and global knowledge providing fair access to knowledge and information to as many as users as possible;

- Offer an inviting and attractive physical space with clean drinking water and toilet facilities;
- Offer proactive services to its user communities;
- Ensure that users are treated with courtesy and respect by library staff;
- Pay attention to the needs of children, women, senior citizens and the physically challenged;
- Optimize its potential to provide access to information and knowledge to all;
- Help users developed information skills to make optimum use of resources;
- Improve its collections and services on continuing basis in consultation with users;
- To work more effectively and efficiently by undertaking every activity in a professional manner;
- To bridge the gap between the information poor and the information rich.

The Commission is organizing discussion forum at different areas for the preparation of its final report, which is expected to be submit to the nation within its stipulated time.

LIBRARY ASSOCIATIONS

The term 'association' is used to denote a group or body of individuals or institutions associated with a common purpose revolving generally for the two main purposes, viz.,:

- Advancement of the service oriented goals of the association, and
- Protection of the interests of the members.

Association may be of different kinds with different objectives and categories, professional or non-professional. However, by considering its nature, Pandey S.K.Sharma defined library associations as 'a group or body of libraries or librarians and users of libraries formed with the common purpose of advancement of library profession including service and also for protection of interests of the members including raising their capabilities to serve more effectively'.

There are more than seventy professional organizations and associations at state level in India. William A Borden went to Baroda in 1910 at the invitation of Maharaja Sayajirao Gaekwar of Baroda and organized the first professional organization of librarians in the country, the Baroda Library Club in 1912.

Other professional associations came up afterwards and some of the national level associations worth to be mentioned for their contributions in public library developments in the country.

USE OF PUBLIC LIBRARY SERVICES

Expert assessment of the nation's health care system suggests that it is slow in translating knowledge into practice and that patient care is not keeping abreast of advances in basic research. The American Medical Informatics Association recently proposed a plan for improving health care delivery. The plan focusses on clinical decision support, which "encompasses a variety of approaches for providing clinicians, staff, patients or other individuals with timely, relevant information that can improve decision making, prevent errors, and enhance health and health care."

The National Library of Medicine (NLM) can make a substantial contribution to improving national health by making a wide range of biomedical resources readily accessible to advanced information technology. There is a large, and growing, amount of online health-related information. Some resources are in the form of text readily accessible only to humans; examples include MEDLINE/PubMed and ClinicalTrials.gov.

Other information is structured and includes biomedical vocabularies, clinical and molecular biology knowledge bases, and model organism annotation databases. Within NLM, examples include the Unified Medical Language System and Entrez Gene.

There are also several specialised biomedical databases, for example the BIND database and PharmGKB, as well as commercially curated drug databases, such as Micromedex DRUGDEX and DrugDigest. The growth of online information resources for biomedicine is outstripping access applications that could allow users to maximally exploit those resources. In order to take full advantage of available resources, the Library needs to provide services beyond traditional information retrieval.

Emerging research provides the underpinnings for developing applications that accommodate the growth in online information. Advanced applications manipulate information, not just text, and provide visualisation of results and interconnections among multiple sources. Some research concentrates on extracting information from text. Other emerging systems focus on using the information extracted; examples include automatic summarisation, question answering, and knowledge discovery.

METHODS AND PROCEDURES

We discuss issues involved in constructing a Biomedical Knowledge Repository and illustrate an emerging Web application that exploits a preliminary version. The SemRep and Sem Gen natural language processing systems will be used to extract information in the form of semantic predications consisting of arguments and a predicate that represent relations between concepts asserted in text. Information in biomedical structured resources will be converted into a common format and all information will be integrated into the repository. Finally, a significant aspect of this project is the development of applications that exploit the Biomedical Knowledge Repository.

Extracting Predications from Text

Two programmes developed at LHNCBC will initially be used to extract semantic predications from ClinicalTrials.gov narrative and MEDLINE/PubMed citations for the repository. SemRep was devised to apply to the clinically oriented research literature, while SemGen addresses the genetic etiology of disease.

SemRep

SemRep is a rule-based symbolic natural language processing system developed for the biomedical research literature. As the first step in identifying semantic predications, SemRep produces an underspecified syntactic analysis based on the SPECIALIST Lexicon and the MedPost part-of-speech tagger. The most important aspect of this processing is the identification of simple noun phrases. In the next step, these are mapped to concepts in the Metathesaurus using MetaMap. Syntactic analysis in table, for example, contains Metathesaurus concepts and semantic types for the sentence in table.

Table. 4.1 SemRep Analysis

Sentence	Phenytoin induced gingival hyperplasia	(1)
Syntactic analysis	[[head(noun(phenytoin)), metaconc('Phenytoin' :[orch,phsu]))], [verb(induced)], head(noun(['gingival hyperplasia')), metaconc(' Gingival Hyperplasia':[dsyn]))]]	(2)
Semantic Network	'Pharmacological Substance' CAUSES 'Disease or Syndrome'	(3)
Semantic Predication	Phenytoin CAUSES Gingival Hyperplasia	(4)

SemRep relies on structures to translate syntactic structures into semantic predications. One aspect of this processing is 'indicator' rules which map syntactic elements to predicates in the Semantic Network. Argument identification rules then find syntactically allowable noun phrases to serve as arguments for indicators. If an indicator and the noun phrases serving as its syntactic arguments can be interpreted as a semantic predication, the following condition must be met: The semantic types of the Metathe-saurus concepts for the noun phrases must match the semantic types serving as arguments of the indicated predicate in the Semantic Network.

For example, in the structure given in table, the indicator *induced* maps to the Semantic Network relation in table. The concepts corresponding to the noun phrases *phenytoin* and *gingival hyperplasia* can serve as arguments because their semantic types match those in the Semantic Network relation. In the semantic predication produced as output, the Metathesaurus concepts from the noun phrases are substituted for the semantic types in the Semantic Network relation.

SemGen

SemGen was adapted from SemRep in order to identify semantic predications on the genetic etiology of disease. The main consideration in creating SemGen was the identification of gene and protein names as well as related genomic phenomena. For this SemGen relies on ABGene, in addition to MetaMap and the Metathesaurus. Since, the UMLS Semantic Network does not cover molecular genetics, ontological semantic relations for this domain were created for Sem Gen. The allowable relations were defined in two classes: gene-disease interactions and gene-gene interactions.

Other Systems

The information submitted to the repository by SemRep and SemGen could be supplemented with output from other natural language processing technologies that produce relationships. Phenotypic information from clinical narrative could be made accessible with the NLP system described by Friedman *et al.*. For molecular biology phenomena, several systems use syntactic templates and shallow parsing to produce a variety of relations, including gene and protein functions, protein interactions, and protein modifications such as phosphorylation. Friedman *et al.* use extensive linguistic processing for relations on molecular pathways, while Lussier *et al.* use a similar approach to identify phenotypic context for genetic phenomena.

Converting Structured Data into a Common Format

Since, relations in structured resources are already represented in some kind of formalism, their conversion to a common format is somewhat easier than extraction from text. However, the challenges in normalising such knowledge are not unlike those encountered with textual data. In both cases, knowledge extraction involves syntactic issues and semantic issues.

Various formalisms are used to represent structured data, including relational databases, tables, graphs, etc. Currently, no universal conversion mechanism is available. Moreover, the semantics of the data is often implicit or limited, for example, to short column names in a database schema. The objective of the conversion is the creation of 'normalised knowledge'. This effort, in the context of knowledge management, is somewhat equivalent to term normalisation. Knowledge normalisation ensures that the same entity referred to in different resources is ultimately identified in such a way that it is recognised as a unique thing. Knowledge normalisation forms the basis for information and data integration.

Description of Resources

Over the past twenty years, NLM has developed many knowledge resources, from various perspectives. Terminological resources such as the *Unified Medical Language System* (UMLS) result from the integration of many existing terminologies and ontologies, represented in a common formalism–UMLS' Rich Release Format—and partially normalised. While synonymous terms are grouped together as names for a given concept, synonymous relationships are typically not identified as such.

Nevertheless, with some 8 million relations, the UMLS Metathesaurus constitutes an important resource, providing mostly hierarchical relations and co-occurrence relations. Another source of structured knowledge is represented by the many databases available under the umbrella of the NCBI's Entrez system. While some databases such as MEDLINE/PubMed and *Online Mendelian Inheritance in Man* (OMIM) are mostly textual resources, many other NCBI databases contain predominantly structured information.

Entrez Gene, for example, is a gene-centric resource in which a record provides gene properties such as names, associated diseases, function, sequence, etc. While numerous links have been created across the resources in the Entrez system for navigation purposes, such links typically require human interpretation and therefore cannot be used for knowledge discovery purposes in high-throughput systems. Finally, structured databases and knowledge bases are also available outside NLM.

One example of large, publicly available genomic resource is represented by the genome annotations for the major model organisms. Here, the existence of a controlled vocabulary—the Gene Ontology—has contributed to developing unified functional annotations, integrated in systems such as the Mouse Genome Database and the Saccharomyces Genome Database. In the clinical domain, the various knowledge bases of drug information constitute important resources about drug-drug interactions, drug kinetics and metabolism, and indications and contraindications. DRUGDEX, produced by Micromedex, is an example of such a resource.

Representing Normalised Knowledge

One of the strengths of the World Wide Web is that it relies on textual information, easily created and interpreted by humans. This is also one of its principal limitations. The absence of explicit semantics prevents agents from being able to make sense of the information on the Web. This is the motivation of the Semantic Web, which aims at creating a vast collections of integrated and interoperable resources.

There is an obvious parallel between the Semantic Web and the Biomedical Knowledge Repository we propose to create. The technologies developed for the Semantic Web offer possible solutions to some of the challenges we face, including selecting a formalism for normalised biomedical knowledge and identification issues for biomedical entities. It is worth noting that some of these issues are still actively being debated in the Semantic Web community, especially in the Semantic Web Health Care and Life Sciences Interest Group.

Formalism

Many of the resources produced by NLM and other organisations are available in XML, the eXtensible Markup Language. However, the semantics of XML is limited. In addition to XML, the World Wide Web Consortium (W3C) has produced the specifications of other formalisms for representing resources.

Collectively know as Semantic Web technologies, these specifications define the building blocks of the Semantic Web. Of particular interest to us is the Resource Description Framework. RDF extends the capabilities of the extensible markup language XML as it enables many-to-many relationships between resources and data. The resulting structure is a graph in which the nodes are resources or data and the edges are relationships.

The basic unit in RDF is therefore the equivalent of a triple, similar to a relation in the UMLS Metathesaurus or a predication extracted by SemRep. RDF integrates limited inference rules, enabling, for example, the definition of subclasses and subproperties.

Some extensive resources such as UniProt have already been converted to RDF. The BioRDF task force of the W3C Semantic Web Health Care and Life Sciences Interest Group currently investigates methods whereby existing biomedical resources can be converted to RDF.

Such methods include XSLT, GRDDL and DB2RDF, among others. The *eXtensible Stylesheet Language Transformation* (XSLT) uses a stylesheet approach to converting XML to RDF. GRDDL specifies associations between markup languages–including XLM–and RDF. Finally, DB2RDF is used to convert databases to RDF.

Identification Issues

In order for RDF triples to form a graph–and for integrated knowledge to be interoperable-entities and relationships must be identified consistently and unambiguously. For example, if the disease *Neurofibromatosis 2* is identified by the code *SNOMEDCT:92503002* in one resource and by the code *MESH:D016518* in another, the RDF triples involving *SNOMEDCT:92503002* and *MESH:D016518* will not come together as expected unless both resource are converted to the other annotation system or mappings are created between the two systems.

For example, the UMLS Metathesaurus could be used to convert or bridge between MeSH and SNOMED CT, in this case through the concept *C0027832*. The predications extracted from the literature by SemRep already use UMLS codes to identify biomedical entities. From a technical perspective, several technologies have been developed by various communities to implement identification mechanisms for RDF.

There are three major identification mechanisms:

- LSID (Life Science Identifier), promoted by the Life Sciences community. Examples of applications using LSID include Taverna and resources created by the BioPathways Consortium;
- Solutions based on the HTTP protocol, promoted by the W3C; and
- ARK (Archive Resource Key), promoted by the Digital Library community.

There are important differences among three mechanisms regarding location independence, backward compatibility, resolution mechanism and versioning. It is unclear at this time what mechanism would suit our needs best.

Pilot Project: Converting Entrez Gene to RDF

As a proof of concept, we converted the Entrez Gene database into RDF. The entire Gene database in its native ASN.1 format was downloaded by FTP from the NCBI web site and later converted to XML using the programme gene2xml provided by NCBI. Using the *eXtensible Stylesheet Language Transformation* (XSLT) approach, we mapped the element tags of the XML representation to more intuitive relationship names manually, and used them during the automatic conversion to RDF. Finally, we stored this RDF version of Entrez Gene in the Oracle 10g relational database management system, which provides support for storing and querying native RDF data. The conversion process is illustrated in figure.

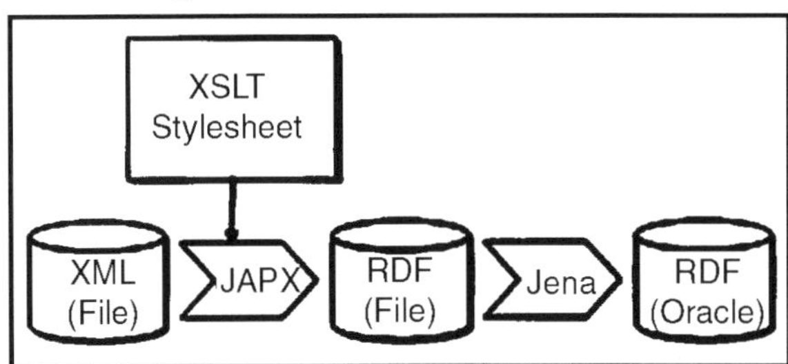

Fig. Overview of the Conversion of Enrez Gene from XML to RDF

Mapping XML Element Tags to RDF Properties

While XML data can be mechanically converted to RDF, the resulting RDF graph would be of limited interest because the semantics of the properties is most often implicit in XML and needs to be made explicit. Starting from one typical Entrez Gene record, we identified all its XML element tags, corresponding to the properties of the gene, as described in the Gene record.

Examples of such properties include *<Genetrack_geneid>* and *<Genetrack_update-date>*, indicating the identifier and the update date of the gene record, respectively. A total of 124 unique elements tags were identified. Because XML element tags represent gene properties, they were transformed into predicates in RDF. For example, *<Genetrack_geneid>* becomes *has_unique_geneid* and relates the gene record to its unique identifier in the Gene database. Note that the RDF property now conveys the notion–implicit in the XML representation–that the identifier is a unique identifier, corresponding to a primary key in a relational database. Converting XML elements to RDF properties requires familiarity with the structure and content of the original record structure and is a key component to the mapping process. After eliminating redundant and superfluous XML element tags, 106 unique RDF properties were created. The mapping of Entrez gene XML element tags to RDF properties is specified formally using the XPath language and constitutes a stylesheet. This stylesheet is specific to the conversion of the Entrez Gene database.

Converting XML to RDF through XSLT

Once the stylesheet is created, it can serve as an auxiliary file for existing programmes realising the XML to RDF conversion. In other words, the major interest of this approach is that no specific code is required for the conversion, because the transformation logic resides entirely in the stylesheet. We used JAXP, the Java *Application Programming Interface* (API) to XML, to implement the conversion. The resulting 411 million RDF triples were then loaded in a store using Oracle 10g using the Jena API.

Lessons Learned, Issues and Challenges

This experiment confirmed the feasibility of converting a large resource from XML to RDF. It also showed that the issues are not technical, but rather lie in the necessity of making explicit the relationships represented implicitly by element tags in XML. This step requires the manual intervention of a domain expert. In our experience, it took less than a week for one person familiar with both bioinformatics and stylesheets to formalise the mapping between XML element tags and RDF properties.

Although the stylesheet created is specific to the Entrez Gene database, it is expected that part of the expertise acquired during this transformation can be applied to transforming other NCBI resources. The major unresolved issue concerns entity identification. If the RDF graph resulting from the conversion of Entrez Gene is to be integrated with clinical or bibliographic information, the diseases associated with genes must be represented not as literals as they currently are, but by their identifiers in the corresponding clinical and bibliographic controlled vocabularies, or with the *concept unique identifier* (CUI) in the UMLS Metathesaurus. Only after such mapping will the RDF graph integrating Entrez Gene and, say, the Metathesaurus, support queries such as *Find all genes associated with neurodegenerative diseases*. The knowledge required in this cases comes in part from Entrez gene and from UMLS.

Integrating Predications: Biomedical Knowledge Repository

The Biomedical Knowledge Repository can be understood as a specialised version of the Semantic Web. It consists of an extensive collection of predications, represented in a common format, processable by computers. Biomedical terminologies and ontologies provide the concepts involved in the facts. Logical reasoners extend the capabilities of the repository by inferring new knowledge. Each fact in the repository is annotated with metainformation regarding its origin, making it possible for applications exploiting the repository to select facts of interest in a given context and for a particular task. Once it is fully populated, the Biomedical Knowledge Repository is expected to comprise several hundred million facts, collected from hundreds of sources.

Origin of the Predications

The Biomedical Knowledge Repository (BKR) comprises predications form three major sources: extracted from the biomedical literature by NLP programmes such as SemRep, converted from existing structured knowledge bases, and contributed by users. In our vision of the BKR, NLM not only contributes to populating the BKR, but also makes it available to the community as a framework for researchers to deposit their predications.

Predications resulting from experiments, from alternative processing of the literature, and inferred from other predictions, for example, can be contributed by members of the community and made available to others. One measure of success of the BKR would be for it to become a standard repository for the knowledge created through biomedical research experiments. In order to maintain the consistency and integrity of the BKR, its developers would have to follow guidelines regarding formalism of the predications and identification mechanism for biomedical entities.

Metainformation Associated with the Predications

Just as few users need all the vocabularies in the UMLS Metathesaurus for a given purpose, it is unlikely that all predications will be equally useful for a given task, such as question answering. Instead, a mechanism supporting the selection of relevant sets of predications is needed.

The metainformation associated with each predication enables this selection and may include the source of the predication, the method of extraction, the date of extraction, in addition to the usual metadata associated with MEDLINE/PubMed citations for predications extracted from the literature.

Researchers contributing predications to the BKR will be requested to annotate them with similar metainformation. Another form of contribution to the repository is to provide not predications, but annotations to existing predications. Such a contribution represents a form of collaborative curation of the repository by the community, similar to the framework developed by the SWAN project for the Alzheimer research community.

Storing the Predications

Several technological solutions, called RDF stores, have been developed for storing information in RDF format, generally implemented on top of some storage system. One such open source RDF database is Sesame. More recently, traditional database management systems have started offering direct support for native RDF triples. For example, version 10g of the Oracle system supports RDF in addition to the relational model. Since, we need to store large amounts of both RDF and traditional information, we started experimenting with Oracle 10g while converting Entrez Gene to RDF last summer. Preliminary results are encouraging although we might face optimisation issues.

Querying the Predications

Analogous to SQL for relational databases, SPARQL is the language for querying RDF. Like SQL, SPAQRL queries have a SELECT and a WHERE clause. However, in a SPARQL query, the WHERE clause follows the pattern of a RDF triple in which at least one element of the triple is replaced by a variable. In the BKR, the predications to be queried would first be selected based on their annotations. For example, a typical query supporting multidocument summarisation would be as follows.

Select all predications from MEDLINE/PubMed returned by a PubMed query on *metabolic syndrome*, restricted to citations from *JAMA*, *Am J Cardiol.* and *J Hypertens.*, published between 2004 and 2005. Additionally, select those predications from the UMLS Metathesaurus and Entrez Gene having at least one node in common with those from the literature.

Integrating Predications

The query example presented above illustrates the interest of integrating knowledge under a unique framework. First, there is a unique namespace for all knowledge in the BKR. As suggested, largely rely on the UMLS for identifying biomedical entities.

Second, once integrated into a graph, the predications can serve as a basis for inferencing, creating additional knowledge along the way. This represents an advantage over traditional database and information retrieval approaches. Finally, complex rules can be written to implement additional reasoning. For example, it is possible to restrict queries to those redundant predications asserted in more than 2 sources and for which the frequency of occurrence is above a certain threshold.

Estimated Size of the Repository

Once fully instantiated, the Biomedical Knowledge Repository is expected to comprise several hundred million predications extracted from the literature, terminological resources and structured knowledge bases. Assuming an average of ten predications is extracted from the title and abstract of each MEDLINE/ PubMed citation, we can expect about 150 million predications from MEDLINE/ PubMed.

The UMLS Metathesaurus records about 9 million relations, either symbolic or statistical. Some seven million functional annotations for the major model organism databases are recorded in the Gene Ontology database. Finally, our conversion experiment with Entrez Gene yielded over 400 million RDF triples. In this experiment, the objective was to systematically represent in RDF all the information present in the original XML file. In fact, part of this information would become metainformation in the context of the BKR, resulting in a significantly smaller number of triples to be actually contributed to the repository.

Exploiting the Repository: Semantic Medline Web Portal

As a pilot project to exploit a preliminary version of the Biomedical Knowledge Repository, we are developing a Web portal, called Semantic Medline, for managing the results of PubMed searches. The portal is designed as a Java-based Web application that seamlessly integrates PubMed, SemRep processing of the results of the search, automatic summarisation, and, finally, visualisation of the results, with links to the underlying citations and relevant additional knowledge in the UMLS Metathesaurus, the Genetics Home Reference, and Entrez Gene. Realtime access is achieved by pre-processing text from MEDLINE/ PubMed abstracts and other sources with SemRep/SemGen and storing the results in a database.

Background

Several recent systems visualise the results of information identified in text as a way of providing users with enhanced access to the information retrieved. Results are often represented as a graph of interrelated relationships. The Telemakus project is based on relationships identified by hand and is meant to enable knowledge discovery through interactive visual maps of linked concepts among documents. Jensen *et al*. constructed literature networks of genes found relevant in gene expression data analysis.

Analysis is based on co-occurrence of genes in MEDLINE/PubMed abstracts. Van der Eijk *et al*. use various relations for literature-based discovery.

The relationships represent co-occurrence of MeSH headings associated with MEDLINE/PubMed citations by a mapping programme. Feldman represent several gene-related relations in a graph. The relations were extracted with a type of underspecified natural language processing. Finally, Tao *et al.* visualise genomic information across both structured and textual databases.

Implementation

Semantic Medline is implemented as a three-tier, Java EE-based Web application. The three-tier architecture allows for the separation of user interface, application logic and data storage, providing improved performance, easier maintenance and scalability. We leverage mature open-source technologies in the development to the extent possible. The prototype runs in a Tomcat servlet container on an Apache Web server. It has been developed using the Apache Struts Web application framework. This framework encourages the use of *Model-View- Controller* (MVC) paradigm to provide a clean separation of application model, navigational code, and page design code through the use of Java Servlet API.

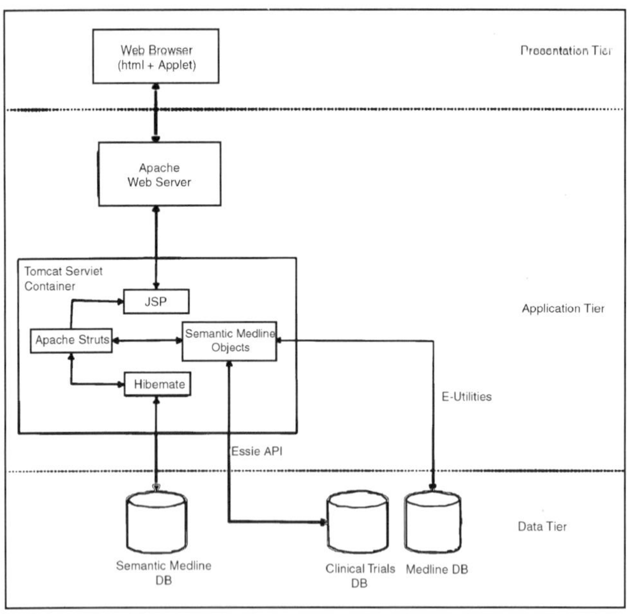

Fig. Semantic Medline System Architecture

The controller is a Java servlet that mediates the application flow; the model comprises Java classes that represent the functionality of the semantic tools and the view is JSP pages that contain dynamic content. A MySQL database is used to store Semantic Medline data, which includes semantic predications extracted from MEDLINE/PubMed abstracts and ClinicalTrials.gov clinical study texts as well as a subset of UMLS Metathesaurus data. The database tables are prepopulated from plain text files that contain SemRep/SemGen output and Metathesaurus data using Perl scripts. Hibernate *object/relational mapping* (ORM) tool is used to programmatically access the database. We use such Hibernate features as database connection pooling and query caching for increased performance.

Using Semantic Medline

MEDLINE/PubMed contains more than 16 million citations drawn from nearly 4,600 journals with biomedical relevance. Searches often retrieve large numbers of items. For example, the query 'diabetes' returns 207,997 citations. Although users can restrict searches by language, date and publication type, results can still be large.

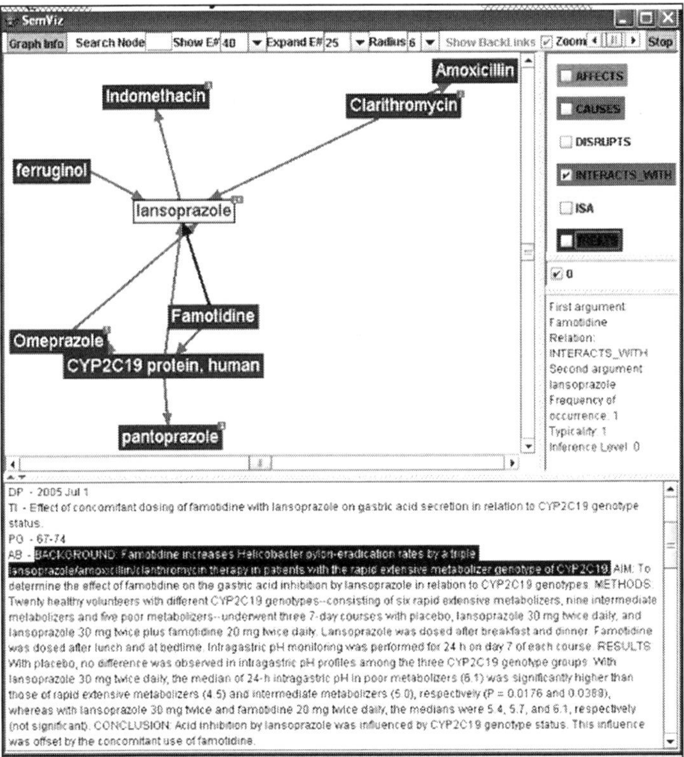

Fig. Summary of 564 MEDLINE/PubMed Citations for Lansoprazole

For example, a query for treatment for diabetes, limited to articles published in 2003 and having an abstract in English finds 3,621 items; limiting this further to articles describing clinical trials still returns 390 citations. It is difficult for a user to effectively exploit the information in this many citations. Semantic Medline addresses this difficulty by allowing users to summarise the results of searches focused on one of several points of view, including diagnosis and treatment of disorders, drug interactions and adverse events, genetic basis of disease, and pharmacogenomics. A clinical scenario based on a summary focused on drug interactions illustrates the potential use of Semantic Medline for taking advantage of the research literature in clinical practice. In a hypothetical situation, a patient presents with peptic ulcer and tests positive for *Helicobacter pylori*. The clinician has tried several standard regimens including two different triple regimens: and; however, the patient still tests positive for *H. pylori*.

In order to gain insight from recent research, the physician uses Semantic Medline to issue a PubMed search for lansoprazole. SemRep extracts 5,971 predications from 564 citations returned by this search, and automatic summarisation for drug interactions involving lansoprazole condenses the final list of predications to 182, which are visualised by the system as the interactive graph in figure. Figure provides an informative overview of recent research on lansoprazole represented as predications asserting INTERACTS_WITH. Each predication is linked to the MEDLINE/PubMed citation that generated it.

Of interest for this case are two predications in the graph: 'Lansoprazole INTERACTS_WITH Famotidine' and 'Famotidine INTERACTS_WITH CYPC19 Enzyme.' SemRep extracted the first predication from a citation with title seen in the first line of table and the second from a citation with in the second line.

Table 4.2. MEDLINE/PubMed Citations

PMID	Title
15963082	Effect of concomitant dosing of famotidine with lansoprazole on gastric acid secretion in relation to
CYP2C19	Genotype Status
15710002	Concomitant dosing of famotidine with a triple therapy increases the cure rates of Helicobacter pylori infections in patients with the homozygous extensive metaboliser genotype of CYP2C19

Both citations discuss the salutary effect of combining famotidine with lansoprazole. In the second citation, which reports on a randomised controlled trial, the authors realised between 63 per cent to 100 per cent eradication of *H. pylori* with the addition of famotidine to a standard triple therapy and conclude that this is a promising option for patients who phenotypically are extensive metabolisers. If the patient in this hypothetical scenario falls under this category, it would be a potentially valuable regimen to pursue.

EVALUATION PLAN

We intend to follow a multifaceted evaluation plan, focusing evaluation activities on specific aspects of the project.

Evaluating Extraction

For this project, effectiveness of information extracted from text crucially depends on the accuracy of SemRep and SemGen. We have performed linguistic evaluation across a wide variety of predicates that includes the clinical as well as the genetic domain. Among the predicates evaluated were Treats, Prevents, Location_of, Causes, Isa, Interacts_ With, Affects, Disrupts, Process_of, Part_of, Manifestation_ of, Associated_With, Inhibits, Stimulates and PREDISPOSES. Recall on the extraction of semantic propositions with these predicates has ranged from 41 per cent to 74 per cent and precision from 68 per cent to 84 per cent. Previous evaluations have been reported in and as suggested, continue this evaluation paradigm.

The framework for evaluating knowledge extraction from terminological and structured knowledge bases is not as well established as the evaluation of relation extraction from text. However, several aspects are particularly important. The rules used for the conversion need to be reviewed independently by several experts for a given knowledge base and integrated across databases in order to ensure consistency of the extraction of the relationships. Key to the consistency of the graph is also the mapping of literals to concepts–the nodes in the RDF graph and their consistent representation by identifiers from authoritative sources.

Evaluating Integration

Ideally, the graph resulting from integrating knowledge from several sources is consistent both structurally and semantically. Therefore structural techniques based on graph theory and semantic approaches similar to reasoning services created for description logics are expected to play a central role in evaluating the quality of knowledge integration in the repository.

However, the UMLS Metathesaurus, while resulting from the integration of a much smaller body of terminological knowledge, is already not always structurally or semantically consistent. Like the Metathesaurus, the Biomedical Knowledge Repository will allow contradictory predications to be represented as long as they occur in the original information sources. However, consistency is expected to be found at both structural and semantic levels on limited subsets of the repository.

Evaluating Applications

When evaluating applications such as automatic summarisation, it is useful to compare results against curated resources. Standard measures of performance can be calculated with respect to the reference standard chosen. For treatment of disease, the British Medical Journal clinical evidence concise is one alternative. For drug interactions and adverse events, Micromedex DRUGDEX, DrugDigest, and the First DataBank's National Drug Data File can be used. A more ambitious method, requiring human experts, is task-based evaluation. Ultimately, user-centred evaluations such as the one described by McKeown must be considered.

PROJECT SCHEDULE

- *Year 1:* Pilot study, processing all of MEDLINE/PubMed, integrating Entrez Gene
- *Year 2:* Integrating UMLS and other NCBI resources
- *Year 3:* Annotating predications, opening the BKR to collaborative development and use
- *Year 4:* Fully integrated ALS system available

PROJECT RESOURCES

This project relies on a range of existing competencies and resources and has the potential to federate research energies throughout the Lister Hill Center. In addition to the efforts of the two core component projects, Semantic Knowledge Representation and Medical Ontology Research, the success of this project relies on collaboration with the Indexing Initiative, the Lexical Systems Project, and ClinicalTrials.gov. The effectiveness of applications drawing on the repository could be strengthened by providing links to Visible Human images where appropriate. In order to accomplish the goals of this project additional staff and equipment are required: staff for creating and populating the repository and servers for providing effective access to the repository. Initially, PubMed and ClinicalTrials.gov will be processed by SemRep and SemGen and the predications extracted will be stored in the repository. Dedicated servers are required to process PubMed for this project.

10

Library Resource Sharing and Networking

The term resource applies to a thing, person or action to which one resorts to in times of need and sharing indicates allotting, apportioning or contributing something that is owned, to benefit others. Resource sharing, therefore, refers to reciprocity, implying a partnership where each member has something useful to contribute to others and which each is willing and able to make available when needed.

Resource sharing is an empty concept, but for the approach permitting resource sharing to work is that which:

- Entails having resources to share
- Having a willingness to share them, and
- Having a plan for accomplishing resource sharing

Resource Sharing is an integral part of modern library services. In the developed countries, no library services can be thought without sharing of resources. In the past, rupee was limited to the interlibrary loan system. In the modern age, with the development of science and technology and innovations of techniques and devices, resource sharing has become easier and fruitful due to the availability of databases, information network, and online sharing facilities. Thus, the resourcesharing system helps one library to access to resources of other libraries.

When resource sharing is agreed upon by participating institutions, then the following aspects must be planned:

- Identify and locate major collections, sources and materials
- Assemble, publish and distribute collective information for all participating bodies
- Workout the basis for sharing, reference service, lending service, copying service, access to materials, delivery service, and lists of holdings
- Establish means of sharing ideas, development and problems in the form of a newsletter
- Plan for new developments in the knowledge of what others are doing
- Developing a National Information Policy

The following are the most important benefits of resource sharing to participating institutions:

- Easy access to materials
- Enables co-operating institutions to extend limited resources
- Allow greater staff specialization
- Improve services to users
- Avoids unnecessary duplication
- Reduces the number of places which will need to go for services
- Improves working relationships between cooperating libraries.

Resource sharing refers to a joint use of resources available on a system or a network by user or peripherals. In the language of information management, when we talk about resource sharing we simply mean collective use of information of all types by various end users from a control coordinating unit or from within a network component at a reduced cost with easy accessibility.

Library cooperation and resource-sharing activity can take place in several forms and can happen at many levels, which include:

- Interlibrary loans/reciprocal borrowing privileges
- Exchange or sharing of expertise, resources, and facilities
- Exchange of publications and photocopies and other reprographic services
- Sharing of bibliographic information
- Cooperative acquisition, cooperative cataloguing, and cooperative collection development preparation of union list of holdings
- Cooperative relationship and network development

The implementation of resource sharing is largely depends on library networking. It gives an easy and wider access to information as members have an expanded information-base and service. A network is a form of arrangement or an administrative structure that links a group of individuals or organizations who have agreed to work together and/or share resources. Information networking entails the sharing of resources so that the information needs of both actual and potential users of information—from the local to national level—of all network participants are met. The network enables the participating bodies to facilitate and expand their users' access to literature and information without corresponding investment in purchase, and processing of information is exchanged through the network on a formal basis. The network may be responsible for coordinating, organizing and providing information and literature support at the national and international level. The main activities and functions of the network are as follows:

Acquisition of materials:

- Joint purchasing of materials
- Assignment of specialization in material acquisition
- Coordinated subscription

- Exchange of duplicate holdings

Technical services:

- Co-operative cataloguing
- Abstracting and indexing services
- Interlibrary loan
- Reciprocal borrowing privileges
- Reference and/or referral services

Publication programme/repackaging information:

- Union catalogue/list of periodicals
- Mutual notification of purchase through lists of new arrivals or acquisition list
- Bibliography development
- Newsletters
- Joint directories of personnel, projects, consultants, resource persons, etc.
- Manuals

Coordination services:

- Clearing house functions
- Retrieval and storage function
- Referral center

Delivery/mailing service:

- Research, training and other special services
  - User interest surveys
  - Joint research projects
  - In-service personnel training
  - Workshops and meetings
  - Translation services.

LIBRARY NETWORKS

Libraries are at the forefront of providing no-fee Internet access to the public. In 1994, just 8.2 percent of public libraries provided this service; as of 2009, 100 percent of libraries do so. While this is a vital role in every community, the library is the only source of no-fee public Internet access in 71 percent of communities.

The core mission of libraries is to connect people with ideas and information. Internet access makes it possible for libraries to fulfill this mission through online resources that can, for example, help people find jobs, improve their skills, access government services, create small businesses, complete school homework, and conduct research. Libraries have reported high demand for Internet access; indeed, in the majority of libraries, the demand for publicaccess computers far outweighs the supply. As demand for public access to the Internet grows, so, too, does the need for higher bandwidth in the library.

In some communities, libraries play the important role of broadband anchor institution; in other words, by obtaining high-bandwidth connections, they drive the deployment of advanced technologies to communities that might be unable to obtain that level of service through residential demand alone.

In short, libraries that are able to meet the demand for no-fee public Internet access play a vital role in serving both their users and their communities. To help libraries achieve this capability, the Bill and Melinda Gates Foundation initiated the Opportunity Online Broadband Grant Programme. This programme provides funding and support to help State Library agencies in seven states—Massachusetts, New York, Virginia, Arkansas, Kansas, California, and Texas—develop leadership and improve library connectivity to the Internet.

The American Library Association's Office for Information Technology Policy (OITP) is participating in this programme, providing research and consulting services to state libraries, as well as developing publications that address key issues salient to the program's goals. The purpose of this publication is to provide a snapshot of five different library networks that provide users with no-fee Internet access.

LEADERSHIP, COOPERATION, AND THE ABILITY TO LEARN FROM PAST SUCCESSES

Strong leadership was an essential element in the development of each of the five networks. At the same time, leadership was distributed among different players at the state, regional, and local levels and was not the exclusive domain of one person or organisation. Moreover, cooperation among these players was a hallmark of the effort. The case studies also illustrate how the various organisations involved often drew on the experiences of other successful cooperative projects to help in the development of their network.

In the formative stage of the Ohio Public Library and Information Network (OPLIN), public libraries that wanted to emulate successful school and academic networks broached the idea of a public library network with the state library association. This association, later called the Ohio Library Council (OLC), assumed a leadership role, and two OLC staff members organised planning and advocacy efforts that led to OPLIN's development.

The West Virginia Network was the first network to centralise the state's computing and data needs. Statewide Library Network (SLN) leadership acknowledged learning from this first statewide network during the project development. Taking a cooperative approach similar to that applied in the development of OPLIN, Wisconsin's local and regional libraries and State Library officials worked together to define the libraries' role in BadgerNet. A past collaborative project to establish a distance learning video network was a key factor in the creation of a 1993 Governor's Blue Ribbon Telecommunications Infrastructure Task Force, which in turn recommended the creation of

BadgerNet. The Maine School and Library Network (MSLN) was also the result of cooperation between statewide library associations and the State Library agency. Finally, the member libraries of California's Peninsula Library System (PLS) developed the Peninsula Libraries Automated Network (PLAN) based on their past success with a common circulation and catalog system. Perhaps the most important factor contributing to the success of PLAN is the spirit and habit of cooperation among PLS members. Since, 1982, member libraries have been cooperating to operate a joint circulation system.

Such collaborations require that libraries engage in significant give-and-take to modify longstanding local policies and procedures so as to accommodate a centralised system. This habit of collaboration led to the success of other collective endeavors, including PLAN.

AGGREGATION OF DEMAND AND SERVICES

Aggregation of demand is an acknowledged successful approach to network management. Among its benefits are:

- Improved planning
- Support for a business case for providers to deploy broadband
- More affordable pricing
- Sharing of costs

Aggregation of demand allowed the establishment of each of the five successful networks profiled here, and its benefits have contributed to the networks' continued success. For example, MSLN aggregates library traffic to two nodes, which results in lower recurring expenses for Internet access. Aggregation offers other, less obvious benefits. An example is streamlining and standardisation of members' E-rate participation. All of the statewide networks profiled here regularly file for E-rate discounts on behalf of their members or offer assistance to members in doing so.

A centralised application relieves the burden on individual libraries. MSLN files an aggregated application for federal E-rate discounts and an application for Maine's state universal service fund. Wisconsin files one aggregated E-rate application that includes every K-12 school district and public library on BadgerNet (about 910 sites), and also completes all the required follow-up.

Considering that the most frequently cited reason for libraries' non-participation in the E-rate programme is the complexity of the process, this is a very real benefit with tangible results. Standardisation is a key requirement for aggregation. OPLIN, MSLN, PLS, and BadgerNet require the same router configuration for every library site; SLN requires that all members have the same network equipment; and every school and library on BadgerNet has the same standard Ethernet interface.

Standardisation avoids the logistical challenges associated with customisation. It also allows for aggregation of technical support services. The benefits of aggregating technical support are readily apparent in West Virginia, where these services are typically beyond the means of individual public libraries with limited budgets and staff expertise. MSLN employs a shared project manager to provide planning guidance to individual libraries, a service that would otherwise be too costly for individual libraries.

USE OF DEMONSTRATIONS

OITP's past research suggests that technology demonstrations are necessary to convince a library's community to support a major new effort such as a regional or statewide network. Such demonstrations, while providing essential training to library staff, also serve a critical outreach and public relations function.

For example, during the initial phase of network development, OPLIN staff members visited libraries around the state to demonstrate how access to the Internet would help their users. While demonstrations can be very helpful in growing network membership, their usefulness does not end with the network's establishment.

OPLIN and SLN representatives continue to provide information on network services and their use at annual conferences and meetings. Other library systems offer ongoing training on new resources provided via the network and on how library staff can use these resources to improve library services and ultimately benefit the library's patrons. Demonstrations can also help achieve the network's sustainability when used as an advocacy tool for continued funding and support of network projects.

ROLE FOR LIBRARY REPRESENTATIVES IN NETWORK GOVERNANCE

The case study networks have widely varying governance and management structures.

For example:

- The Maine Public Utilities Commission (MPUC) governs MSLN.
- Wisconsin's Department of Administration manages BadgerNet.
- The West Virginia Library Commission administers SLN.

All of these networks are dependent on the network's information technology (IT) staff for ensuring the day-to-day management of network operations. But just as there are differences in network management (*e.g.,* some may be outsourced), there are also differences in overall network governance and how much input the library community has to make decisions or to set network policy. For example, the OPLIN governing board in Ohio consists solely of member library representatives. Wisconsin's BadgerNet Advisory Council includes representatives of all network users including libraries, K-12 schools, higher education and state government. The Advisory Council advises the state Administration Department in areas like member bandwidth needs and planning for the next generation network.

California's PLS allows the technical staff of member libraries to be involved with network issues through a committee structure.

NETWORKING THROUGH COMPUTERS

A computer is emerging and no one could keep himself/herself away from it any longer. But, what are the types of a network within the arena of computers? Those are LAN, MAN and WAN. Not only this, there are certain topologies associated with it and there are certain components which carry out these functions. We need to acquaint ourselves with these technical words and their usages when we move to the area of networking through computers and extend its use in reaching out to adult learners.

Types of Network

Based on geographical dispersion of computers there are mainly three types of network.

- Local Area Network (LAN)
- Metropolitan Area Network (MAN)
- Wide Area Network (WAN)

Local Area Network

In this type of network computers and other communication devices are in a small area and are connected together (networked). The area can be single building, cluster of buildings in the same campus. Examples can be Local Area Network of Lab in which you may be working or a library which you may be using.

Metropolitan Area Network

A Metropolitan Area Network is basically a bigger version of LAN and normally uses similar technology. It might cover a group of nearby corporate offices or it can be in a city. It can be private or public.

Wide Area Network

Computers can be farther apart like covering cities, countries or even continents. The computers are connected by telephone lines or radio waves or optical fibres.

Network Topologies

Topology refers to the shape of a network or network's layout. How different nodes in a network are connected to each other and how they communicate is determined by the network's topology. There are four most common network topologies, namely,

- Bus Topology,
- Star Topology,

- Ring Topology and
- Mesh Topology.

Star Topology

All devices are connected to a central hub. Nodes communicate across the network by passing data through the hub.

Bus Topology

All devices are connected to a central cable, called the bus or backbone.

Ring Topology

All devices are connected to one another in the shape of a closed loop, so that each device is connected directly to two other devices, one on either side of it.

Mesh Topology or Point to Point Network

Devices are connected with many redundant interconnections between network nodes. In a true mesh topology every node has a connection to every other node in the network.

Network Components

The following are essential components for computer networking.

- Network hardware
- Transmission media
- Network software

Network Hardware

The basic component of computer network hardware is a computer. Computers on a network can be divided into two categories,

Server is the computer of higher power, and speed. It costs more. To this computer resources are attached. And the clients, also known as nodes access, are the resources which are attached to server. In peer to peer computer networks there are no servers.

Transmission Media

Communication of data propagation and processing of signals is called transmission. Signals travel from transmitter to receiver via a path. This path is called medium. Medium can be guided or unguided.

Guided Media

In guided media, data is sent along a physical path *i.e.* cables. There are several types of cables used in network. The type of cable chosen for a network is related to the network's topology protocol and size. Different types of cables:

- Coaxial cable looks like cable that brings the cable TV signal to television.
- Twisted pair copper wire cable looks like phone cable. Twisted pair cables come in two varieties, a. shielded and b. unshielded.
- Optical fibre cable

Unguided Media

Here no wire is installed. The data communication is predominantly sent by radio waves and microwaves.

Network Card

We will discuss about networking software. But hardware has also to be connected. Most important part of connection is the network card. This is the middle part of connection.

These cards are 8 bit cards, 16 bit cards and 32 bit cards. Each card has its own method of sending information (network protocol) through the cable. The most commonly used is Ethernet Protocol.

A network card is called Interface card, network adapter, a NIC etc. It is a circuit board or chip which allows the computer to communicate to other computers on a network.

Modem (MODulator / DEModulator)

A modem converts digital signals (computer signals) from the computer into analogue signals for transmission and vice versa for reception over a telephone line. There are four basic types of modems for a PC:

- External,
- USB,
- Internal and
- Built-in.

External and USB are set on your desk outside the PC, while as Internal and Built-in are inside the PC. Present day modems have 56 kilobites per second speed. ISDN (Integrated Services Digital Network) circuits are digital. In this conversion from digital to analogue is not required.

Switch

Switches are basically bridges, but usually have multiple ports. Switches connect network segments, using a table of addresses to determine the segment on which a packet needs to be transmitted.

Hubs

A hub is used to connect multiple computers and devices via a dedicated cable. It is cheap and connections are easy. It generally has 4, 8, 12, 24 ports.

Router

These are used to connect networks and to determine the optimal path along which the network traffic should be forwarded. They are occasionally called gateways. There are other network devices like repeaters, bridges, ports, etc.

Network Operating Software

Network operating software (NOS) is a collection of software and associated protocols that allow a set of autonomous computers, which are interconnected by a computer network, to be used together in a convenient and costeffective manner. It is similar to any other operating system like windows, DOS, etc. except it operates over more than one computer. It controls operation of the network system, including who uses it, when they can use it, what they have access to, and which network resources are available. At a basic level, the NOS allows network users to share files and peripherals such as disks and printers. They provide data integrity and security. The examples can be categories of NOS: The NetWare, LAN Manager, Solaris and Windows 2000 etc. The main categories of network software are:

- Peer to peer software and
- Client / Server-based

Peer to Peer Software

In peer to peer networking operating software users can share resources and files located on their computers and can access shared resources on other computers. There is no central server. All computers in the network are equal. They have similar capabilities and resources. Examples of Peer to peer network software are Windows XP, Windows 98. When you are working in Microsoft Office Word under Windows environment, you can share the shared documents. It is possible because Windows XP is peer to peer networking software.

Client Server Based (Two Tier)

This software is in two parts. One part which includes functions and services resides in one or more exclusive (dedicated) computers. This part is called server. It provides security and access to resources. Another part called 'client' resides on other computers (nodes / client). They access resources on the server. The network operating system allows multiple users to simultaneously share the same resources irrespective of physical location. Examples of Server based networking software are: Novel Netware, Windows NT, UNIX, Window 2000 etc.

Client Server Based (Three Tier) Here a client-software is split into two parts.

- Browser (user-interface) (thin client)
- Logic.

Thus two tier client-server becomes three tier architecture. The logic which describes how to access and process data is moved to a new server. This new server is server for thin client. Nothing changes in the server side.

LAN

Standards for LAN are Ethernet, LocalTalk (for Macs), Token Ring, the most popular in Ethernet Protocol. It allows for linear bus, star or tree topologies. Data can be transmitted over twisted pair, coaxial or fibre optic cable at a speed of 10mbps.

NETWORK CLASSIFICATION

The following list presents categories used for classifying networks.

Connection Method

Computer networks can be classified according to the hardware and software technology that is used to interconnect the individual devices in the network, such as optical fibre, Ethernet, Wireless LAN, HomePNA, Power line communication or G.hn. Ethernet uses physical wiring to connect devices. Frequently deployed devices include hubs, switches, bridges and/or routers.

Wireless LAN technology is designed to connect devices without wiring. These devices use radio waves or infrared signals as a transmission medium. ITU-T G.hn technology uses existing home wiring (coaxial cable, phone lines and power lines) to create a high-speed (up to 1 Gigabit/s) local area network.

Wired Technologies

- Twisted pair wire is the most widely used medium for telecommunication. Twisted-pair wires are ordinary telephone wires which consist of two insulated copper wires twisted into pairs and are used for both voice and data transmission. The use of two wires twisted together helps to reduce crosstalk and electromagnetic induction. The transmission speed ranges from 2 million bits per second to 100 million bits per second.
- Coaxial cable is widely used for cable television systems, office buildings, and other worksites for local area networks. The cables consist of copper or aluminum wire wrapped with insulating layer typically of a flexible material with a high dielectric constant, all of which are surrounded by a conductive layer. The layers of insulation help minimize interference and distortion. Transmission speed range from 200 million to more than 500 million bits per second.
- Optical fibre cable consists of one or more filaments of glass fibre wrapped in protective layers. It transmits light which can travel over

extended distances. Fibre-optic cables are not affected by electromagnetic radiation. Transmission speed may reach trillions of bits per second. The transmission speed of fibre optics is hundreds of times faster than for coaxial cables and thousands of times faster than a twisted-pair wire.

Wireless Technologies

- *Terrestrial Microwave:* Terrestrial microwaves use Earth-based transmitter and receiver. The equipment look similar to satellite dishes. Terrestrial microwaves use low-gigahertz range, which limits all communications to line-of-sight. Path between relay stations spaced approx. 30 miles apart. Microwave antennas are usually placed on top of buildings, towers, hills, and mountain peaks.
- *Communications Satellites*: The satellites use microwave radio as their telecommunications medium which are not deflected by the Earth's atmosphere. The satellites are stationed in space, typically 22,000 miles (for geosynchronous satellites) above the equator. These Earth-orbiting systems are capable of receiving and relaying voice, data, and TV signals.
- *Cellular and PCS Systems*: Use several radio communications technologies. The systems are divided to different geographic areas. Each area has a low-power transmitter or radio relay antenna device to relay calls from one area to the next area.
- *Wireless LANs*: Wireless local area network use a high-frequency radio technology similar to digital cellular and a low-frequency radio technology. Wireless LANs use spread spectrum technology to enable communication between multiple devices in a limited area. An example of open-standards wireless radio-wave technology is IEEE
- Infrared communication, which can transmit signals between devices within small distances not more than 10 metres peer to peer or (face to face) without any body in the line of transmitting.

Scale

Networks are often classified as local area network (LAN), wide area network (WAN), metropolitan area network (MAN), personal area network (PAN), virtual private network (VPN), campus area network (CAN), storage area network (SAN), and others, depending on their scale, scope and purpose, *e.g.*, controller area network (CAN) usage, trust level, and access right often differ between these types of networks. LANs tend to be designed for internal use by an organization's internal systems and employees in individual physical locations, such as a building, while WANs may connect physically separate parts of an organization and may include connections to third parties.

Functional Relationship (Network Architecture)

Computer networks may be classified according to the functional relationships which exist among the elements of the network, *e.g.*, active networking, client–server and peer-to-peer (workgroup) architecture.

Network Topology

Computer networks may be classified according to the network topology upon which the network is based, such as bus network, star network, ring network, mesh network. Network topology is the coordination by which devices in the network are arranged in their logical relations to one another, independent of physical arrangement. Even if networked computers are physically placed in a linear arrangement and are connected to a hub, the network has a star topology, rather than a bus topology. In this regard the visual and operational characteristics of a network are distinct. Networks may be classified based on the method of data used to convey the data, these include digital and analog networks.

TYPES OF NETWORKS BASED ON PHYSICAL SCOPE

Common types of computer networks may be identified by their scale.

Personal Area Network

A personal area network (PAN) is a computer network used for communication among computer and different information technological devices close to one person. Some examples of devices that are used in a PAN are personal computers, printers, fax machines, telephones, PDAs, scanners, and even video game consoles. A PAN may include wired and wireless connections between devices. The reach of a PAN typically extends to 10 metres. A wired PAN is usually constructed with USB and Firewire connections while technologies such as Bluetooth and infrared communication typically form a wireless PAN

Local Area Network

A local area network (LAN) is a network that connects computers and devices in a limited geographical area such as home, school, computer laboratory, office building, or closely positioned group of buildings. Each computer or device on the network is a node. Current wired LANs are most likely to be based on Ethernet technology, although new standards like ITU-T G.hn also provide a way to create a wired LAN using existing home wires (coaxial cables, phone lines and power lines). All interconnected devices must understand the network layer (layer 3), because they are handling multiple subnets (the different colours). Those inside the library, which have only 10/

100 Mbit/s Ethernet connections to the user device and a Gigabit Ethernet connection to the central router, could be called "layer 3 switches" because they only have Ethernet interfaces and must understand IP. It would be more correct to call them access routers, where the router at the top is a distribution router that connects to the Internet and academic networks' customer access routers. The defining characteristics of LANs, in contrast to WANs (Wide Area Networks), include their higher data transfer rates, smaller geographic range, and no need for leased telecommunication lines. Current Ethernet or other IEEE 802.3 LAN technologies operate at speeds up to 10 Gbit/s. This is the data transfer rate. IEEE has projects investigating the standardization of 40 and 100 Gbit/s.

Home Area Network

A home area network (HAN)is a residential LAN which is used for communication between digital devices typically deployed in the home, usually a small number of personal computers and accessories, such as printers and mobile computing devices. An important function is the sharing of Internet access, often a broadband service through a CATV or Digital Subscriber Line (DSL) provider. It can also be referred as Office area network(OAN).

Campus Network

A campus network is a computer network made up of an interconnection of local area networks (LANs) within a limited geographical area. The networking equipments (switches, routers) and transmission media (optical fibre, copper plant, Cat5 cabling etc.) are almost entirely owned (by the campus tenant/owner: an enterprise, university, government etc.). In the case of a university campus-based campus network, the network is likely to link a variety of campus buildings including; academic departments, the university library and student residence halls.

Wide Area Metwork

A wide area network (WAN) is a computer network that covers a large geographic area such as a city, country, or spans even intercontinental distances, using a communications channel that combines many types of media such as telephone lines, cables, and air waves. A WAN often uses transmission facilities provided by common carriers, such as telephone companies. WAN technologies generally function at the lower three layers of the OSI reference model: the physical layer, the data link layer, and the network layer.

Global Area Network

A global area network (GAN) is a network used for supporting mobile communications across an arbitrary number of wireless LANs, satellite coverage areas, etc. The key challenge in mobile communications is handing off the user communications from one local coverage area to the next. In IEEE Project 802, this involves a succession of terrestrial WIRELESS local area networks (WLAN).

Enterprise Private Network

An enterprise private network is a network build by an enterprise to interconnect various company sites, *e.g.*, production sites, head offices, remote offices, shops, in order to share computer resources.

Virtual Private Network

A virtual private network (VPN) is a computer network in which some of the links between nodes are carried by open connections or virtual circuits in some larger network (*e.g.*, the Internet) instead of by physical wires. The data link layer protocols of the virtual network are said to be tunneled through the larger network when this is the case. One common application is secure communications through the public Internet, but a VPN need not have explicit security features, such as authentication or content encryption. VPNs, for example, can be used to separate the traffic of different user communities over an underlying network with strong security features.

A VPN may have best-effort performance, or may have a defined service level agreement (SLA) between the VPN customer and the VPN service provider. Generally, a VPN has a topology more complex than point-to-point.

Internetwork

An Internetwork is the connection of two or more private computer networks via a common routing technology (OSI Layer 3) using routers. The Internet is an aggregation of many internetworks, hence its name was shortened to Internet.

Internet

The Internet is a global system of interconnected governmental, academic, corporate, public, and private computer networks. It is based on the networking technologies of the Internet Protocol Suite. It is the successor of the Advanced Research Projects Agency Network (ARPANET) developed by DARPA of the United States Department of Defence. The Internet is also the communications backbone underlying the World Wide Web (WWW). Participants in the Internet use a diverse array of methods of several hundred documented, and often standardized, protocols compatible with the Internet Protocol Suite and an addressing system (IP Addresses) administered by the Internet Assigned Numbers Authority and address registries. Service providers and large enterprises exchange information about the reachability of their address spaces through the Border Gateway Protocol (BGP), forming a redundant worldwide mesh of transmission paths.

Intranets and Extranets

Intranets and extranets are parts or extensions of a computer network, usually a local area network. An intranet is a set of networks, using the Internet Protocol and IP-based tools such as web browsers and file transfer applications, that is under the control of a single administrative entity. That administrative entity closes the intranet to all but specific, authorized users. Most commonly, an intranet is the internal network of an organization. A large intranet will typically have at least one web server to provide users with organizational information. An extranet is a network that is limited in scope to a single organization or entity and also has limited connections to the networks of one or more other usually, but not necessarily, trusted organizations or entities—a company's customers may be given access to some part of its intranet—while at the same time the customers may not be considered trusted from a security standpoint. Technically, an extranet may also be categorized as a CAN, MAN, WAN, or other type of network, although an extranet cannot consist of a single LAN; it must have at least one connection with an external network.

Overlay Network

An overlay network is a virtual computer network that is built on top of another network. Nodes in the overlay are connected by virtual or logical links, each of which corresponds to a path, perhaps through many physical links, in the underlying network. For example, many peer-to-peer networks are overlay networks because they are organized as nodes of a virtual system of links run on top of the Internet. The Internet was initially built as an overlay on the telephone network. Overlay networks have been around since the invention of networking when computer systems were connected over telephone lines using modem, before any data network existed. Nowadays the Internet is the basis for many overlaid networks that can be constructed to permit routing of messages to destinations not specified by an IP address. For example, distributed hash tables can be used to route messages to a node having a specific logical address, whose IP address is not known in advance.

Overlay networks have also been proposed as a way to improve Internet routing, such as through quality of service guarantees to achieve higher-quality streaming media. Previous proposals such as IntServ, DiffServ, and IP Multicast have not seen wide acceptance largely because they require modification of all routers in the network. On the other hand, an overlay network can be incrementally deployed on end-hosts running the overlay protocol software, without cooperation from Internet service providers. The overlay has no control over how packets are routed in the underlying network between two overlay nodes, but it can control, for example, the sequence of overlay nodes a message traverses before reaching its destination. For example, Akamai Technologies manages an overlay network that provides reliable, efficient content delivery (a kind of multicast). Academic research includes End System Multicast and Overcast for multicast; RON (Resilient Overlay Network) for resilient routing; and OverQoS for quality of service guarantees, among others.

INTERNET TECHNOLOGY AND ITS SERVICES

The Internet has revolutionised our society, our economy and our technological systems. Over the past century, important technological developments have created a global environment that is drawing people of the world closer and closer together. About fifteen years ago, most of the world knew little or nothing about the Internet. The Internet was then a private network accessible only to computer scientists and researchers who used it to interact with colleagues in their respective disciplines. It is estimated that about 60 million host computers on the Internet today serve about 200 million users in over 200 countries and territories. Also, the total numbers of host computers and users have been growing at about 33 per cent every six months Since, 1988 – or roughly 80 per cent per year. The Internet has revolutionised the computer and communications world like nothing before. The invention of the telegraph, telephone, radio, and computer set the stage for this unprecedented integration of capabilities. The Internet is at once a world-wide broadcasting capability, a mechanism for information dissemination, and a medium for collaboration and interaction between individuals and their computers without barriers of geographic location. The Internet represents one of the most successful examples of the benefits of sustained investment and commitment to research and development of information infrastructure. Beginning with the early research in packet switching, the government, industry and academia have been partners in evolving and deploying this exciting new technology. Today, terms like 'Yahoo' and 'Google' are common part of our vocabulary. Internet-based communication services, content creation and delivery tools applicable in libraries.

INTERNET-BASED COMMUNICATION SERVICES

Libraries use Internet-based communication system while attending their day-to-day routine works. An Internet-based communication system allows communication between computer users hooked into a network. Internet-based communication system is used for communication between person-to-person, person-to-group and group-to-group. A document or message sent through electronic system may contain text, graphics, image, speech as well as other types of information.

Electronic Mail (E-mail)

Electronic Mail, or e-mail, is a fast, easy and inexpensive way to communicate with other Internet users around the world. It is the most popular and widely used services of the Internet. E-mail is the term given to an electronic message, usually a form of simple text message that a user types at a computer system and is transmitted over some form of computer network to another user, who can read it. E-mail offers speedy and economical transfer of messages anywhere in the world. Sending e-mail messages are virtually free even to long-distance destinations. Most integrated library system support e-mail-based communication to library users (for circulation and acquisitionrelated activities) and to the vendors/ publishers (for placing orders, reminders, cancellation, etc).

Listserv

Listservs are electronic groups that typically centre around broad topics such as Digital Libraries or Reference Service, ,etc. Listservers of IFLA with the name IFLA-l, Digilib-l LIBJOBS-l are good example of this. Every e-mail message sent to the listserv is distributed to all members of that listserv, which is potentially hundreds or thousands of people.

It does not cost anything to subscribe to a listserv, but simply requires that the user sends an e-mail message to the appropriate address with the message: subscribe (listserv) Firstname Lastname. Each Listserver has one address where a user sends requests to subscribe, un-subscribe, search the archives, etc., and another address to send actual questions or responses to the readers of the list. Apart from organising discussions, job announcements and conference announcements are popular usage of Listservs.

Chat or Instant Messengers

Chat refers to any live discussions conducted using the Internet, usually between more than two persons using their keyboard to communicate. Chat Programmes allow users on the Internet to communicate with each other by typing in real time. It is a feature offered by many online services or Web sites that allows users to 'chat' by typing messages which are displayed almost instantly on the screens of other users who are using the chat room at a given time. After entering a chat room, any user can type a message that will appear on the monitors of all the other users. Chatting is one of the most popular uses of the Internet. Generally the users remain anonymous by using nicknames or pseudonyms to identify themselves online. A variation of chat is the phenomenon of the instant messenger. Instant messaging can be used to communicate privately with friends, relatives or co-workers.

To send and receive instant messages, a user needs a connection to the Internet and instant messaging software such as Gmail Messenger, Yahoo Messenger and MSN Messenger. The instant messaging software enables a user to set up a list of contacts who also use the same Programme. Once this list is set up, one can see each contact as they come online. A chat session can be started with them quickly and easily. Most conversations are typed text messages that are sent back and forth, though more advanced users can exchange voice, video, files and more.

Conferencing

One of the most exciting features of Internet is to communicate, talk, and see groups of people in different locations around the world, without the expense of travel. Conferencing can take many forms, such as web chat, audio conferencing, video conferencing, multimedia conferencing, screen-sharing, etc.

The conferencing Programmes, such as the popular CU-SeeMe, allow workgroups to use the Internet to see each others' faces in small windows on the computer screen and to hear their voices through computer speakers. One can use desktop video and audio simultaneously or audio can be used alone, or just use the screen-sharing capability without either audio or video.

Audio Conferencing or Internet Telephony

Internet telephony also called IP telephony is a combination of hardware and software that allows the Internet to be used as a telephone carrier. Internet telephony is the conversion of analogue speech signals used on current telephone systems into digital data, allowing calls to be sent over the Internet, bypassing long distance charges. While the Internet was first devised as a way of transmitting data, it is now being used to make voice calls. Internet telephony is projected to explode as the costs plummet. After the costs of initial set-up and access to an Internet Service Provider, long-distance voice calls can be made via the Internet free of charge, but current quality of voice transmission over the Internet is not always as good as direct telephone service.

There are also PSTN/ Internet gateways that allow regular telephone callers to make Phoneto- Internet-to-Phone connections. There are PC-to-Phone connections and Phone-to- PC connections.

Video Conferencing

Video conferencing is one of the most exciting areas of development in telecommunications, with applications ranging from business to government to education to home and family. Video conferencing involves sending video signals as well as audio and computer data signals. Conferencing can be done one-to-one, one-to-many (called multicast), and many-to-many (called multipoint). While video conferencing, one can talk as well as see the people sitting miles away as if all are discussing in one room facing each other.

One of the most popular applications is transmission on news from various locations by the TV news channels. It also has enormous potential for enhancing communications for small and mid-sized companies, as well as distance learning. However, video conferencing requires sufficient bandwidth to transfer video files of acceptable quality. Desktop conferencing, therefore, is not yet widely implemented for business and educational use. As bandwidth increases, desktop video conferencing is expected to blossom. The PictureTel and Vtel are two of the largest companies that sell video conferencing equipment.

NetMeeting

Microsoft NetMeeting facilitates a new way of talking, meeting, working and sharing over the Internet. It uses Internet phone voice communications and conferencing standards to provide multi-user applications and data sharing over Intranets or the Internet.

Two or more users can work together and collaborate in reach time using application sharing, whiteboard, and chat functionality. NetMeeting can be used for common collaborative activities such as virtual meetings. It can also be used for customer service applications, telecommuting, distance learning, and technical support. The product is based on ITU (International Telecommunication Union) standards, so it is compatible with other products based on the same standards. NetMeeting supports text chat, video shared whiteboard, transferring of files, directory of connected users. Files, such as documents or pictures, can be exchanged. One of the problems with net meeting is the break-up in audio that sometimes becomes inaudible when using it on the Internet, though it works fine over a high-speed company network.

News Groups

Another Internet service similar to listservs is a newsgroup. News Groups are like an International bulletin board. Each group is a forum for a different subject, where a subscriber can post his/her questions or answers.

There are thousands of groups covering just about every area of interest. The difference between listserv and news group is that when a user joins a group, the mail is no longer automatically deposited into his mailbox. Instead a user is expected to go to the newsgroup himself to read it. Some listservs can also be accessed as a newsgroup. A good analogy to a newsgroup is a bulletin board, *i.e.,* one can go to it, as opposed to having mail delivered to his/ her desk. The mails from newsgroup does not get cluttered and it can be easily regulate how often messages are read. A drawback of a newsgroup lies in the fact that a user must remember to go out to the newsgroup to look for the information. There are hundreds of newsgroup communities. They centre around topics such as computing, news, recreation, social, and 'alternative' topics. There are newsgroups dealing with virtually every topic under the sun and new newsgroups appear every day.

INTERNET-BASED CONTENT PUBLISHING AND DELIVERY SERVICES

The World Wide Web- know as WWW, W3 or simply, the Web help people to publish, organise and provide access to information on the Internet. The

WWW can be defined as a hypertext, multimedia, distributed information system that provides links to hypertext documents, as well as to many other Internet tools and databases. The Web serves as a platform for several specialised content publishing and delivery services. Some of the important tools for content publishing and delivery services applicable to libraries and information centres are described here.

Blogs

A blog (an abridged form of term web log) is a Web site, usually maintained by an individual, with regular entries of commentary, descriptions of events, or other material such as graphics or video. Entries are commonly displayed in reverse chronological order. Blogs are considered as lightweight publishing tools. Blogs provide control to an individual or group of individuals for publishing contents or making commentary on it. Technologically, blogs are easier to use, platform-independent, and accessible online over the Internet. Broadly, blogs can be said to be online dairies, however, thousands of blogs are maintained by experts in different subject areas who are willing to share their knowledge, understanding and opinions with other people. Michael Casey, who coined the term 'Library 2.0', for example maintains a blog on Library 2.0 called LibraryCrunch. The most obvious application of blogs for libraries is to use it as a tool for promotion, publicity and for outreach services. Libraries can disseminate information to their users, make announcements for its new resources and events through its blogs. Blogs can be used to initiate debates and interaction amongst users and staff. Moreover, library staff and user can be encouraged to use Library blogs to get to know each other and interact at personal level.

Wikis

A wiki is a collection of web pages designed to enable anyone who accesses it to contribute or modify content, using a simplified markup language. Wikis are often used to create collaborative Web sites and to power community Web sites. For example, the collaborative encyclopaedia, Wikipedia is one of the best-known wikis, that has broken down one the golden rules of librarianship, *i.e.,* content validation and authenticity of information. Wikis are also used in businesses to provide affordable and effective Intranets and for knowledge management. Ward Cunningham, developer of the first wiki software, WikiWikiWeb, originally described it as "the simplest online database that could possibly work". Wikis can essentially be equated to open web-pages, where anyone registered with it can publish on to it, add to it, amend it and change it. As in case of blogs, Wikis do not have reliability as traditional resources.

Inspite of this, their value as information resource cannot be undermined. Wikis are not only popular but de-facto source of information for people inspite of the fact that it is not validated or authenticated. The lack of peer review and editorship in case of Wikis is a challenge to librarians. Wikis as items in a collection, and the associated instruction of users in their evaluation, is certainly an important task for libraries. Libraries can use wiki as a communication tool to enable social interaction among librarians and patrons.

Users can share information, ask and answer questions, and librarians can do the same within a wiki. Moreover, a record of these transactions can be archived for perpetuity. Transcripts of such question-answer sessions would serve as a resource for the library to provide as reference. Furthermore, wikis will ultimately evolve into a multi-media environment, where both synchronous and asynchronous audio and video collaborations will take place.

Podcasting

The word 'podcasting' is derived from two words, namely 'broadcasting' and 'iPod' (popular MP3 player from Apple Computer). Podcasting is defined as "process of capturing audio digital-media files that can be distributed over the Internet using RSS feeds for playing-back on portable media players as well as computers. Users can subscribe to such feeds and automatically download these files directly into an audio management Programme (such as iTunes, Windows Media Player or MusicMatch) on their PCs. When a user synchronises their portable audio device with their personal computer the podcasts are automatically transferred to that device to be listened to at the time and location most convenient for the user. Podcasts can be used with a variety of digital audio formats and play on almost any MP3 player or portable digital audio device - as well as any brand of desktop computer or laptop. Though podcasters' web sites may also offer direct download or streaming of their content, a podcast is distinguished from other digital media formats by its ability to be syndicated, subscribed to, and downloaded automatically when new content is added, using an aggregator or feed reader capable of reading feed formats such as RSS or Atom. Several libraries use podcasts to support library orientations programmes. Taking advantage of podcasting and other consumer technologies (*e.g.,* PDAs, iPods and other MP3 players) as a deliver media of Library's content and services is a great leap forward for library profession.

Vodcasting

The 'VOD' in Vodcasting stands for 'video-on-demand'. It is identical to podcasting. While podcasting is used for delivering audio files, vodcasting is used for delivering video content. Like podcast content, vodcasts content can be played either on a laptop or on personal media assistant (PMA).

RSS Feeds

RSS stands for Real Simple Syndication or Rich Site Summary. The technology, on one hand allows a web site (or e-publisher) to list the newest published updates (like table of contents of journals, new articles) through a technology called XML, on the other hand, it facilitates a web user to keep track new updates on chosen Web site (s). Like a personal search assistant, RSS feed readers visit pre-defined web sites, look for updated information and fetch it automatically on to the user's desktop.

It provides users a way to syndicate and republish content on the Web. Users republish content from other sites or blogs on their sites or blogs, aggregate content on other sites in a single place, and ostensibly distil the Web for their personal use. Libraries are already creating RSS feeds for users to subscribe to, including updates on new items in a collection, new services, and new content in subscription databases. They can also republishing content from other scholarly web sites on their sites.

THE GENESIS OF LIBRARY NETWORKING IN INDIA

In India during the late 1980s and 1990s there was a move-ment to establish city and regional-based library networks by NISSAT (National Information System for Science and Technology), a body under Dept of Scientific and Industrial Research (DSIR), Government of India. It provided some financial assistance for the setting up of these library networks.

This has lead to the mushrooming of various city library networks in India including:

- BONET (Bombay Library Network),
- CALIBNET (Calcutta Library Network),
- DELNET (Delhi Library Network which later became Developing Library Network in 2000),
- PUNENET (Pune Libary Network).

The University Grants Commission (UGC) has also developed INFLIBNET (Information and Library Network) in 1991 to network the University Libraries in the country. Only a few networks were able to work on the self sustainable model and continued to exist after the initial phases of implementation and functioning. DELNET, started as a project in 1988 became a national library network in India by the year 2000. UGC continued funding INFLIBNET to provide the support to the University Libraries in the country. The remaining city library networks due to the lack of planning for developing the networked resources and its functions soon perished from the networking scene of the country.

DELNET-DEVELOPING LIBRARY NETWORK

DELNET-Developing Library Network is a major operational resource sharing library network in India connecting more than 1597 libraries in 30 States and UTs in India and seven other countries. DELNET was conceived as a city based library network in Delhi in 1988 and was known as Delhi Library Network, networking the libraries of the Delhi region. It got registered as a society in 1992. With the availability of DELNET services on the World Wide Web, the accessibility soon was transformed from the local dial up connectivity for the Delhi region institutions to the global access through the Web. This gave a great boost to DELNET and soon DELNET crossed the geographical boundaries within the country and also became accessible outside. It was on 13th September 2000 that the name of DELNET got changed from DELNET-Delhi Library Network to DELNET-Developing Library Network. The main objectives of DELNET is to promote resource sharing among the member-libraries by collecting, storing and disseminating information and by providing networked services to the researchers and scholars to supplement their research activity.

FIVE Cs-FUNCTIONAL PARAMETERS OF DELNET

We would like to mention the five Cs of the Library Networking which is essential for an operational library network and governs its functionality.

These five Cs are:

1. Connectivity;
2. Cost;
3. Computers;
4. Client; and
5. Content.

Connectivity

The connectivity is a life line for the smooth functioning of a library network. There is an availability of the leased-line, wireless, broadband, VSAT and Wifi connectivity in the libraries. The DELNET services are accessible through the World Wide Web by the registered member libraries. The DELNET databases are hosted on Basis Web server and are connected with a 11 mbps RF link offered by National Informatics Centre, Ministry of Communications and Infor-mation Technology, Government of India. The network remains functional on 24/7 basis. The web tracking software installed at DELNET servers gives a day to day picture of the usage of the DELNET services by the member libraries.

It is quite heartening to note that the access to the servers hosting the databases are being made by the researchers and scholars of the member libraries at different times starting from midnight to early morning besides the usual peak hour network access. The survey conducted among the member libraries have shown very encouraging figures regarding the availability of the dedicated links in the libraries. ninety per cent of the respondents have confirmed the availability of the dedicated Internet facility in their libraries.

The University Libraries have the largest availability of the dedicated Internet facility with 95.2 per cent affirmed the availability of the dedicated link, followed by 90.7 per cent in Institutes, 89.7 per cent in Research/Special

Libraries and 86.7 per cent in the Colleges. The survey results shows that Internet has been able to penetrate well among the organisations in the country and the libraries have the Internet bandwidth availability with them. It is found that in 97.3 per cent of the organisations, the faculty has Internet facility at their own desk. It is quite essential to have the direct internet access in order to utilise the library network's resource and services to the fullest.

Cost

The cost of membership to the library network and the resources provided through them are important for the sustainability of a library network. DELNET membership charges are quite nominal, it is ₹ 7500 per annum for the libraries in India and SAARC nations, the non-SAARC members pays USD 500 per annum. The membership fee is kept same for all Institutional Members whether it is a University, an Institution, an R and D organisation, a specialized library or a school library. The democratic approach, an unbias one, helps in promoting the resource sharing. Also it leaves an impression of being equal in their participatory roles in a network for resource sharing.

It is worth reporting that some of the library networks in India could not grow and sustained themselves due to the exorbitant membership charges rates and different categori-zation of the members on the basis of their collections, etc. DELNET charges for the actual courier charges for sending the books on Interlibrary loan and the member-institutions and their researchers finds it an affordable one. In a developing country like India, Cost of getting the desired material plays a crucial role. Herein, the researchers and scholars for higher research are not being helped financially to a reasonable extent through scholarships, grants, etc. contrary to their counterparts in the Western world.

Computers

In order to facilitate the optimum use of the library network resources and services, the researchers, scholars and faculty of the member institutions should have adequate availability of the computers. Through the survey conducted, it was found that 43.2 per cent of the libraries have upto 10 computers in the library whereas 59.1 per cent of the University Libraries have more than 20 computers in the library and only 32.2 per cent of the respondents have more than 20 computers in their libraries. It is quite evident that the libraries are not better equipped with the availability of the computers in their libraries though there may be separate computer labs or the computer departments but they are not the part of the libraries.

Client (Member-Libraries)

The more diverse the library network has the coverage, the more effective would be the resources of such a library network. In DELNET, the participating libraries are from various disciplines and they pool their resources together and share them across the network. I would like to mention the fascinating scenario of resource sharing wherein a technical book required by a S and T Library will be available in a library specialising in Commerce discipline rather than being available in the best technical libraries.

The resources and the collections becomes more trans-parent for the act of resource sharing. The survey results have shown that 92 per cent of the member-libraries are aware about DELNET services and 61 per cent are the frequent users of the DELNET services. It would like to mention that DELNET organizes one day orientation programmes in member-institutions located in various parts of the country. This enables in better promotion and spreads awareness about DELNET and helps in popularizing the services among the users, faculty and researchers of the member-libraries.

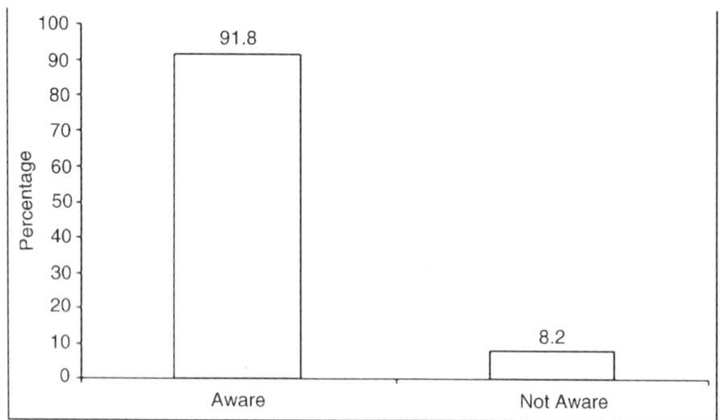

Fig . Awareness about DELNET Services among the Library Users.

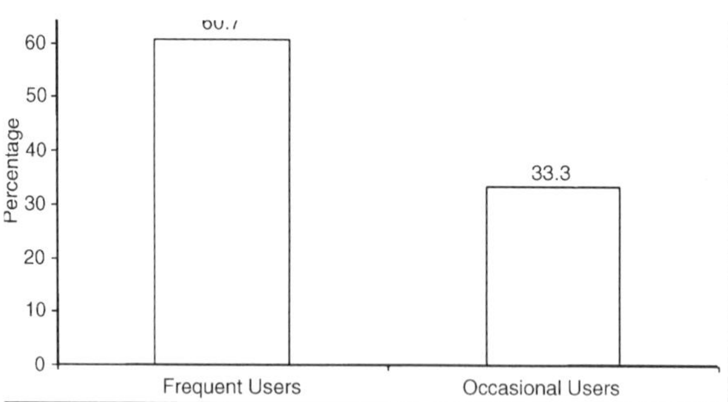

Fig . How Often do you Use DELNET Services.

Bibliography

Ajit Singh: *Information Technology and Library Sciences*, Ancient Publications, Delhi, 2011.

Arunima Baruah: *Library Science: Prospects in 21 Century*, Kilaso Books, 2004.

B.K. Prasad: *Encyclopaedia of Teaching of Library Science (2 Vols- Set)*, Anmol Publications, Delhi, 2003.

Bhagwan Das: *Current Tools and Techniques in Library Science*, Cyber Tech Publications, Delhi 2007.

Bidyut Mal: *Library Sciences and Documentation*, Shree Publications, Delhi, 2004.

H.R. Chopra, U.C. Sharma and M.K. Srivastava: *Library Science and its Facets (2 Vols-Set)*, Ess Ess Publications, Delhi, 1998.

Hasnain Qureshi: *Principles and Practices of Library Science*, Anmol Publications, Delhi, 2006.

J.B. Sharma: *Professional Leadership in Library Science*, Book Enclave, Jaipur, 1998.

K S Dhawan: *Readings in Library Science (4 Vols-Set)*, Commonwealth Publications, Delhi, 2001.

K.G. Rastogi: *Acquisition and Collection Development in Library Science*, Alfa Publications, Delhi, 2006.

K.G. Rastogi: *Reference Services in Library Science*, Alfa Publications, Delhi, 2006.

K.G. Rastogi: *The Functions of Cataloguing in Library Science*, Alfa Publications, Delhi, 2006.

Kamla Sinha: *Concept of the Library Science and Librarianship*, Ankit Publishing House, Delhi, 2011.

A.A.N. Raju: *Facets of Library and Information Science*, Ess Ess Publications, Delhi, 2012.

Amjad Ali: *Ane's Encyclopedic Dictionary of Library and Information Science*, Ane Books India, Delhi, 2006.

B S Aggarwal: *An Introduction to Library and Information Science*, ABD Publication,

Delhi, 2005.

B.P. Shrivastava: *Library and Information Science Education in Indian Universities*, Commonwealth Publication, New Delhi, 2002.

Bhupendra Narayan Singh: *Encyclopaedia of Library and Information Science in the Digital Age Vols. I to III*, Anmol Publication, Delhi, 2011.

Bikika Laloo Tariang: *Essays on Library and Information Science Education*, Ess Ess Publications, Delhi, 2012.

C K Sharma; Rakesh Kumar and Akhil Kumar Singh: *Library and Information Science (3 Vols-Set)*, Atlantic Publication, Delhi, 2008.

C Lal and K Kumar: *Descriptive Questions in Library and Information Science,* Ess Ess Publication, Delhi, 2010.

C.D. Sharma: *Advances in Library and Information Science Vol. 1: Computer Applications*, Scientific Publication, Jaipur, 1995.

C.R. Karisiddappa: *Current Studies in Library and Information Science*, Manak Publication, Delhi, 1994.

Cherian Mathew: *Dynamics of Library and Information Science*, Cyber Tech Publicaitons, New Delhi, 2011.

D.B. Patil and M.M. Kooganuramath: *Library and Information Science*, APH Publication, Delhi, 2011.

D.C. Ojha and D.V. Kothari: *Advances in Library and Information Science : Vol. 5. Digital Libraries*, Scientific Publication, Jaipur, 2005.

G. Devarajan: *Applied Research in Library and Information Science*, Ess Ess Publication, Delhi, 2005.

H.K. Srivastava: *Foundation of Library and Information Science*, Mohit Publication, Delhi, 2011.

I.M. Goswami: *Encyclopaedia of Library and Information Science (5 Vols-Set)*, Commonwealth Publication, New Delhi, 1997.

Jogender Singh Burman: *Encyclopaedic Survey of Library and Information Science : Principles and Practices (5 Vols-Set)*, Rajat Publication, Delhi, 2006.

K.A. Isaac: *Glimpses of Library and Information Science*, Ess Ess Publication, Delhi, 2001.

K.L.M. Swaminathan: *Encyclopaedia of Library and Information Science (3 Vols-Set)*, Sarup and Sons, Delhi, 2001.

Index

L

M

N

O

P

Q

R

S

T

U

V

W